Art Therapy with Children

Art Therapy with Children: From Infancy to Adolescence takes the reader through the child's development by describing the specialist work of the art therapist in each developmental stage. This passionate and exciting book demonstrates the wide theoretical base of art therapy, presenting new areas of clinical practice.

New to the literature is innovative work with mothers and babies, a study of the sibling bond in looked-after children, transgenerational work in kinship fostering, gender disorder and multi-family work with anorexic young people.

The detail of clinical process brings alive the significance of the relationship between the art therapist, child and the art forms made. More general topics include:

- the value of art for the pre-verbal child;
- the preventative role of art therapy in schools;
- the development of imagination in 'hard to reach' and dyspraxic children;
- the importance of working with the family and professional network in the different settings of the health, social services, education and voluntary sectors.

Art Therapy with Children will inspire the student, encourage the clinician and interest an international readership of all professionals working with children and young people.

Caroline Case is an analytical art therapist working in private practice with children and adults. She is also a child and adolescent psychotherapist working in a child and family mental health service in the NHS in Bristol.

Tessa Dalley is an experienced art therapist and child and adolescent psychotherapist, working in an adolescent unit and the Anna Freud Centre, London.

Art Therapy with Children

From Infancy to Adolescence

Edited by Caroline Case and
Tessa Dalley

Routledge
Taylor & Francis Group

LONDON AND NEW YORK

First published 2008 by Routledge
27 Church Road, Hove, East Sussex BN3 2FA

Simultaneously published in the USA and Canada
by Routledge
270 Madison Ave, New York, NY 10016

*Routledge is an imprint of the Taylor & Francis Group,
an Informa business*

Typeset in Times by
RefineCatch Limited, Bungay, Suffolk
Printed and bound in Great Britain by
MPG Books Ltd, Bodmin, Cornwall
Paperback cover design by Lisa Dynan

British Library Cataloguing in Publication Data
A catalogue record for this book is available from the British Library

Library of Congress Cataloging in Publication Data
Art therapy with children : from infancy to adolescence / edited by
Caroline Case and Tessa Dalley.
     p. ; cm.
  Includes bibliographical references and index.
  ISBN 978-0-415-38629-6 (hbk) – ISBN 978-0-415-38630-2 (pbk)
1. Art therapy for children. 2. Art therapy for teenagers.
I. Case, Caroline, 1948– II. Dalley, Tessa.
  [DNLM: 1. Art Therapy. 2. Mental Disorders–therapy.
3. Adolescent. 4. Child. 5. Infant. WS 350.2 A784 2007]
  RJ505.A7A78 2007
  618.92'891656 – dc22

                                     2007011518

ISBN: 978-0-415-38629-6 (hbk)
ISBN: 978-0-415-38630-2 (pbk)

Peace

Peace is eye blinding white,
It smells like the sweet, loveliest flower.
Peace tastes like French vanilla,
It sounds like the dreamiest voice of an opera singer,
It feels like the feather of a dove.
Peace lives in the clouds and heavens of love.

Jay Peterson (9)
St Colomba's School,
Prep Department, St Albans

Contents

Illustrations

Plates

Figures

Permissions

The quotation from A.A. Milne's *The Complete Collection of Stories and Poems* ([1926] 1973) in Chapter 6 comes from *Winnie-the-Pooh*, 'In which Eeyore has a Birthday and gets Two Presents', © The Trustees of the Pooh Properties, reproduced with permission of Curtis Brown Group Ltd, London.

Chapter 11. The quotation from "East Coker" in *Four Quartets*, copyright 1940 by T.S. Eliot and renewed 1968 by Esme Valerie Eliot, Reprinted by permission of Harcourt, Inc. (US rights) and Faber and Faber Ltd (UK, Europe and Australia).

Dali, Salvador (1904–1989): The Persistence of Memory (Persistance de la memoire), 1931. New York, Museum of Modern Art (MoMA). Oil on canvas, 9½ × 13" (24.1 × 33 cm). Given anonymously. 162.1934. © 2007. Digital Image, The Museum of Modern Art, New York/Scala Florence.

Introduction

Caroline Case and Tessa Dalley

The idea of this book grew out of our shared and continuing interest in working with children, young people and their families. Our last book *Working with Children in Art Therapy* (1990) presented the innovative practice of the day in the three statutory areas of education, health and social services, with particular focus on the latency child. Since then, there has been significant expansion of art psychotherapy with children in different settings in the UK, particularly in education and private practice.

The chapters in this book reflect these theoretical and clinical developments in contemporary art therapy practice, and the different styles of writing demonstrate various ways of thinking about this work. We have decided to focus attention on normal developmental processes of the child – from infancy, young childhood, latency, adolescence to adulthood – and consider the work of art therapists with children and their families in each of these developmental stages. This developmental model is helpful in understanding how each period of mental life affects each subsequent phase in contributing to the move from infancy to adulthood. This framework reflects our dual qualifications as art psychotherapists as well as child and adolescent psychotherapists.

In this introduction, the main developmental stages of childhood are outlined. Each stage has to be negotiated by the growing child. Both progressive and regressive pulls are in evidence in the balancing act of continuous development, which can be precarious. Developmental progress does not necessarily take place smoothly, but often through leaps in physical, emotional and cognitive achievement (Stern 1985). It is helpful to consider that progress represents a gain for the child, but also loss of the previous stage, and it is not unusual for the child to regress at times of anxiety and uncertainty.

Failure to achieve a particular stage signals an interruption in development. This may be due to internal conflicts within the child or external factors such as trauma, serious illness, loss, abuse or a combination of these. Either way, the child's progress will falter and difficulties will manifest themselves in a multitude of ways, affecting behaviour, emotional and social relating, cognitive development and learning. Some children, such as those who are learning disabled or on the autism spectrum, may need particular help to maintain developmental progress. The art therapist works within the framework of understanding the significance of these developmental processes, paying attention to the internal world of the child, attachment issues and early infantile experience. Psychoanalytic theorists such as Freud, Klein, Anna Freud and Winnicott, among others, have made significant contributions to the developmental stages of our understanding. We also acknowledge the importance of new theoretical developments in neurobiology, attachment theory and parent-infant psychotherapy which continue to inform our work (Case and Dalley 2006). Please note that we use 'he' to refer to 'the child' or 'the adolescent' in order to avoid the rather clumsy 'he or she'.

The parents and pregnancy

As a couple become parents it is a time of great psychic upheaval and possible re-evaluation of their relationship during the pregnancy. Each also re-evaluates their relationship as the child they are to their parents (Raphael-Leff 1993). During the pregnancy, an imaginary baby exists, fantasised in each parent's inner world. Increasing evidence shows how babies, *in utero*, are sensitive to the mother's emotional state and responsive to the surroundings into which they will be born (Piontelli 1992, 2002). When the baby is born there are further changes as the baby becomes recognised as an individual and hopefully the fantasy of the baby disperses.

Several external factors may significantly affect parents, such as social and economic circumstances, a sense of belonging to a particular community, and physical and mental well-being. Internally, their own experiences of being parented will influence and affect their capacity to parent their new baby. In their paper 'Ghosts in the nursery', Fraiberg *et al.* (1975) explore how a mother's past – her own experience of being mothered and fathered – influences the mother she will become. This can be particularly damaging if there has been trauma such as physical, sexual or emotional abuse in either of the parents' past. If a parent cannot remember the trauma in childhood, he or she may be drawn to re-enactment, with devastating consequences for all the family. Fonagy *et al.* (1992) have shown how remembrances of suffering can become a form of protection to the new baby. One good experience amidst many neglectful, violent and emotionally impoverished ones can be internalised, that is, become a working model that can be drawn on very positively: 'The parents' "reflective function" or "mentalising stance", expressed in the way they reflect upon their own and their baby's inner experience, is linked to secure attachment in their infants, even in adverse conditions' (Baradon 2000: 17).

Mothers and babies

The practice of baby observation (Bick 1964; Miller *et al.* 1989; Reid 1997) and the work of parent-infant psychotherapy has developed our understanding of early attachment influences in the first years of the mother and baby couple (Baradon 2000). Attachment is the central relationship that develops between an infant and caregiver (Bowlby 1969, 1973; Carlson and Stroufe 1995). The quality of this attachment relationship influences all aspects of development (see Chapters 2 and 3 of this volume). The baby has a sense of omnipotent functioning in his expectations that all his needs will be met. In turn, the mother is emotionally attuned to the demands of her baby. The baby is absolutely dependent on the caregiver, for physical care and emotional care, which helps his psychic development. Babies are particularly receptive to feeling states and sensitive to the mother's emotional tone, and in this way seek out affective interactions with others.

This absolute dependency makes the baby extremely vulnerable and where there is not 'good-enough' mothering (Winnicott 1960) or maternal containment (Bion 1962) this exposes the baby to states of overwhelming helplessness. Without a good enough parent, the baby's emotional states disrupt the developing sense of self. Affect regulation is fundamental (Schore 1994) as the infant's evolving sense of self, who he is, becomes a central organising process in psychic development (Stern 1985). The baby's social-emotional relatedness of the early environment is the setting in which the infant's inner world is constructed.

The task for the mother and baby is to establish a relationship within which the baby can feel safe and secure in order to learn and grow (Hindle and Smith 1999). As this happens, the transitional space between mother and baby develops and the baby begins to experience 'me' and 'not me' as an important developmental step. In this space the capacity for play emerges through the baby's innate creative potential as well as the mother allowing her baby to move away in accordance with what the infant can manage as an 'experience of disillusionment' (Winnicott [1953] 1971).

Toddlers

The toddler stage, between the ages of 1 to 2, is a time of first steps, first words and the beginning of exploration away from the mother. There is a need for the parents to be united as a parental couple, as the toddler negotiates the next developmental stage towards separation and individuation. This can be a stage of temper tantrums, frustration with dependence and a wish for control. By 2, the child has a primary sense of gender, and can be preoccupied with his anatomy. There is a growing sense of agency through affirmation of identity in the notion of 'me'. Language is developing alongside the capacity to symbolise, to use words for the expression of needs rather than enactment through the body of early infancy. Play with objects has not acquired symbolic content but, with engagement in fantasy, focuses on tactile exploration – pulling, pushing, stacking and knocking over, with an ability to be 'alone in the presence of an object' (Winnicott 1958).

In connection with moving away from the mother, the use of transitional objects (a special toy, teddy or cuddly blanket) helps the developing toddler with his mother's absence in the forward moves towards independence. The 'intermediate area of experience' (Winnicott [1953] 1971: 2) is the perception of separateness from the mother which is linked to the capacity for symbolisation and the ability to play. Relationship with siblings and the different handling by the father help to expand the toddler's world. The importance of painting in mother and baby groups in working with attachment issues and establishing the intermediate space between mother and child is of growing interest for art therapists (see Chapter 1).

Using video, Hosea (2006) shows the interaction of mothers and their infants painting together and how this positively affects their relationship by building up an experience of connectedness. The video interaction technique is becoming integral to parent-infant work, both as a sensitive therapeutic tool and also to enable a positive reflective space for mothers (Woodhead et al. 2006).

Play is a diverse activity as it involves working out anxiety and conflict, exploring fantasy and reality with social and cognitive experimentation. Through play, the child makes sense of his world. As the toddler gradually assigns symbolic meaning to his toys, play becomes more social and inter-active with others. First play is 'alongside others' but soon the child pro-gresses to play 'with' others. The child begins to hold things, develop manual dexterity, to make the first marks on paper. As the child manipulates the environment, and the materials around him, he can begin to use basic draw-ing materials such as crayons, Playdoh etc. His first scribbles are attempts at reproduction of himself and his world (Matthews 1989, 1999). The develop-ment of these creative activities is an important part of the play repertoire that helps the child grow in his imagination, curiosity and mastery of the world.

Between the ages of 2 and 4, there is an explosion of learning. The young child is moving on in his separation and independence, acquiring more skills, such as sleeping, toilet training and dressing, and experimenting with social situations in play using a secure base of home from which to venture out (Bowlby 1988). Social life continues to expand, especially with attendance at playgroups and nurseries as sibling relationships and friends become more important. With greater awareness of other children and adults there may be feelings of competitiveness, rivalry and anger and a difficulty in moving on to the next stage, in losing the closeness of the maternal relationship. As well as experimenting with sensory and tactile play, scribbling, making 'mud-pies' with water and sand play, the increased motor control of the toddler improves his efforts to draw something at a representational level. There may be the first circle or attempts to draw a face (Dubowski 1990).

Art therapists have an important contribution to this work with under 5s. The young child's capacity to communicate his feelings remains largely pre-verbal through behaviour such as crying, soiling, collapsing, withdrawing, biting and so on. Important first steps to give meaning to these emotional states can be facilitated through engagement with art materials, sand, water and play.

The Oedipus complex

The Oedipal phase and its resolution is important to the child's development as it involves renouncing the intense emotional relationship with the mother. Classically, the boy's rivalry and ambivalence towards his father is relin-quished by an acceptance of a father who can be emotionally available to him. For the girl, in the turning away from the mother to a passionate rela-tionship with the father, the renouncement of him as a partner enables iden-tification with the mother. More recently there is a growing view that the significance of the Oedipal resolution lies in the realisation for the child that he is part of a three-person relationship. The child has to come to terms with the sexuality of his parents who are also partners. For the child in a single parent family, the idea of a parental relationship is important. Through reso-lution of this conflictual stage, the child turns away from parents to focus on external peer relations and further learning of new skills which sets the scene for entering latency. Where there is no resolution of Oedipal conflicts, the relationship between mother and child remains enmeshed and interrupts forward development, with some serious consequences either in delay in moving into latency (see Chapter 4), or in later life during adolescence (see Chapter 9).

Latency

Between the ages of 4 and 5 comes the transition from home to school which happens earlier in the UK than in some other European countries. The latency period, which traditionally brings the peer group into prominence, roughly spans the ages 5 to 11, although some girls are reaching puberty earlier. During this stage, the passions of the Oedipus complex lie dormant while the child gathers resources in preparation for the major psycho-sexual changes to come at puberty: 'The laying down of this emotional provision is the central undertaking of these years' (Waddell 1998: 74).

There is a gradual emergence into latency. The residues of infant life per-petuate at this transitional point of change and remain within the person-ality: 'The quality of the struggle and resolution that has preceded this stage will lie at the heart of the child's capacity to change, adapt, and expand: to learn and grow in the new environment' (Edwards 1999: 71). Latency is seen as a pause in the evolution of sexuality, with an accompanying decrease or de-sexualisation of object relations and emotions. The reorganisation of internal defences against the passions of infant longings gives the latency period a sense of stability. The sexual components of the Oedipus complex go into social feelings and into building up barriers against sexuality.

Sublimation, one of the important latency defences, is at the centre of symbol formation and psychological development as libidinal energies and drives are diverted into curiosity about the world and learning. Winnicott (1965) referred to sublimation as the 'facilitative split' which is essential for learning to take place. This helps to preserve the good earlier experience of a creative parental couple and allows the child to embark on the next stage.

Latency is a period of social integration and developing a peer group. Attachment relationships become internalised as working models and, socially, there is a move from 'egocentricity to companionship' (Freud 1965). In object relations terms this requires a move from dependency to libidinal investment in people outside the family, ideals and interests. In latency, there is a hunger for information, facts and lists of things (Meltzer 1973). It is normal to have hobbies, to collect things such as sets of cars, cards or collectable toys, or sets of numbers, as in train-spotting or bird-watching. Identification with heroes and idols is central for both boys and girls. At this time children tend to play with their own sex in which clubs, groups and games with clear rules are important with a rigid perception of right and wrong. The sublimation of sexual feelings can be seen in children's games – rhythmic skipping games, rough and tumble, 'kiss chase' and so on as they establish a sense of body boundaries in preparation for the advancement of puberty.

Latency can be a very creative time for both boys and girls in their capacity to draw, paint, act, mime and play music. Traditionally, latency drawings are careful, rule-bound and figurative. Many art therapists work with latency children in schools, with Child and Adolescent Mental Health Service (CAMHS) teams, social services or in private practice. Their images or art forms help to communicate at a symbolic level many of the conflicts and anxieties that are difficult to put into words. Fantasy can offer an important outlet, and regression, as at all stages, can give a child temporary relief from the stresses of a particular stage. Some children may retreat and be very hard to engage in latency because of the closing down of infant experience. The challenges of the outside world can be worrying as well as stimulating. Also, internal situations can feel dangerous, unmanageable and uncontrollable. This can lead to timidity or obsessionality, inhibit the child from exploring or taking the initiative, and limit the imaginative side of the self (see Chapters 6, 7 and 8). In Chapter 5, Reddick helpfully illustrates how interruptions in latency can affect learning and how addressing issues of gender splits and rivalries in the whole class setting enables understanding to take place.

Latency years that are successful can give inner strength to embark on the conflict of adolescence.

Adolescence

Adolescence is a time of transition, of change, of intense emotional experience. This period of life has a crucial part to play in the young person's whole development, especially in his development to adulthood. As every adolescent experiences stress at some time, the question is how they deal with this stress and whether their behaviour or worries are normal or show signs of more serious psychological disturbance.

The adolescent has the task of separation from primary relationships and development of identity which can be characterised by emotional confusion, unhappiness and distress. The body undergoes rapid changes which are both frightening and exciting. Early onset of puberty among latency peers can be as disturbing as the late developer who fears he is permanently different as no changes have happened. It is a period of comparison of sizes and fears about social and sexual abnormality.

Blos (1967) describes adolescence as the 'second individuation process', the first one having been completed toward the end of the third year of life with the attainment of object constancy. What in infancy becomes a 'hatching from the symbiotic membranes to become an individuated toddler . . . becomes in adolescence the shedding of family dependences, the loosening of infantile object ties in order to become a member of society at large or, simply, of the adult world' (Blos 1967: 163).

Adolescence heralds the revival of early infantile states of mind and sexual feelings. Failure in friendships and relationships is felt acutely as intimacy once again becomes a pressing issue. As in infancy, there is a need for a containing adult with the capacity for thinking about emotions. A parent's capacity to contain anxieties may be affected by unresolved adolescent difficulties of their own. The adolescent, who now has a sexually functioning body, takes ownership of both his changing body and also his mind. The privacy of the adolescent's thoughts and feelings is held sacrosanct in order to negotiate an appropriate distance from adults to manage these enormous changes, and gain respite from infantile feelings and the pressures to be adult. Additional external pressures are placed on the adolescent through target-setting and aspirations to achieve in education. Other pressures from adults who do not understand an adolescent's predicament are commonplace.

Many adolescents, who were able to keep potential trouble areas in some precarious balance during childhood, fail with the demands of adolescence. The challenges of managing these pressures can lead to collapse of earlier ways of managing situations and precipitate adolescent breakdown. The adolescent presents as someone made helpless by forces over which he has no control. Laufer and Laufer (1968) highlight the establishment of final sexual organisation as the main developmental function of adolescence. Adolescent breakdown manifests itself in the relationship to the body and through the unconscious rejection of the representation of the body as sexual. Hatred of the body can now turn to action against the self or others which results in disorders such as attempted suicide, anorexia, delinquency and drug-taking. Impulsive, aggressive and confused feelings are expressed through extreme behaviours such as acting out through alcohol and substance misuse, violent mood swings, cutting and other self-harming behaviour.

Risk-taking is reminiscent of the omnipotence of the toddler years and can be dangerous as the function of self-preservation is lacking. Where the adolescent has had poor or disrupted early attachments without good enough parenting, there is no secure emotional base from which to move away towards independence. This makes the adolescent task for looked-after children, who may have had many different carers in their life, even more complex (see Chapter 3). For the adopted child, who has experienced a rupture in the relationship with the birth mother, moving away from adoptive parents sets in train the possibility of searching for and finding her once again, which can be a necessary part of the establishment of identity (Dalley and Kohon in press).

Gradually the mixed peer group becomes central and forms a background to the development of personal and sexual identity. The breakdown of the more stable experience of the latency period is replaced by feelings of vulnerability and uncertainty, with a fluctuating sense of self. Meltzer (1973: 51) describes the adolescent world as a social structure: 'The inhabitants of which are the happy/unhappy multitude caught betwixt the "unsettling" of their latency period and the "settling" into adult life'. He describes how the *centre of gravity* of the experience of identity shifts wildly in the same person. In the group, various parts of the self are externalised into the various group members. The adolescent can find relief from the different parts of his personality, which may be contradictory, as it is harder to differentiate internal experiences from external ones, between adult and infantile feelings, good from bad and male from female.

The use of the group in mid-adolescence provides the same function as the relationship with the close same-sex friend in early adolescence. As attempts to get approval from parents are no longer as effective, the adolescent turns to a peer group, but has to perform and behave in a way that is acceptable to them. Mirroring obtained from peers is important and conformity to group identity provides an external identity while the internal processes are so in flux. In his writing on adolescence, Meltzer (1973) says that the group, no matter how delinquent or antisocial it may appear in relation to the adult world, is holding together the splitting process. Deutsch (1968) suggests that adolescents can be in 'mutual imitation' or form an identity as 'we'. Group life can provide a set-apart place but also provide a cover for anxieties.

Many of the characteristics of adolescent life are present in Shakespeare's *Romeo and Juliet*. Adolescent gangs find pleasure in the indulgence of polarisation and provocation, which gives free rein to aggressive and sexual impulses (Copley 1993). The young lovers seek 'the other' who represents the unknown as an unfulfilled part of the self: the experience of falling in love. Adolescent relationships gradually increase in depth, becoming based on true intimacy, with love for the other because of who they are. It is normal for there to be uncertainty about sexual orientation, and for young people to experiment, some eventually settling on a partner of the opposite sex and some for a partner of the same sex. There are particular difficulties in this final sexual organisation for those children who have been sexually abused. Where a destructive part of the personality is dominant, perverse relationships may develop (see Chapter 9).

Art therapists work with adolescents, individually and in groups, in both day and inpatient settings. Internal conflicts can be processed non-verbally through images which helps to make sense of thoughts and feelings that are negated, split off into action or repressed. The adolescent's fear of being out of control as well as underlying fantasies and anxieties are embodied in the art work and brought into the therapeutic relationship. Five chapters in this book (Chapters 9, 10, 11, 12 and 13) cover a range of adolescent problems such as anorexia, gender disorder, school refusal, bullying, the pressures of achievement and the difficulties of being on the margins of a group. These chapters give a sense of the complex treatment issues surrounding adolescence in working towards a 'stability of identity', described as the point, in late adolescence, at which the young person is able to move on into adulthood (Tyson and Tyson 1990).

Acknowledgements

We would like to thank our colleagues, supervisors and patients for teaching us so much on the way, our families for their love and support and also our fellow contributors for their hard work and commitment to this book.

The chapters and contributors

The first three chapters are concerned with attachment relationships and the advances in neuroscience in the understanding of early infant development.

Chapter 1: Painting together – an art therapy approach to mother-infant relationships

Penelope Hall describes the evolution of her interest in mother and baby painting groups. The aim of the group is to improve the relationship between mother and baby in the context of postnatal depression and 'ghosts in the nursery' (Fraiberg *et al.* 1975), which may be preventing a closer bond. All participants, including the organisers, paint on the floor and the feeling of equality that this produces is reflected in the valuing of all art productions, however young the participator. Moving vignettes describe her work, which spans over two decades, in a CAMHS team and more recently working for SureStart. The theoretical grounding of her work is set within the framework of new thinking about infant development and the importance of parent-infant relating.

Penelope originally studied sculpture and qualified as an art therapist at St Albans in 1980. A special interest in attachment and relationship issues was explored in her MA project of 1991, based on art therapy workshops for parents with young children, which led to work in CAMHS in Norwich and Cornwall. In recent years she has run painting groups for postnatally depressed mothers and their children with SureStart, North Cornwall. She has a private practice (art therapy and supervision) at her home near Bodmin, coordinates the Truro art therapy foundation course and for many years was a committee member for the Champernowne Trust (for Jungian psychotherapy and the arts) summer course.

Chapter 2: Attachment patterns through the generations: internal and external homes

Frances O'Brien discusses the trans-generational transmission of disorganised attachment in her simultaneous individual work with a grandmother and grandchild. This chapter encompasses kinship fostering, and early relational trauma, as well as a helpful account of the contribution of neuroscience to our understanding of how an infant processes early experience. This provides an introduction to thinking about memory and dissociation and how this impacts on certain children, particularly those who are looked after. The clinical description demonstrates how use of art therapy images as well as verbal images from psychotherapy are vivid and alive in the work.

Frances works in a CAMHS team with children, adolescents and their carers, and in private practice with adults and as a clinical supervisor. Her interest in early life experience including rejection and abuse formed the basis of her research into understanding how the development of the brain is affected by poor relationships and insecure attachment in infancy, and how art psychotherapists can work with this. She has published papers in *Inscape*, the *Journal of the British Association of Art Therapists*, and has spoken at conferences and universities. Frances trained as an art psychotherapist at the University of Sheffield and completed the advanced training and MA in art psychotherapy at Goldsmiths College.

Chapter 3: 'I'm the king of the castle': the sibling bond – art therapy groups with siblings in care

Teresa Boronska provides a much needed theoretical discussion on the bond between siblings. Working in a social services setting of child protection she discusses art therapy groups for siblings in care. The siblings have a shared experience of neglect, physical and/or sexual abuse which strains the normal relationship towards pseudo-parenting and sibling-sibling abuse. The children are temporarily stable in foster homes but are in emotional crisis due to loss and transition. Like Penelope Hall, she co-works with other professionals, finding the added perspective essential in this demanding work. In her discussion she redresses the normal perspective where siblings are seen as rivals by thinking about the sibling as potential for support, companionship, attachment, confidante and playmate, and how important this is for the development of a more secure sense of identity.

Since qualifying as an art therapist in 1989, **Teresa** has worked mainly with children and young people with behavioural and emotional difficulties, at first in special schools and over the last ten years in the area of child protection. Her practice has developed to include joint working with other professionals, specifically family therapists with children and families. Other areas have included children in care, liaising with both foster carers and residential staff, training, consultancy and supervision. She has found attachment theory and research of particular value in understanding the needs of children, specifically where they have suffered abuse and multiple loss. Since 1992 she has been part-time tutor at Goldsmiths College, working on both the foundation and postgraduate training courses in art therapy.

Chapter 4: The use of clay as a medium for working through loss and separation in the case of two latency boys

Tessa Dalley focuses on the problematic move into latency for two boys living with the experience of maternal unavailability due to major loss before their birth. Working in CAMHS, she describes individual work with two 6-year-old boys who present with symptoms connected with bodily products – soiling and phobias about vomiting and eating. The style of writing in the third person provides the theoretical overview to the clinical vignettes which illustrate how the clay was used as a central part of the treatment for both boys. This enabled concrete representation of experience, 'an unknown thought', that could not be put into words. Tessa furthers our thinking about siblings as well as attachment issues with a theoretical exploration into the experience of twinship – particularly the loss of a twin at birth.

Tessa is an experienced art therapist and child and adolescent psychotherapist. She works in an inpatient adolescent unit and in the Parent-Infant Project at the Anna Freud Centre, in private practice and as a clinical supervisor. She has published a number of books and articles on art therapy and is currently on the editorial board of the *International Journal of Art Therapy: Inscape*.

Chapter 5: Working with the whole class in primary schools

Dean Reddick takes us to the heart of the latency experience. Working from research findings from his own thesis, he discusses an innovative way of working with the whole class in a primary school setting where defensive class dynamics were preventing the class from learning. His work is in keeping with current government policy as outlined in *Every Child Matters* (DfES 2003) and the Children's Act 2004 which advocate the emotional health of every child. He shows how making and working with images from everybody, i.e. children, teachers, assistants, as well as his own, and using the health of some children in the class enables defences to be understood and lessened. The dynamics in the class change, allowing normal social interactions to take their place and learning to develop.

Dean currently works in primary schools and at a nursery and children's centre in London. He completed the MA in Advanced Clinical Practice in Art Psychotherapy at Goldsmiths College in 2006, where he specialised in working with children and families. He has worked with children, with and without disabilities, in a variety of settings including the Child and Adolescent Mental Health Service (CAMHS), a special educational needs secondary school and the voluntary sector.

The next two chapters encompass the important transition from primary to secondary school which can be developmentally challenging for many children.

Chapter 6: Playing ball: oscillations within the potential space

Caroline Case describes the development of play and creative work with a girl aged 10, diagnosed with dyspraxia. On referral she had difficulties with tantrums, and was not able to play or make friends. Part of the accompanying family work involved thinking about 'ghosts from the past' and ongoing maternal depression. Essential to the therapeutic process were the use of Winnicott's squiggle game and the paintings of Salvador Dali, which gave permission to play. The clinical work, which took place in a CAMHS, demonstrates how the growing relationship with the therapist allowed internalisation of liveliness that then transferred to relationships outside the family, and led to successful transition to secondary school.

Caroline is an experienced art therapist and child and adolescent psychotherapist working in a CAMHS team, in private practice and as a clinical supervisor. She has published a number of books and articles on art therapy and is a reader for the *International Journal of Art Therapy: Inscape*, and the *Journal of Child Psychotherapy*.

Chapter 7: From 'beanie' to 'Boy'

Zara Patterson works in a country-wide service for autism, which has resource bases attached to host primary and secondary schools. Two further chapters (Chapters 10 and 13) cover the theoretical aspects of autism, allowing Patterson to focus on the detail of the clinical material and the images that tell the moving therapeutic story of 'The Boy'. She respects his request for the reader to know 'what' he is rather than 'who' he is and the immediate style of writing preserves the poignancy of this work and what it is like to be 'The Boy'. His struggles are expressed and shared through his 'beanie world'. By staying alongside and entering the beanie world, Patterson beautifully brings alive the therapeutic relationship, over four years, with a young boy who was a twin, and had speech and language difficulties, difficulties with attention, motor control and perception (DAMP) as well as being on the autistic spectrum. He was referred because high anxiety and accompanying defensive behaviour were preventing him learning. As 'lists' of beanie babies changed to beanies in a landscape, she shows how shifts in his internal world allowed play, narrative, pretending and humour to develop in their relationship, allowing her to support his difficult transition into secondary school.

Zara began her career as an art teacher and instructor working in schools, the UK National Health Service (NHS) and social services. From this work, with a variety of client groups, she has since specialised and spent 14 years working for a county-wide service for children with autism. Initially teaching and managing one of the resource bases, she changed her role to art therapist upon qualifying in 1995. Becoming a member of the senior management team, she eventually held the position of service manager before leaving in 2006. During her time in The Service for Autism, she developed therapy provision, enabling primary- and secondary-aged students, across all the autism resource bases, to have access to the creative arts therapies and psychotherapy.

Chapter 8: Growing up can be so hard to do: the role of art therapy during crucial life transitions and change in the lives of children with learning disabilities

Barrie Damarell and Dot Paisley continue the theme of transitions in the context of learning disability. Working in a joint project between a school for children with moderate to severe learning disabilities and CAMHS/learning disability services, they write with the two voices of supervisor and therapist respectively. This rich association explores the effects of changes in the family, particularly due to family illness, on the anxieties of the learning disabled child approaching adolescence. Jack had a communication disorder as well as neuro-developmental delay. The clinical material illustrates the inevitable process of developmental change which combines with the impact of loss due to the premature ending of the therapy. The chapter sensitively addresses problems of telling children the 'truth' about difficult situations and how living with fantasies can be much more disturbing. There is also a recognition of the use of string in the symbolic negotiation and control of the therapeutic relationship which can be a regular theme in working with children (see Chapter 9 and Dalley 1993).

Barrie has over two decades of experience in the field of learning disabilities. He trained at St Albans and later completed his advanced training and master's degree at Goldsmiths College. The latter institution has become the venue for his research into the relationship between geographical space and the learning disabled person's object-making and use of the art psychotherapy studio. He is currently a member of the editorial board of the *International Journal of Art Therapy: Inscape* and is the professional lead for the arts therapies for a south-western NHS trust.

Dot trained and worked as a social worker with a children and families team before qualifying as an art psychotherapist at QMUC in Edinburgh in 2002. She is a practising stained glass artist and is in the midst of exploring the symbolic potential of using glass in therapy as the subject of her master's dissertation. She is employed by a Learning Disability Partnership in the south-west of England and works with both adults and children.

The remaining five chapters focus on different aspects of working with young people in adolescence.

Chapter 9: Gender disorder in the treatment of a young person in care

Sue Retford-Muir returns to thinking about looked-after children and, in particular, consideration of the needs of looked-after boys in the care system. The context of Retford-Muir's work is a residential therapeutic community. She describes six years of work with a young man aged from 10 to 16. He had been neglected and repeatedly sexually abused, and arrived both incontinent and mute. As the therapy accompanies him into adolescence, the challenge in this chapter is describing the complexity of this work over such a long period of time. Retford-Muir focuses on development of gender identity and allows the reader into the countertransference dilemmas of this work in the building of the therapeutic relationship, which at times was chaotic and disturbing. The images graphically illustrate this process and the predicament of this young man, struggling with the normal adolescent task of independence and separation, as his final sexual organisation emerges into consciousness.

Retford-Muir draws extensively on the literature on perversion, gender formation and transsexual identity and takes into account the need for external containment provided by the institution when a crisis necessitated moving to a secure unit.

Sue is an art psychotherapist with 12 years' experience of working within adult mental health services, with children and young people in care and with children and families in private practice. She trained in fine art (painting) and then went on to teach fine art and run art groups within various care settings. She trained at Hertfordshire University in 1993 (MA in art therapy) and then at Goldsmiths College on the advanced art psychotherapy course in 2000. For the last few years she has specialised in children and young people, within Bedford CAMHS, on a specialist team working with looked-after children and their carers.

Chapter 10: Paranoia and paracosms: brief art therapy with a youngster with Asperger's syndrome

Working in an assessment and diagnostic service, **Robin Tipple** presents a model of brief art therapy in work with a 16-year-old adolescent, recently diagnosed with Asperger's syndrome. He discusses theoretical approaches to brief therapy and the need to find an agreed focus. The young man presented as isolated, quirky, bullied, depressed and with limited interests. He engaged, as far as he was able, in thinking about his interpersonal relationships through discussion about images of the 'Warhammer' world. This world presented both as a defence against the outside world but also, when engaged in imaginatively, proved to be a way in to the narrative of his experiences.

Robin studied painting and printmaking at Norwich School of Art and Reading University. He spent some time working as a mural artist in Bethnal Green Hospital and this led to his interest in art therapy. He trained at Goldsmiths College in 1983 and subsequently returned to complete an advanced diploma and MA. He has worked with adults who have learning disabilities, children in residential care, and children and young persons with developmental disorders. He has published papers on his work with adults who have learning disabilities with Open University Press and in the *International Journal of Art Therapy: Inscape*. At present he is engaged in Ph.D. research which explores the role of art therapy in diagnostic assessment. He is interested in developing his awareness of how art therapists respond to the production of art in clinical settings and how this influences practice.

Chapter 11: Seen and unseen: art therapy in a girls' comprehensive school

Carole Welsby presents an art therapy service as part of the pastoral system in a multi-ethnic, mainstream secondary school for girls. The art therapist has strong links to educational psychology and CAMHS, but her school-based practice maintains the work in Tier 1 which prevents further referral on to Tier 3 or Tier 4 services. In this chapter, as in Chapter 7, the process of therapy is beautifully shown, unfolding, allowing the images to speak to the reader, unpunctuated by theoretical discussion, which is available in other chapters. The close detail of the therapeutic work is presented primarily through the images, firstly with a 14-year-old girl whose father was seriously ill, and died during the course of the work. The therapeutic relationship and use of images highlight the importance of working through her bereavement and loss up to the first anniversary of her father's death. Secondly, with another 14-year-old girl, a school refuser, who presented as isolated, lonely and unseen. The presenting dynamics had an intergenerational pattern, where discord between parents led to parent/child dyads and consequent difficulties in growing up to form healthy couple relationships. For a time, the art therapy session became the only aspect of school life that felt safe enough and tolerable for this young person to attend.

Carole was an art teacher for many years in secondary education, working with pupils both within and outside mainstream schooling. Experience gained in classrooms led her to train as an art therapist and since qualifying in 1992 she has been able to develop and establish art therapy provision for needy adolescents in school. As well as promoting the benefits of on-site therapy to all those in education who will listen, Carole also joins with other involved professions (until recently she was the British Art Therapy Association's representative on the Young Minds Council) in working for the improvement and accessibility of good mental health provision for all young people.

Chapter 12: 'I wonder if I exist?': a multi-family approach to the treatment of anorexia in adolescence

Tessa Dalley provides an introduction to the relatively new approach of multi-family work in the treatment of anorexia. Working in a multi-disciplinary CAMHS team, the art therapist takes the lead in introducing creative activity as part of the overall planned therapeutic programme. Through a discussion of different theoretical models in understanding anorexia, the chapter explores the challenges of working with this client group who are so resistant to change and how the use of a non-verbal medium can assist the process of reflection and develop the capacity for thought. In the modelling of a family sculpt using clay, the concrete form enabled articulation, and also understanding by the whole family, of the bleakness of the anorexic experience in a daughter's attempts to maintain control of her eating, her relationships and development of a female identity.

Chapter 13: 'Other people have a secret that I do not know': art psychotherapy in private practice with an adolescent girl with Asperger's syndrome

Julia Meyerowitz-Katz describes long-term individual work in private practice with a young girl of 15, Sally, who had been diagnosed with Asperger's syndrome. The clinical material brings alive what can be deadening or mind-numbing work as the therapist is receptive to contact from young people who are sometimes described as being excluded from human ordinariness. The early images convey a sense of control and a degree of artistic talent for drawing cartoons. Shifts in Sally's internal world and capacity to develop relatedness are illustrated by changes in her image-making. Working with her unconscious through the images enabled Sally to fully enter adolescence and further maturity. This work was crucial in helping establish a sense of identity. Consultations with her parents supported them to find a way of working together as a couple in order to think about their daughter. The complication of working in private practice, without a team of colleagues to do this supportive parent work, is discussed.

Julia was born in South Africa where she obtained a degree in fine art. After several years of teaching art, she moved to the UK where she trained as an art therapist and worked in a range of settings including the NHS, private practice and as a lecturer on the MA in art therapy at the University of Hertfordshire. She currently lives in Sydney, Australia, and is working as a supervisor and art therapist in private practice as well as a visiting tutor on the MA in art therapy at the University of Western Sydney. She is training to be a Jungian analyst with the Australian and New Zealand Society of Jungian Analysts and is a member of the editorial board of the *International Journal of Art Therapy: Inscape*. She continues her involvement in her own art-making as a potter.

References

Baradon, T. (2000) *The Practice of Psychoanalytic Parent-Infant Psychotherapy: Claiming the Baby*. London: Routledge.

Bick, E. (1964) Notes on infant observation in psychoanalytic training, *International Journal of Psychoanalysis*, 45: 558–66.

Bion, W.R. (1962) *Learning from Experience*. London: Heinemann.

Blos, P. (1967) The second individuation process of adolescence, *Psychoanalytic Study of the Child*, 22: 163–85.

Bowlby, J. (1969) *Attachment and Loss, Vol 1: Attachment*. London: Academic Press.

Bowlby, J. (1973) *Attachment and Loss, Vol 2: Separation*. London: Hogarth.

Bowlby, J. (1988) *A Secure Base: Clinical Applications of Attachment Theory*. London: Routledge.

Carlson, E. and Stroufe, L.A. (1995) Contribution of attachment theory to developmental psychopathology, in D. Cicchetti and D.J. Cohen (eds) *Developmental Psychopathology, Vol 1: Theory and Methods*. New York: Wiley.

Case, C. and Dalley, T. (eds) (1990) *Working with Children in Art Therapy.* London: Routledge.

Case, C. and Dalley, T. (2006) *The Handbook of Art Therapy*, 2nd edn. London: Routledge.

Copley, B. (1993) *The World of Adolescence: Literature, Society and Psychoanalytic Psychotherapy.* London: Free Association Books.

Dalley, T. (1993) Art psychotherapy groups, in K. Dwivedi (ed.) *Group Work with Children and Adolescents: A Handbook.* London: Jessica Kingsley.

Dalley, T. and Kohon, V. (in press) Deprivation and development: the predicament of an adopted adolescent in the search for identity, in D. Hindle and G. Shulman (eds) *Psychoanalytic Approaches to Adoption.* London: Routledge.

Deutsch, H. (1968) *Selected Problems in Adolescence.* London: Hogarth.

DfES (Department for Education and Skills) (2003) *Every Child Matters.* London: DfES.

Dubowski, J. (1990) Art versus language: separate development during childhood, in C. Case and T. Dalley (eds) *Working with Children in Art Therapy.* London: Routledge.

Edwards, J. (1999) Kings, queens and factors: the latency period revisited, in D. Hindle and M.V. Smith (eds) *Personality Development: A Psychoanalytic Perspective.* London: Routledge.

Fonagy, P., Steele, M., Moran G., Steele, H. and Higgett, A. (1992) Measuring the ghost in the nursery: an empirical study of the relation between parents' mental representations of childhood experiences and their infants' security of attachment, *Journal of American Psychoanalytical Society*, 41(4): 957–89.

Fraiberg, S., Adelson, E. and Shapiro, V. (1975) Ghosts in the nursery: a psychoanalytical approach to the problem of impaired infant-mother relationships, *Journal of American Academy of Child Psychiatry*, 14: 387–422.

Freud, A. (1965) *Normality and Pathology in Childhood.* New York: International Universities Press.

Hindle, D. and Smith, M.V. (eds) (1999) *Personality Development: A Psychoanalytic Perspective.* London: Routledge.

Hosea, H. (2006) 'The Brush's Footmarks': parents and infants paint together in a small community art therapy group, *International Journal of Art Therapy: Inscape*, 11(2).

Laufer, M. and Laufer, M. (1968) The body image, the function of masturbation and adolescence: the problems of the ownership of the body, *Psychoanalytic Study of the Child*, 23: 114–37.

Matthews, J. (1989) How young children give meaning to drawing, in A. Gilroy and T. Dalley (eds) *Pictures at an Exhibition: Selected Essays on Art and Art Therapy.* London: Routledge.

Matthews, J. (1999) *The Art of Childhood and Adolescence: The Construction of Meaning.* London: Falmer Press.

Meltzer, D. (1973) *Sexual States of Mind.* Strath Tay: Clunie Press.

Miller, L., Rustin, M., Rustin, M. and Shuttleworth, J. (eds) (1989) *Closely Observed Infants.* London: Duckworth.

Murray, L. (2005) *The Social Baby.* London: CP Publishing.

Piontelli, A. (1992) *From Fetus to Child: An Observational and Psychoanalytic Study.* London: Brunner-Routledge.

Piontelli, A. (2002) *Twins from Fetus to Child*. London: Routledge.

Raphael-Leff, J. (1993) *Pregnancy: The Inside Story*. London: Sheldon Press.

Reid, S. (ed.) (1997) *Developments in Infant Observation: The Tavistock Model*. London: Routledge.

Schore, A. (1994) *Affect Regulation and the Origin of the Self: The Neurobiology of Emotional Development*. Hillsdale, NJ: Laurence Erlbaum.

Stern, D. (1985) *The Interpersonal World of the Human Infant*. New York: Basic Books.

Tyson, P. and Tyson, R.L. (1990) *Psychoanalytic Theories of Development: An Integration*. New Haven, CT: Yale University Press.

Waddell, M. (1998) *Inside Lives: Psychoanalysis and the Growth of the Personality*. London: Duckworth.

Winnicott, D.W. ([1953] 1971) *Transitional Objects and Transitional Phenomena in Playing and Reality*. Harmondsworth: Penguin.

Winnicott, D.W. (1958) *The Capacity to be Alone in the Maturational Processes and the Facilitating Environment*. London: Hogarth.

Winnicott, D.W. (1960) The theory of the parent-infant relationship, in D. W. Winnicott (ed.) *The Maturational Process and the Facilitating Environment*. New York: International Universities Press.

Winnicott, D.W. (1965) *The Family and Individual Development*. London: Tavistock.

Woodhead, J., Bland, K. and Baradon, T. (2006) Focusing the lens: the use of digital video in the practice and evaluation of parent-infant pscyhotherapy, *Infant Observation*, 9(2): 139–50.

Chapter 1

Painting together: an art therapy approach to mother-infant relationships

Penelope Hall

Introduction

This chapter is about art therapy groups for mothers and young children. It is the personal account of a way of working which has evolved over many years. My interest, which originated in student enquiry leading to experimental workshops, has developed as part of the early years work of a mainstream Child and Adolescent Mental Health Service (CAMHS) child and family centre. My most recent experience in a specialised group, targeting postnatal depression is sponsored by SureStart, a government-funded initiative, aimed at improving public services for families with young children.

In these groups, mothers and young children spend time using simple art materials, painting and playing together. The focus of this work is the mother-child relationship. I shall describe how, over the years, the groups have evolved with changing contexts. However it has been interesting to realise that the theoretical base for the effectiveness of this way of working has been confirmed through advances in the research into early child development (Stern 1985; Brazelton and Cramer 1990). Latterly this has been backed up by evidence from neurobiology (Schore 1994).

Mothers, children and art materials

As an art therapist my concern is with the effect of engaging with the creative process through the use of art materials. In the context of family art therapy I have seen how interest is awakened and relationships strengthened when parents and other family members or carers join with children to work creatively together. This has also been my experience with the painting groups, in which mothers with toddlers and even babies participate. I would suggest that reasons for this probably date back to our earliest history, as mark-making has been a feature of human society from the beginning. Most people will have observed the delight that children take in investigating the qualities of the different substances surrounding them in the environment. From infancy, exploring texture and taste, smearing and generally messing about is pleasurable. Indeed, to be denied such opportunity results in impoverishment. The process of mark- and image-making becomes more interesting, and will be engaged with as the child develops.

Art-making is an activity which many adults and children enjoy and one which is natural to them. Another dimension is added when this activity takes place in the context of the first relationship and is shared by a mother and her child. There is evidence to show that infants have an innate ability to bond with their primary carer. Murray (2005) and Trevarthen *et al.* (1981) observed that when working with mothers and babies one can rely on having an active partner in the work in the form of the baby. It is now recognised that a secure and warm attachment to the mother or primary carer is an indicator of the potential for stability and resilience in the future adult. If this is the case then the implications reach beyond the individual, to be influential on the welfare of the family and, taking the long view, on the local community and wider society. Fraiberg (1980: 53), explaining how she took the decision to work in the homes of mothers and babies who desperately needed psychological help ('psychotherapy in the kitchen') wrote, 'No baby can wait for the resolution of a parental neurosis which is impeding his own development.' These realisations have added urgency to this work, because the formative baby and toddler years are so short and missed opportunities can reverberate down the generations.

Right from the start it has been noticeable that children are unfailingly interested in being involved with their mothers in the painting groups and that the mothers respond with interest. I have seen how making and looking at their own images can strengthen a mother and child's sense of identity and belonging. Making a handprint, knowing that 'it's mine' and announcing that 'I made this!' are proud claims of ownership by little children (Plate 1), while possessively taking charge of 'mine', 'my mum's' or 'our picture' also carries a powerful message. The direct expression of feelings can be recognised through both the content and the manner of execution of art work and this can help mother and child to know and understand each other better. Pictures can be taken care of and kept as memories of activities that brought them closer together. Joint image-making brings equality, especially when everyone present works on the floor together. It is noticeable that even very young children are as capable of producing striking images as any adult. Visual images make an impact, even if they are not talked about and an impression may be created that cannot be put into words. Mothers and children playing together with art materials are practising attunement and discovering different ways of relating to one another. Sharing these activities in an environment where no demands are made on them gives them the chance to learn about each other in new ways.

In certain circumstances, mutual sharing of interests and friendly interaction between mother and child may need special encouragement at first if, for some reason, the time around the birth of the child has been particularly difficult for the family. For instance, in the case of postnatal depression, which will be mentioned later, a mother may not have been able to be fully present for her child. It is worth noting that in art therapy activities for mothers and their children there will be considerable physical contact between them. Young children's reactions to the materials tend to be physical and direct, often involving the whole body. The mother's sensitive response is required to prevent the experience from becoming overwhelming. The taste of paint may be investigated (later causing a colourful nappy), and freely investigating the spread and wet sticky texture of paint leads to the invention of new and unusual ways of using it. As the children develop, the growth of their abilities for symbolic play and story-making adds richness to the shared experience. The mother's latent playfulness may be awakened, but it is important for a balance to be kept, as art materials are unpredictable substances the unstable nature of which requires a reliable adult to be ready to take control.

History of this approach

It was as an art therapy student at St Albans in 1980, at the point when individual experience was beginning to mesh with theoretical aspects of course teaching, that I began to wonder about the feasibility of an art therapy approach for mothers with their young children. Following qualification a fellow graduate and I decided to explore my interest in the early years. Over the next five years we ran occasional events together, which we called 'mother and baby painting workshops' in which parents with children under 5, drawn from a network of interested families, spent a weekend together, playing, using art materials and reflecting. The presence of my colleague's own young children aligned her with the mothers, while I was inclined to receive indications of a grandmotherly transference. These first experimental workshops provided valuable learning experience from which I was able to draw in the future. The painting workshops for mothers and children have since evolved as they encountered new influences and moved into different contexts. The fundamental principles remain the same and may be summarised as follows.

Everyone present is expected to paint. This includes mothers, children and organisers, who all join in the art-making together. The art therapist and others involved in organising and facilitating must be careful not to come between a mother and child or tell them what to do. Resisting the temptation to take over, unless there is actual danger, ensures that parents retain responsibility for their children and find their own way of doing things. The art work made by everyone is valued equally, given serious attention and taken care of. This may be recognised as a symbolic way of showing respect for people of all ages and their inner world.

Convinced of the benefits that this way of working could bring to other families, including those experiencing more serious problems (Hall 1991), I wanted to develop this in CAMHS or a similar setting. In 1991 I joined the well established art therapy department at the Bethel Child and Family Centre in Norwich. As well as working individually and in groups with school-age children and adolescents, I began to use art therapy in family work with under 5s in company with a clinical psychologist colleague who was developing new methods of working with young families. Systemic family therapy had a strong presence in the clinic and my colleague received supervision in using a video interaction guidance technique in Holland. Sluckin (1999) recounts how the founders of 'Video Home Training' had been inspired in the 1980s by the work of Colwyn Trevarthen. His groundbreaking research into mother-infant interaction was forging ahead at that time, leading to developments described by Biemans (1990). Our work, filling a gap in the clinic's early years service, included many referrals for 'multi-problem chaotic families', who had poor records of attendance at the child and family centre. For these families, bonding between mother and child could be an issue. We evolved a way of working with art materials in our clients' homes, using brief video recordings of the parents' and children's interaction. The art images produced became instruments for change.

Catton Grove painting group

In 1993 I was able to develop art therapy work with mothers and young children with a health visitor whom I had met during the course of community-based work. She was interested in offering the mothers in her deprived inner-city patch an alternative, primarily non-verbal way of relating to their children through art and play. When we joined forces I found that her specialised knowledge and professional expertise considerably broadened the scope of the painting group which we launched together. She also found helpful new perspectives on her clients, as she watched them engaging in an enjoyable art activity with their children, while she painted alongside them.

The large baby clinic room was opened up to a weekly gathering of mothers and children and we decided to call it simply, 'The Painting Group' (Hall 1997). A sheet of polythene protected the floor, and on it everyone who came engaged with simple art materials. Painting was followed by a time when all the morning's art work was collected and spread out together on the floor, to be looked at and admired. At first I found it strange that the phenomenon of a shared talking time, which had been important in the first painting workshops, did not happen in the baby clinic, but I came to realise that it was in the nature of this open group that the pictures were shared, and held the group identity. As participation was open to all in the local community, for reasons of confidentiality, personal revelation was restricted to friends or took place individually, with chosen professionals. Great care was taken of all the pictures and they were taken home when dry. I occasionally took photos of art work and, influenced by video interaction guidance techniques, tried to catch 'moments of good contact' between mother and child, which they could keep. The baby clinic painting group was well attended by those referred through the health visitor's informal system. It was found to attract families who had been resistant to other approaches and often led to their involvement in other clinic and community activities. Families joined and ceased coming to the painting sessions in their own time and other family members were welcome.

Hosea (2003, 2006) used an ethnographic and participative approach in her study of six mothers and children painting together. The evidence produced by the positive findings of her research, which included video footage of the interactions followed by interviews with the women in her sample, provided a sound foundation on which further investigation could be based. Working in Cornwall I approached a local SureStart agency with a proposal for a painting group in the area they served. This was well received and in 2002 a mothers and children painting group came to be launched into a third environment.

Theoretical background

The theoretical background to this work is grounded in an interest in the relationship with the real, tangible mother as well as in aspects of unconscious fantasy which might be glimpsed through the media of art materials, imaginative play, myth and fairytales (Jung 1959; Von Franz 1970). Winnicott began as a paediatrician before becoming a psychoanalyst, and his emphasis on the interdependent nature of the mother-infant relationship as 'primary relatedness' seemed particularly relevant. With many other arts therapists we shared the feeling that the 'potential space' (Winnicott 1971) provided us with a creative working framework. As I was interested in the origin of the infant's sense of self, my dissertation reviewed psychoanalytic theories of child development from Freud (1912), Jung (1959), Klein (1932), Fordham (1985) and baby observation Bick (1964), noting how research was focusing in, ever closer, on the 'nursing couple': the mother and her baby. In my study, using the concept of the current, transference, projective and primordial levels which operate in groups (Foulkes 1964) I observed interactions between mothers and children using clay together (Hall 1991).

Stern (1985, 1990) introduced me to advances in ideas about infant development which were the result of the meeting of psychoanalytic theory and developmental psychology. The integration of these ideas was a major shift in the understanding of the nature of the mother-infant relationship. These developments stemmed from the influential work of Bruner (1986), a developmental psychologist who brought a natural history approach to human development, bringing prominence to the ways of thinking about mother-child relationships.

Psychoanalytic theory of infant development had long recognised the gravitas of an infant's early experience (Klein 1932; Winnicott 1971). Stern

(1985), Brazelton and Cramer (1990) and others were able to access previously unobserved details, recognising the nature of the first relationship as a 'working partnership'. Video playback and frame-by-frame analysis (Trevarthen *et al.* 1981), for example, made fleeting moments repeatable and revealed a dynamic relationship between two individuals interacting from the start. Very young babies were seen to be seeking active engagement, instigating exchanges themselves and not merely responding to their carer's signals. There was overwhelming visual evidence that infants wanted, and actively sought, social engagement and play, as well as good feeding experiences. What were described as 'now moments' and 'vitality affects' by Stern (1985) and Trevarthen (2001), and captured on video, were immediately recognised as important, while their full significance in the acquisition of speech and the development of thought came to be understood later.

Evidence of early mutual attunement seen on video aroused interest in observing the way babies and their caregivers begin to communicate with each other, even in the first hours after birth. The simple, instinctive patterns of behaviour were revealed. These develop, through reliance on tone of voice, rhythm and timing, into the 'proto conversations', which Trevarthen identified in many cultures and which he considers to be universal. Sluckin (1999) noticed that even the first, simplest, games, like 'peek-a-boo', which can be recognised as having what Wittgenstein termed 'emergent rules' are an essential precursor to language development(Cronen and Lang 1994). This also holds the potential for understanding and facilitating other aspects of communication in families and other areas of adult life. Babies were more competent and played a more active role than had been considered possible before through 'intersubjectivity': the quality of mutuality in a relationship between two 'subjects', rather than one 'subject' that acts and an 'object' that is acted upon.

Stern (1985) asserted that the infant's core self was present from birth or before. He saw no evidence of a state of fusion existing between a mother and her newly-born infant. This observation is in line with Jung's belief in the presence of a primal self from birth or before, a potential wholeness which holds the possibility of being realised through the lifelong process of individuation (1959). It is interesting to note that Fordham (1985) arrived at the idea of 'an original self ingrate, without phenomena' and also that Trevarthen (2001) identified 'intrinsic motive formation', which means that the baby is born already predisposed to relate and be sociable in ways that further its healthy development. These are all ideas that could be understood as evidence of an archetypal pattern at work.

In *The Motherhood Constellation* (1995), Stern looked at the ways in which therapeutic approaches operating from different theoretical starting points, cited as 'ports of entry', were able to achieve good outcomes for difficulties in early mother-baby relationships. They could be thought of as altering the representations mother and baby hold of each other, but by taking different routes. All involved a sensitive approach and required 'positive regard' for the mothers and fathers themselves. Stern also identified a 'good grandmother' transference, which reminded me of my relationship with the young women in the first mother and baby workshops and which I would recognise again in the SureStart painting group.

Bowlby's Attachment Theory (1988) was influential in providing a tool for gathering evidence about the long-term effects of different styles and qualities of maternal caregiving and relationship. Using video, interview techniques and psychological testing, the types of bond or attachment between mother and child were examined and categorised and the results over months and years analysed and recorded. Connections between impaired attachment and a mother's mental health problems, borderline personality, postnatal depression and also the child's exposure to different types of abuse, the affect of absent fathers, working mothers or extensive nursery care were calibrated (James 2003).

Three strands of investigation into early child development came together when the ideas of developmental psychologists and psychoanalytically-orientated therapists received endorsement from biochemical and neuro-biological research (Schore 1994). Gerhardt (2004) provides an account of the integration of the neurological aspects with the psychological implications. As a psychoanalytic psychotherapist with long experience in parenting work, she credits Schore (1994) as being instrumental in integrating aspects of brain, psychological and emotional development. Exposure to violence and neglect cause biochemical reactions which adversely affect brain development, whereas sensitive loving care, experienced in the early months, triggers the development of the baby's 'social brain' which starts after birth, and without which the potential for the development of empathy and many other abilities is impaired.

Aspects of these findings related directly to the arts therapies, as it appeared that connections within the brain that received stimulation through creative activity were strengthened, possibly even repaired. The gathering body of art therapy research reinforced my belief in the effectiveness of an approach which engages mothers and their children in the creative process together. In particular I was interested in evidence that supported the idea of art-making as an essential human activity (Mithen 1999; Dissanyake 2000).

The importance of the child's early experience, with a focus on attachment issues, has had an impact on clinical services where specific early years services have been set up. Government initiatives, such as SureStart, Home Start and others, demonstrated an awareness of the value of preventative work in strengthening the family's inner and outer resources. For example, the Solihull Approach, the result of collaboration between a child psychotherapist and health visitors, offers health professionals practical ways to help strengthen the families' own resources (Douglas 2002).

SureStart painting group

This group began with a pilot project. The mothers gave very positive feed-back. The children had enjoyed themselves and the local health visitors were enthusiastic. Since then, painting groups have taken place in both locations of SureStart North Cornwall, which covers a large area in which pockets of both rural and urban deprivation are to be found.

As anticipated, introducing the mother and child painting group into a new environment meant changes. Some of these were attributable to the SureStart ethos. In the current climate, the aim 'To strengthen bonding and to foster the growth of a healthy relationship between the mothers and their young children through creative work' ensured the continuity of my focus and was acceptable to SureStart guidelines. However, a specific 'evidence of need' in the community was required before we could begin. This was provided by local health visitors and parents who testified to the lack of specialised services for treating postnatal depression in the district.

As a result, closed, time-limited groups were planned for women suffering from postnatal depression, but who were not in acute crisis, and their children. Referrals were received from health visitors and other health workers. The women all shared a common diagnosis and this, I was aware, would allow a different dynamic to develop. For assessment and audit, my health visitor colleague, who had a special interest in the subject, used the Edinburgh Post Natal Depression Scale (EPND) which she completed with the women before and after participation in the group. Scores of 12 or higher, generally regarded as the point at which further intervention is recommended, was our agreed criterion for inclusion.

The more intense nature of a closed group proved to be beneficial for these mothers and children. The women wanted help as they were aware that damage was being done to their families and the quality of their lives. The hope of finding new ways of enjoying being with their children made them willing to risk engagement. Though an important talking time resurfaced in the SureStart painting groups, it could be sensed that some unspoken, perhaps unspeakable, issues still remained held in the art work, perhaps to be silently present in the moment when everyone looked at the paintings together, face-to-face with images, not people. A time that acknowledges that 'at the heart of every picture is the mystery that serves to remind the artist that "there is more to life than the immediate moment" ' (Pearce and Cronen 1980: 21).

Postnatal depression

Information about postnatal depression is now readily available (Shaw 2001; Mind 2006). The overriding effect of postnatal depression is an inability to cope with the huge life change which results from pregnancy and giving birth. These are risky processes in themselves. Whatever the outcome, the woman's life will never be the same again. To enter into this uncharted territory already burdened with unresolved issues can be quite devastating for the woman, and her family, and serious for the development of her baby. Socioeconomic stresses, understandably, have been shown to exacerbate the problems. The women who came to the group were in this state of mind. They were all highly individual but the women's personal stories shared a common theme of being stuck in some aspect of their lives, which they felt powerless to change. There was a sense that for them, at this time, the future had shut down. Untreated, it is known that this state of affairs can last for many years. However, the prognosis is not entirely negative, because research indicates that although while it continues, postnatal depression can hamper the building of the relationship between the mother and baby, even relatively simple interventions can make a difference in the quality of relationship, owing to the speed with which a baby will respond to a more friendly and receptive mother (Gerhardt 2004). Except in serious cases of bonding failure, which are rare, the downward spiral can be halted as a mother becomes more sensitive to her baby or child's needs, wishes and individual character (Robson and Kumar 1980).

Vignette of a typical SureStart painting group

A number of women with young children gather in a large room. Soon they have formed a rough circle on a sheet of blue polythene which has been spread on the floor and are engaged in an absorbing activity. The sound of their voices, which vary from low serious tones to loud laughter, rises and falls as they work. Bright flashes of colour appear as paint is transferred from bottle to palette to the paper, on which images are quickly forming. For the most part the women, having settled, remain in their own space, while the activity of the children ebbs and flows around them. Moments of close involvement between adult and child alternate with times when distance opens up between them. A little figure may break away, striking out boldly, before turning to look back to mother. Another, after circulating, will perhaps approach and enjoy a playful exchange with others. Sometimes a quiet moment of watching takes place or painting alone for awhile, before rejoining the main body of the group. Sometimes an adult leaves the protected area of blue to fetch something to satisfy an infant's needs from the area where bags and buggies are stored. The occasional flash of a camera evokes little response. Regularly, wet paintings are carried to other parts of the room where they can dry away from interference. Gradually, the appearance of the room changes and brightens, becoming more colourful as time passes. When painting time is over, the activity of the group shifts from the centre to the end of the room, for refreshments. Talk among the women, sitting on a low platform and cushions, is animated and at times becomes general. The children romp and play around them, coming in and out of the focus of conversation. As the ending approaches, energy levels drop, faces are wiped clean of paint and crumbs, nappies are changed and tired tumblers are comforted with hugs. Next, the day's paintings are laid out on the floor, to be looked at together and commented on. Finally, last week's art works come out of the big portfolio and are handed out to be taken home. When coats have been put on and buggies loaded up, calling out goodbyes to each other, the group disperses. Soon the clearing up is completed and the polythene folded away. After a short time of reflection for the three remaining adults, the door is shut and the room returns to its former state.

Clinical examples

Holly and Jack

It is often assumed that babies will be too young to benefit from a painting group and indeed, at the start, mothers themselves wonder if this is true. The experience of a teenage mother and baby illustrates involvement from the early days. Holly was 16 and living with her boyfriend's family in a tiny, overcrowded house, when she was introduced to the group with her son Jack, then 6 weeks old. Dominant relatives had taken over Jack's care and Holly had become withdrawn, hardly even touching him any more. The health visitor who made the referral was surprised at her passivity. Before the birth she was an assertive young woman and said she was happy to be pregnant.

During her first week in the group Holly seemed frozen and made no contact with anyone, but she watched and was able to attend to her baby's needs in peace. At the next session the baby slept and it was suggested that she might like to paint on her own. This appealed to her and over the next weeks she painted and took home simple images with beautiful colour combinations. Reluctant to miss her painting time when Jack was restless, she evolved a way of rocking him in his carrying seat with one hand while wielding her brush with the other. The glowing colours spread over the paper and her baby gazed at her as he fell asleep. Coming to sessions regularly, her lively and outgoing nature gradually reasserted itself. She became a lively member of the group, made friends and played with older toddlers and children. Jack was thriving. He was a handsome and responsive baby, who seemed to enjoy being passed around for extra cuddles. At 4 months of age Holly decided that Jack was old enough to start painting himself. She sat on the floor with legs apart, supporting him in front of her, encouraging him to feel paint which she put on paper before them. Jack, warmly enclosed in this way by his mother, became engrossed in moving his fingers in the sticky substance and the delicate little scrabbling lines which he left on the paper, which she greeted as his first paintings, became a valued possession. By the end of the 20 weeks Holly's confidence had returned, she had reconnected with her former social life and mother, father and baby were about to move into their own housing association accommodation.

Hannah and Leo

A baby with a less straightforward inheritance was Leo. His mother Hannah came with a high EPND score. Hannah had an easy, sociable manner which concealed complicated feelings about babies and dependence, the result of her own troubled childhood. A psychotic episode with hospital admission followed the birth of her first child and her ambivalence about her next pregnancy increased when the expected baby was a boy. While both children were well cared for and Hannah's decorative paintings had a style all their own, she hovered uncertainly between breast- and bottle-feeding and her underlying feelings were expressed in disquieting ways, such as her habit of leaving Leo on his own, lying flat on the cold, hard, floor while she went off to another part of the room.

Over time Hannah came to find the group congenial. She enjoyed the company and valued talking to another mother, to whom she felt close. She also confided in the SureStart health visitor during home visits, being able then to talk openly about her most personal concerns. In sessions Leo was good-natured and popular with the other children, and his first rolling over on the blue plastic was celebrated. He responded obligingly to Hannah's matter-of-fact approaches, as she made prints of his hands and feet. She did not talk to him much, but as he grew older she began to experiment with other ways of involving him. One of the most successful was placing him on his tummy, with paint spread out on paper within arm's reach, while she painted beside him. One day when the paint had been green, as she began to clean him up, I heard her say that he was 'like the Hulk'. Remembering how that mutant superhero transformed with uncontrollable rage, it felt as if that chance remark could be understood as an involuntary glimpse into a primitive inner world. Gradually, seeing them repeatedly together, it became clear that Leo was becoming more of an individual to his mother and serving less as the recipient of baleful projections. In the last weeks of the group Hannah, whose recent weight loss had released a burst of energy, devised a playful new method of painting, first with her son and later with other children, who clamoured for a turn. Bending over and gripping Leo round the middle, she swung him vigorously between her legs, while his outstretched fingers trailed in wet paint which was waiting on paper below them, and he chuckled uproariously. These were called 'swing paintings'. By varying the colours and the sweep of the swing, interesting results could be achieved, which were much admired. Leo and his mother were united in enjoyment of this wild activity. A photo taken around this time shows them sitting together on the floor, with her body curled protectively around him. At her follow-up interview Hannah said that she now 'loved Leo to bits' and indicated that she felt more confident about the future, for herself and her children. However realistically, we are aware that although substantial progress had been made, this was only a beginning. Hannah herself knew that it may not always be easy for her to access the help she may need to resist the temptation she sometimes felt, to run away or to self-medicate with drugs and alcohol. We very much regret that it is unlikely that long-term psychotherapy, which ideally we would recommend, will be available for Hannah in the area where she lives.

Faye and Robin

Robin was nearly 2 when he came to the group with his mother Faye. Although we soon discovered that he was a very active and agile child, she persisted in carrying him into the group in a baby seat, with a dummy in his mouth. Faye was very anxious to make a good impression. She had a bright fixed smile on her face and maintained that everything in her life was 'wonderful'. When it became obvious, even to her, that this was unconvincing, it then shifted to being hilariously amusing and 'crazy'. It was quite painful to listen to this and to watch her struggling to keep up the performance. It made it hard for others in the group to share their more tentative feelings.

At the start, painting time was not easy either, as it appeared that Faye was also determined that she and Robin were going to be the perfect mother-son painting duo. Keeping up a rousing commentary and with loud cries of 'Come on fella!' she tried to organise Robin and the art materials into cohesive action. Her expectations proved unrealistic; Robin joined in with this manic activity for a while, but then, craving more freedom, he went off to find other children. Faye's pursuit turned into a devilish winding-up game which she was never going to win. On our advice she took the opportunity of time and space to paint for herself. Later on, when she had found that she enjoyed this very much, Faye was joined by Robin. He had returned to see what she was doing and stayed to help. After that breakthrough mother and son would spend quite long periods of time harmoniously together. One could see that they shared a love of colour and texture. They most enjoyed working alongside each other on separate pieces of paper. They shared palettes, which gave a family resemblance to their images, though naturally, owing to their age difference, they were very different in form and content. This was the beginning of a change which allowed Faye to relax her relentless pursuit of unattainable perfection, which she herself related back to the critical and exacting mother of her own childhood. She realised that she did not have to convince people that she was 'super mum'. She said, 'I do not have to stay in my shiny shell.'

Sarah and Rosie

Rosie was almost 3 when she came to the group with her mother Sarah, a quiet young woman, with a pleasant though sad manner, and who seemed to have many regrets. She was a single parent, had chosen to live far from her family and had little local support. Rosie held back shyly at first, but soon felt at home in the group. She was friendly, showed interest in everyone and joined in rumbustious play with a boy of a similar age. Sarah had no difficulty in engaging Rosie with the art materials, but it soon became apparent that she felt overwhelmed by her daughter's demands and sheer energy and Rosie herself began to show a tyrannical side. She clearly found her mother giving attention to others very hard to bear. She also became angry when Sarah wanted to have time for herself, throwing tantrums, which Sarah dreaded. We learned that this was causing problems at home, as their financial survival depended upon Sarah looking after other children for part of the week. Sarah needed time to sort out her feelings but Rosie needed reassurance that her mother was not withdrawing from her.

In retrospect, it is possible to see the spontaneous repetition of this drama in the group every week, as a renegotiation of terms. Each session included time for Sarah to paint her private, introspective picture, which we encouraged her to defend from Rosie's attacks. Meanwhile the little girl, keeping an eye on her mother, painted and played with the other adults and children, being part of many positive interactions with all the different age groups, which Sarah equally was aware of. This did not always go smoothly. Sarah's own dependent feelings made progress slow, but gradually she began to have more idea of what she wanted from life and the time when they came together to do art work in the group took on a joyous quality. In particular they evolved one special technique, admired by all and which gave them shared enjoyment. Sarah covered the soles of Rosie's feet with thick paint and then, kneeling, lifted her up higher than she could jump, bringing her down again so that an imprint was made on the paper where she landed. This was repeated, varying the colours until they were both satisfied with the result. This was called 'dancing feet'. Some of the footprints were later cut out and I am told that Sarah stuck them round a doorway in their home to good effect.

Conclusion

In this chapter I have traced my interest in an art therapy approach to working with mothers and young children which has stretched over two decades. It tells the story of how what in the beginning stemmed from an intuitive feeling about the importance of the mother-child relationship and the wish to explore it through a primarily non-verbal modality of images, gathered theoretical underpinning which gradually revealed the depth and profundity of the ideas beneath the surface of its simple form.

The implications of research from developmental psychology, psychoanalytically-orientated therapies, biochemistry and neurobiology continue to pursue their multidimensional study of the beginnings of human beings. This can now be seen to extend into domains that not long ago appeared to be unrelated areas of inquiry. Three writers I would recommend and who have taken me forward are Hobson, *The Cradle of Thought* (2004), with ideas about the development of the ability to think and to arrive at a theory of mind; Mithen, *The Pre-History of the Mind* (1999), which explores the concept of cognitive fluidity; and Damasio, *The Feeling of What Happens* (2000), which is concerned with the origin of consciousness. The significance of their ideas has made an impression on me which will influence my work in the future.

Acknowledgements

The process of writing has brought vividly to mind the many people who have shared and supported my work. That I owe enormous gratitude to my colleagues, the other art therapists, health visitors and clinical psychologist, will have become clear as the narrative unfolded. They have all informed my thinking and practice from their individual perspectives. I have been influenced by their different backgrounds and trainings, while retaining my basic art therapy identity.

I should like specifically to acknowledge the presence in this chapter of the art therapists, Julia Ryde and Hilary Hosea, and health visitors, Anne Pringle, Sharon Fielder and Vicky Rodgers, who have been my companions in the various stages of the work. I would like to thank Joy Schaverien, who supervised my MA and also Anne Gilespie and Fiona Foster, my fellow students on that course, for taking me to a memorable lecture by Daniel Stern. Finally, I want to acknowledge my gratitude to Andy Sluckin, Clinical Psychologist, whose generous help, encouragement and unswerving belief in the power of the visual image made him a most rewarding working partner.

Finally, I would like to remember all the participants of the mother and baby painting workshops and painting groups, and also my own children and grandchildren who never cease to amaze me.

References

Bick, E. (1964) Notes on infant observation in psychoanalytic training, *International Journal of Psycho-Analysis*, 45: 558–66.

Biemans, H. (1990) Video Home Training: theory, method and organisation of SPIN, in J. Kool (ed.) *Innovative Institutions*. Ryswijk, Netherlands: Ministry of Welfare, Health and Culture.

Bowlby, J. (1988) *A Secure Base: Clinical Applications of Attachment Theory*. London: Routledge.

Brazelton, T.B. and Cramer, B.G, (1990) *The Earliest Relationship: Parents, Infants and the Drama of Early Attachment*. Cambridge, MA: Perseus Books.

Bruner, J.S. (1986) *Actual Minds, Possible Worlds*. Cambridge, MA: Harvard University Press.

Cronen, V. and Lang, P. (1994) Language and action: Wittgenstein and Dewey in the practice of therapy and consultation, *Human Systems: The Journal of Systemic Consultation and Management*, 5: 43.

Damasio, A. (2000) *The Feeling of What Happens: Body, Emotion and the Making of Consciousness*. London: Vintage.

Dissanyake, E. (2000) *Art and Intimacy: How the Arts Began*. Seattle, WA: University of Washington Press.

Douglas, H. (2002) *Solihull Resource Pack*. Unpublished.

Fordham, M. (1985) *Explorations into the Self*. London: Academic Press.

Foulkes, S.H. (1964) *Therapeutic Group Analysis*. London: Karnac.

Fraiberg, S. (1980) *Clinical Studies in Infant Mental-Health: The First Year of Life*. London: Tavistock.

Freud, S. (1912) *The Dynamics of Transference*, Standard Edition, vol. 12. London: Hogarth.

Gerhardt, S. (2004) *Why Love Matters: How Affection Shapes a Baby's Brain*. Hove: Brunner Routledge.

Hall, P. (1991) Exploring the mother-child relationship: an art therapy workshop, unpublished art therapy MA dissertation, University of Hertfordshire, St Albans.

Hall, P. (1997) *Phantastic Families: Art Therapy and Community Development*. Champernowne Trust Summer Course Year Book, private publication.

Hobson, P. (2004) *The Cradle of Thought: Exploring the Origins of Thinking*. London: Pan Macmillan.

Hosea, H. (2003) The Brush's Footmarks: parents and infants paint together in a small community art therapy group, unpublished art psychotherapy MA dissertation, Goldsmiths College, University of London.

Hosea, H. (2006) 'The Brush's Footmarks': parents and infants paint together in a small Ccmmunity art therapy group, *The International Journal of Art Therapy: Inscape* 11(2): 69–79.

James, O. (2003) *They F*** You Up: How to Survive Family Life*. London: Bloomsbury.

Jung, C.G. (1959) *The Archetypes and the Collective Unconscious, Collected Works*, 9 Part 1. London: Routledge.

Klein, M. (1932) *The Psychoanalysis of Children*. London: Hogarth.

Mind (2006) Out of the blue: understanding postnatal depression: Mind week theme 2006, motherhood and depression, www.mind.org.uk.

Mithen, S. (1999) *The Prehistory of the Mind: The Cognitive Origins of Art and Science*. London: Thames & Hudson.

Murray, L. (2005) *The Social Baby*. London: CP Publishing.

Pearce, B. and Cronen, V. (1980) *Communication, Action and Meaning: The Creation of Social Realities*. New York: Praeger.

Robson, K.M. and Kumar, R. (1980) Delayed onset of maternal affection, *British Journal of Psychology*, 136: 347–53.

Schore, A. (1994) *Affect Regulation and the Origin of the Self*. Hillsdale, NJ: Lawrence Erlbaum.

Shaw, F. (2001) *Out of Me: The Story of a Postnatal Breakdown*. London: Virago.

Sluckin, A. (1999) Humans are conversational from birth: systemic therapy, developmental psychology and the artistic metaphor, *Human Systems: The Journal of Systemic Consultation and Management*, 10(1).

Stern, D. (1985) *The Interpersonal World of the Infant: A View from Psychoanalysis and Developmental Psychology*. London: Karnac.

Stern, D. (1990) Lecture given at the Middlesex Hospital, London.

Stern, D. (1995) *The Motherhood Constellation: a Unified View of Parent-Infant Psychotherapy*. New York: Basic Books.

Trevarthen, C. (2001) Intrinsic motives for companionship in understanding: their origin, development and significance for infant mental health, *Infant Mental Health Journal*, 22(1): 2.

Trevarthen, C., Murray, L. and Hubley, P. (1981) Psychology of infants, in J. Davis and J. Dobbing (eds) *Scientific Foundation of Clinical Paediatrics*. London: Heinemann Medical Books.

Von Franz, M.L. (1970) *The Interpretation of Fairy Tales*. Dallas, TX: Spring.

Winnicott, D.W. (1971) *Playing and Reality*. Harmondsworth: Penguin.

Chapter 2

Attachment patterns through the generations: internal and external homes

Frances O'Brien

Introduction

Early relational trauma continues to misshape attachment long after the original trauma and the relationships involved in it may have ceased to exist, with consequences throughout the infant's future life. In writing about three generations of a family whose lives have been blighted by trauma related to insecure attachments, I describe the creative ways the art psychotherapy process has been used to find meaning through the art of the child and the verbal images of his grandmother who looked after him and whom I saw simultaneously. Working with both the child and his grandmother, the therapeutic goal was to change the attachment pattern of both and intervene in the transgenerational transmission of disorganised attachments.

I have written previously (O'Brien 2004) about early development and how the brain actually takes shape through relationship. I would now like to focus on attachment: how the infant becomes attached to the parents, and how insecurity can develop when parents are unable to foster healthy attachment. I will briefly summarise how neuroscience has provided understanding of how experience is processed in early life and how memory is burned into the developing limbic system and continues to effect expectations and relationships throughout life.

Children and their families who are experiencing difficulties that affect their emotional, behavioural, educational or social well-being are referred through general practitioners (GPs), social services and others to Child and Adolescent Mental Health Service (CAMHS) teams within the National Health Service (NHS). Their difficulties may be specific and effect only one child, or may be more pervasive and involve the functioning of the whole family. This chapter concerns one family, but other families have similar experiences.

Within CAMHS, it is the child who is referred but parents, siblings and other involved adults are also seen. The child who is the subject of this chapter had attended art psychotherapy for some time while a colleague saw his grandmother. Changes within the team led to loss of support for the grandmother, but anxiety developed within social services and school as difficulties were noted concerning her parenting ability. Although I was aware that working at depth with two people in the same family is usually considered inappropriate within psychodynamic psychotherapy, as no other clinician was available to work with the grandmother I started working weekly with her. In writing about both I am weaving the story of my work, moving from one to the other as the story emerges, and describing theory as the container that made our experience meaningful.

Relational trauma

Case (2005) describes the crucial role parents play in creating an environment in which the baby's emotional life is reflected on by them to find meaning, thus promoting the development of mind in the baby. I use Schore (1994, 2003), Gerhardt (2004) and Wilkinson (2006) to help me explain the quite complex information gathered from research into developmental brain activity. Attachment styles are secure or insecure depending on early and current life experiences. Insecure attachments may be divided into avoidant, anxious or disorganised. Schore (2003) suggests that the complex disorganised/disoriented attachment pattern is found most often in infants who are abused or neglected and he reminds us that this is associated with severe difficulties in stress management and dissociative behaviour throughout life.

Schore (2003) explains that the abusive caregiver repeatedly frightens her infant[1] and is unable to protect him from the frightening behaviour of others. As this caregiver has probably not experienced attachment to her own mother, she does not know how to play with her infant and cannot 'read' or understand his expression of stress. She may experience it inappropriately and may respond angrily, intrusively or not at all. She is unable to help her infant regain his sense of continuity and increases his stress by heightening emotional distress through abuse or deepening his despair by neglecting his needs, causing him to dissociate to escape the pain of abandonment. The infant cannot transform this distress alone, he needs help to regulate his emotions. If recovery and repair are not available to the infant his heightened stress will continue for extended periods of time, becoming longer and with less reason for each episode of distress. Schore reminds us that this stress is 'accompanied by severe alterations in the biochemistry of the immature brain, especially in areas associated with the development of the child's coping capacities' (2003: 181). We know that the response to traumatic experience in later life has a poorer outcome if the initial attachment is insecure (Pynoos *et al.* 1996).

---

1   I use the pronoun 'her' for the parent and 'his' for the child throughout.

Early history

I will briefly introduce the family history before returning to the literature to provide understanding of its ongoing effect. The child, whom I call Peter, was 9 years old and on the point of being excluded from school when he started art psychotherapy. His mother had abandoned him after making many threats and attempts to gain respite by sending him to stay with different aunts, who also had insecure attachment difficulties. He was encapsulated in an isolated world where he was attached to no one. He desperately wanted love, but was unable to feel secure, having been abandoned several times previously, and was now in the care of his grandmother whose insecure attachment patterns resonated with his own.

The grandmother, whom I call Pearl, was in her early 50s. She was sexually abused by her father and neglected by her mother throughout her childhood. She was raped at 14 by an older man and had her first daughter at 15. She lived in a mother and baby residential home for two years before marrying the man who raped her. Her experience of this and of life with her subsequent five children born at yearly intervals, was of isolation, violence and ridicule. She was unsupported and had little idea of what a baby might need. We can be fairly certain that her children also had a disorganised attachment pattern, and there was some suspicion that their father may have sexually abused their daughters. Peter's mother is Pearl's fourth child. Initially he lived alone with his mother. When he was 3 she married and had two daughters. She and her husband rejected Peter. Her sisters looked after him for a while, but his behaviour expressed his painful loss and he was left in care at age 8. At this point his grandmother, who saw in him similarities to herself as a child, took him in, hoping she could help his life turn out differently.

Pearl had loved her own children and wanted to care for them in ways she had not experienced, but she did not know how. She had no relationship with her own mother who she felt had betrayed and neglected her and colluded in her sexual abuse. She had been physically and sexually abused, first by her father and then by both her husbands. She had fallen out with all her children as they reached maturity and during the early years of therapy she had little contact with them. At times of stress, when Peter did not comply with her wishes, she was unable to be certain that her grandson was not her abuser, and she responded to his developing masculine traits with fear and threats of abandonment. Pearl was quite unable to help him learn how to resolve difficulties or conflict in his relationships. Mollon (2001) tells us that what characterises healthy relationships is a pattern of re-establishing attunement after it has been lost. He discusses the disruption and repair managed by the good-enough caregiver where the carer has the capacity to monitor and regulate her own affect, especially negative affect. Gerhardt (2004) also emphasises this, suggesting that rupture and repair are the key to secure relationships. In the early years of therapy there was often an aroused quality to Peter's and Pearl's play in the waiting room, which suggested that Pearl was unable to provide appropriate boundaries or to know how to regulate her own or Peter's emotional state. Throughout the therapy it often seemed that the capacity for regulation or repair was missing.

The importance of relationship

Infants are born with the brain in a receptive state to develop fully. The genome is instrumental in forming the brain up until birth, it continues to develop throughout infancy and on into childhood and even into adulthood (Carter 1998; Wilkinson 2006). Trevarthen (1995) reminds us that the continuing development is dependent on relationship with interested adults rather than on a set of instructions contained within the genetic code. How others relate to the infant is of paramount importance. This relating prunes or retards development of neural pathways when relations are impoverished or abusive, but in secure attachment relationships neural pathways grow and form clusters that become memory, enabling the development of thinking and of the mind.

From the earliest stage in life, babies interact with their environment, both initiating and responding to the voice, touch and face of interested others. The securely attached infant is related to with looking at and looking away; with greeting, laughing and making sounds; with turn-taking, attention and responsiveness. The infant will gradually know that his need to be fed, warm and dry will usually be met, and that play feels nice and he is not left alone for long periods. The insecure child has no such consistent experience. He may be neglected for long periods or be expected to attune to his parents' needs. Teicher (2000: 54) wrote, 'We know now that our genes provide the foundation and overall structure of our brain, but that its myriad connections are sculpted and moulded by experience.' Disturbingly, he also informs us that 'maltreatment is a chisel that shapes a brain to contend with strife, but at the cost of deep, enduring wounds. Childhood abuse isn't something you get over, it is an evil that we must acknowledge and confront . . .' (p. 67). Teicher explains, 'the trauma of abuse induces a cascade of effects, including changes in hormones and neurotransmitters that mediate development of vulnerable brain regions' (p. 54). Abuse of all sorts, including psychological abuse and neglect, as well as the more visible sexual and physical abuse, cause what Teicher terms 'enduring negative effects on brain development' (p. 51), with specific kinds of brain abnormalities seen in patients who were abused as children.

Conscious and unconscious memory

Before the left hemisphere, with its language and its structure of time and place, has fully developed at around the age of 3, infant memories are held in the process-dominated, emotional, limbic and cortical areas of the developing right hemisphere. The infant uses his senses to gain information about his environment, and this becomes a template for future understanding of the world and other people. Wilkinson (2005: 486) reiterates Schore's explanation:

> when trauma with its associated fight, flight and freeze responses has been experienced in the context of the earliest attachment relationship, then it becomes burned into the developing limbic and autonomic systems of the early maturing right brain . . . [it becomes] part of implicit memory, and [leads to] enduring structural changes that produce inefficient stress-coping mechanisms.

Because these memories are stored before the hippocampus lays down conscious long-term memories (Carter 1998) and before speech has developed, there is no conscious memory of the fear and depression of relational trauma. This does not mean that the traumatised child is not continually effected by these experiences in future relationships. Wilkinson (2005: 487) describes early memory as:

> implicit, unconscious, emotional and inaccessible, arising out of right hemisphere processing of information, and is on line from birth. It stores acquired skills, conditioned responses and emotional responses that at an unconscious level manifest themselves in the person's most fundamental ways of being and behaving.

The difficulty in accessing memories laid down at this time is apparent; there is no attached verbal narrative and as memories are known implicitly, but not explicitly, they take time and patience to reach.

We are reminded by Turnbull and Solms (2003) that conscious and unconscious remembering are entirely different, and that memory traces are activated without a corresponding conscious narrative being available. Memories might manifest themselves in many ways, somatically, behaviourally and emotionally. They will be present in all relationships, often playing their part destructively, sabotaging future attempts to gain love. Understanding this is key for the art psychotherapist as art work is produced and feelings evoked that appear to have no meaning and are full of pain. These states reflect the earliest experience of relating. Art psychotherapy processes contain clues about what has happened. Memory that cannot be brought to mind consciously is apparent in the unconscious communication during the therapeutic process.

The patterns of fear that become established in response to emotional arousal are seen in the child in therapy who cannot speak, but whose art work betrays his retreat from relating. Patterns seen in practice may involve paints, mixed and spread over hands, paper and table in ways that feel hard to contain; clay and sand are used similarly. Constructing an image is difficult to even conceive of – the only process available at this stage is the bodily felt chaos of dissociated feelings in the making of sloppy mixtures or disconnected marks. This seems to reflect the lack of structure in the mind when relationships have been abusive; the child attempts to keep safe by using activity to ensure thinking cannot happen. Adult patients may not express themselves so graphically, but similar fragmentation and dissociation may be present. Wilkinson (2005) reminds us that at this time the therapist does not engage with the anxiety state or impulsive hyperactivity of the child, but maintains calmness, lowering rather than raising the voice and staying emotionally attached so as to help regulate the child's emotional arousal and keep him in the relationship of 'now' rather than the bodily felt experience of 'then'.

Therapists may experience countertransference to the dissociated child with feelings of being overwhelmed by chaos, loss of skill and disconnectedness during the apparently mindless play brought to therapy. There are clues within the play that can be seen as metaphors for the original experience, but there is no intended communication because the experience is not in the more accessible parts of the mind; it is a playing out of early experience or implicit memory. The art process is a right-brain activity, it accesses the right hemisphere's emotional memory of abuse and neglect; at the same time the relationship with the therapist activates the left hemisphere. Words are found by the therapist to make meaning, gradually integrating left and right hemispheres and unifying the explicit construction of a narrative that accompanies the implicitly emotional experience of 'making' in art psychotherapy.

I have been considering the effects of early relationship and how this is carried forward into the life of the child and subsequently to the life of the adult. What has happened in the earliest relationship becomes indelibly inscribed in the mind, shaping and organising how the person will continue to attempt to make sense of all further experiences. These attachment patterns are transmitted through the generations, as parents use their own experience as a template for parenting their children.

I will now turn to clinical sessions to show how this theory helped me understand Peter's communications.

Early sessions

Peter came into art psychotherapy when he was 9 years old. I worked with him individually until he was 16 and established a strong therapeutic relationship with him. Initially Peter found it very hard to be in relationship with me. He believed that I would repeat his experience of rejection and was hypervigilant and hyperactive. He tried to control me by giving orders and getting angry when they were not carried out. Gradually he relaxed and used the sessions differently.

The art room is large and bright with windows along one wall with a door to the garden at the end of the room and a carpet on the floor. Tables and storage cabinets provide working space and the sink and sand box are easy to reach. There are large cupboards, filled with paints and modelling materials which can be accessed at any time. In early sessions Peter often pulled the box of sand to the centre of the room and added water. As the sand became saturated it gradually overflowed, spreading around him and leaking onto the carpet. One day Peter decided to add brown paint to the mixture. His activity became more impulsive and insistent and I knew I had little chance of stopping him. He squirted copious amounts of brown paint into the sand; then, filling his mouth with saliva, he loudly expelled spit into the sand. He added more and I watched with feelings of disgust as he spread it over his hands and arms. I began to feel contaminated as he told me that he wanted to put it on my arms too. He wanted to show me just how he felt by concretely enacting it and I could envisage how his inner world was contaminated and poisoned. I wanted to convey that I would not be spoiled by his mess and could tolerate it. By not wanting him to see my revulsion, or to experience my rejection of what he did, I began to understand his painful experience of rejection, of not being nice enough for his mother to want him. He attempted to keep the mixture contained by spreading it on the table but wet sloppy sand fell to the floor. He put it into trays, but somehow it fell over the sides.

Although he provided such a clear picture of an inner world with no structure or boundaries, Peter was unable to know consciously what he felt. He was expressing implicit memory, a trace of early relating that felt toxic. I discovered later that his recent contact with his mother had been distressing. She did not come to see him when arranged and would not talk to him on the phone. She did not want to be informed when he ran away from his grandmother unless he had been missing for more than 24 hours. She went on an expensive holiday with his half-sisters but said she had no money to provide for his needs. She angrily demanded that his grandmother put him into care as he was too difficult to manage.

Psychic pain expressed in tiny amounts through images

Alvarez (1992: 153) describes how the abused child may need to remember in 'a million tiny integrations' and that unwanted feelings might need to be contained for the patient for long periods. Although Peter resisted talking about his painful experience, he described it in his use of materials, and seemed to know that if he allowed a flood he could be overwhelmed. He made dams of clay and sand that were put into trays to retain water; he instinctively knew that releasing that which was not conscious must be done slowly. He put small 'houses' in the end of the tray and made little breaches in the clay dam, watching as the water slowly saturated the dry sand. If it came through too fast he rushed to stem the flow, mindful to make sure his houses at the end were safe. Terr (1996) describes how children become walled off from intimate relationships by their abusive experiences. Instead of the confidence of knowing that others are interested in them and will provide food, comfort, warmth and love, they may repress desire for this and develop a second skin of self-dependency and an omnipotent belief that they can be self-sufficient.

Gradually the images changed. Peter no longer added water to the sand but pushed it to one end in the box. He tunnelled into it, using broken pieces of wood or plastic to shore up the soft and collapsing sand. The images reminded me of searching inside his mother's body, repeatedly making passages through sand that was fragile and easily fell down, like his relationship with mother. When it did hold its shape he delighted in the canals made by pushing his hand and arm through the sand, being 'born' into my view and excitedly asking if I could see him. I wondered what his mother's first response had been to him. Was she pleased to see him and delighted in his birth? It seemed that this experience was needed in therapy.

Peter made mounds of sand on the floor, circular with a dark centre, a breast like image with a nipple in the middle, made by placing a round brown bowl of water into the peak of the sand. This sand-image seemed like a container to hold his longing for a mother. He made a road and used the baby cars to explore this shape, every week returning to make another. He painted lines to show the way from the edge to the centre; he lay on the floor, driving around the breast, exploring and finding 'food' in it. He parked his cars, nestling at the edge, and seemed to be moving psychically from the unformed internal space of the womb to the external nurture of the breast.

Containment

In the early stage of his therapy, Peter's communication was about the chaos of his internal world. Schaverien (1992) speaks of the picture made in the presence of the therapist; she suggests that the edge of the paper creates a boundary that 'permits potentially unmanageable images to be contained' (p. 71). The early images made by Peter used the edges of the room as their boundary, the pictures had no structure, and his inner world seemed unformed. Schaverien tells us that when an image is made within a therapeutic relationship, 'the transference to the therapist is likely to be woven into the picture' (p. 127). Peter's changing image shows his developmental needs being met in therapy, probably for the first time. It was still too dangerous to show his anger that the breast was withheld but he began to be able to show his love and desire for the breast, and to have hope that he too could be loved.

Peter made secluded spaces constructed of paper and furniture so that he could lie down inside and ask me to tell him stories. They were dark and warm and he placed cushions inside. A children's tale would spring to mind, and I sat outside his den as he lay still and attentive inside, listening to stories that helped him to make sense of his feelings and gave him a structure for his own story. Children may deliberately suppress, or unconsciously repress, memory. They may dissociate, using a sort of self-hypnosis in which they fail to register or take in memory of their trauma. They may let the memories slip away by displacing their attention onto something less awful (Terr 1996).

Peter's awareness of his experience was lost to his mind; he needed to construct a narrative but he could not find a direct route to access it. He made several blackboard images, carefully constructed with brushes and pots like an artist's easel standing securely on its tripod, a blank canvas or little sculpture, a space for his transference to be placed, his story written or a window into other children's work.

Points of change

A house was started soon after beginning therapy. It was modified through-out, sometimes months elapsing between periods of work on it and finally left a little unfinished. A new home on wheels was built during the ending period and carried home gleefully. Each sequence of change had its own conclusions and the house encapsulated the alterations in Peter's inner world.

The first house seemed a pitiful expression of a home. It had neither shelter nor comfort. It was shaped like a footprint. At one end was a curved wall, bent over slightly at the top to make the bedroom. At the other end was a wood and wire arch. In the middle, a settee was placed, with a twig acting as a tree beside it. Peter wanted to make a strong structure but used soft paper straws and soft wire in the clay floor that seemed to weaken rather than strengthen it. The house was placed on a pedestal, shaped like a column of ancient architecture; it conveyed desirability and importance but made the home unstable and impossible to reach. Schaverien (1992) speaks of pictures being made as a substitute for something desired but unobtainable; this image was initially an unconscious plea for home and mother but the model in his mind was bleak, cold and perilous.

Peter became dissatisfied with a home of such paucity and insecurity; he dismantled it. He told me the owner had lived there for three years (the same duration that Peter had been in therapy) and wanted change. Peter's inner world was changing, his isolation was less and he began to symbolise relationship with the use of animals.

He rebuilt the structure. The pedestal was removed and the floor placed onto a sheet of hardboard, symbolically more secure and grounded. He built new and stronger walls. He made a fence around the outside and a new aliveness became apparent in him as he placed reptiles underneath the house, domestic animals nearby, wild animals further away. Although the house was quite small, there was a feeling of space. Case (2005) writes of the many ways animals are used by children in therapy. She explores the meaning they have as expressions of the self or other and describes ways children may process experience through them.

I understood that Peter was deepening his access to his unconscious and to me through placing the animals in relation to the house. Reptiles are cold-blooded creatures; while underground no rays of the sun can warm them, corresponding to the coldness of his emotions that his mother could not warm. Could he have known that the most primitive part of the brain, controlling the autonomic nervous system which keeps heartbeat, breathing, digestion and other involuntary life supports active and is responsible for the flight and fight reflex is colloquially known as the 'reptillian brain'? Not in words, but the process of therapy throws up an intuitive knowing that is creative in its communication. As Peter's need for fight and flight diminished his use of reptiles disappeared.

Peter's attachment needs were expressed through animals. When he was still in primary school he would wander away from home to the fields where the horses grazed. He excitedly told me about foals born there, and for a period enacted being a horse during therapy sessions. He made a bridle for himself and, on all fours, he pranced and kicked and neighed, behaving like a wild horse. He had taken on the persona of the horse, moving and identifying himself with it. He wanted me to hold the bridle and calm his frightened neighing until, like a young horse, he was schooled to become a tame and useful animal in a peaceful pastoral scene. He could not ask me to hold him for himself, but could ask that the horse be soothed and held. Case (2005) describes troubled children taking on the identity of an animal, perhaps hoping to increase attachment through this. Within his model Peter placed horses and foals, cows and calves, donkeys and goats in the garden. These mother and infant pairs remained important throughout the early years. Initially he kept a cow and calf in his drawer in the therapy room. He checked them every session until they joined the other animals by his house. For many years, he also kept a cow and calf model on the floor of his bedroom at home. It seemed that they symbolised a positive transference, enabling him to hold me in mind when at home, and to experience maternal warmth and his longing for relationship while in sessions.

The wilder animals such as giraffe, lion and bear stood further away from the house. Sometimes these seemed to be protective; to keep danger outside, to patrol the boundary and ensure nothing got through to the vulnerable inside. Sometimes they seemed more like parts of himself: wild; impulsive and uncontrolled, dangerous and unpredictable and reflecting his own tendencies, which were eventually diagnosed as attention-deficit hyperactivity disorder (ADHD). The wildness might also denote the unpredictability he felt in relation to his experience of people in his life and his actual or imagined effect on them. He was experienced as so wild by his mother that she rejected him, and attempted to make his grandmother reject him too.

A containing 'electric' fence was carefully constructed to create a safe boundary that could not be penetrated. It surrounded all and included a gate that opened. Peter needed to control his environment. He wanted a strong barrier around himself so that his grandmother's chaotic attachment pattern would not impinge too much and his mother and stepfather could not hurt him. In the transference he attempted to control the flow of interpretation, keeping it to a minimum but choosing sometimes to sit on the edge of the table to listen to what I might say. Our relating was almost wholly through the non-verbal interaction of attunement, gesture and projection similar to the pre-verbal child and his parent. Verbal interpretation was often blocked but enough was understood through non-verbal communication to create a feeling of warmth, reflected in the order and care in his model. The original house had become incorporated into an entirely different structure. As structure developed in the artwork meaning became available, giving structure in which to develop a narrative.

Simultaneous psychotherapy

Simultaneous therapy with carers is discussed by Chazan (2003). She explores how clinicians frequently embark on this hidden part of the work with children and families without discussing it explicitly in the literature. In addition to art psychotherapy with Peter, Pearl also attended weekly, seeing me for verbal psychotherapy on her own. Pearl talked about her experience of childhood and her care of Peter. I imagined her as a small and confused child who was isolated and neglected and who escaped from reality by living in a tiny part of herself that played in the park or street and who was always happy and smiling. It is almost impossible to describe Pearl's family boundaries because they are so tangled. Pearl herself could not unravel them, but thought they were normal. She felt confused but attributed this to others telling her lies. It was many months before we both began to understand who was who. Her father was apparently married to her mother, but he was also the second husband of her grandmother; he was the brother of her grandmother's first husband, and Pearl's mother was his niece. This demonstrates the chaos of Pearl's world. Pearl's father was also her great uncle, and her step-grandfather. Pearl's grandmother lived with Pearl and her parents until she died when Pearl was 4. Pearl spoke of her with affection, and felt favoured by her. She had memories of the family splits between her grandmother and mother and spoke of her own animosity to her mother.

Her father had served a prison sentence for sexually abusing one of his daughters from his first marriage, but no one seemed to be concerned that he might abuse another daughter. Pearl described the neglect and abuse of her early life and her feeling that no one knew or cared about what was happening to her. The 'welfare officer' told her that she should be grateful to have a father and her mother told her to stay out of the house when he was at home alone. If she got home before her mother, her father was awaiting her. She would escape through a toilet window and stay on the streets. She wondered why other children had to go home for tea. Her memory of her childhood was patchy; she seemed to have grown up unaware of how or why anything happened. Her world was frightening and unpredictable and she attempted to reduce her fears by keeping everything out of mind. At 14 she became pregnant by an older man whose sister had befriended her. She knew so little about her body that she had no notion of her situation until her mother saw her changing shape. Even then she was too afraid to ask questions and did not understand the attempted home abortion, or why her mother took her to the police, or her subsequent custody in what she thought was a remand home. She felt constantly punished and confused about why she was 'bad'. Terr (1996) describes how trauma is split away from awareness, so that the 'good' part of the self has no knowledge of the bad experiences held within the 'bad' part they feel themselves to be.

She married the man who had raped her. He beat her and divorced her after the birth of her sixth child. Then she married a man who had seemed kind but who also beat her, hitting her so hard that she was frequently knocked across the room and over furniture. The physical injuries she sustained at this time continued into the present, making her subject to ongoing pain. He insisted the children were all brought into the room to witness their mother's beating and locked her in the coal shed to punish her. It is against this background that Pearl attempted to care for six children. She wanted to keep them as playthings that would be safe and would comfort her, but she was unable to tolerate their attempts to separate. She divorced when her children were adolescent and they left her. Her fragile attachments and difficult relationships continued during the early part of therapy.

The therapeutic relationship gave a foundation on which thinking and trusting could begin. Pearl was able to describe the sexual and emotional abuse and to realise that it really happened. She was able to look at her ways of relating to Peter and tried to separate him from her inner world of abuse. Gradually Pearl's developing feeling of safety and of being understood and held for the first time meant that she was less destructive in her relationships. She reconnected with her family and developed a warm relationship with a half-sister and with one of her sons, although unstable relationships continued with her daughters.

Containment was an essential element of Pearl's therapy. When there were breaks an upsurge in feelings of fear and emotional turmoil erupted. In my absence, social services were often contacted and threats of abandonment made to Peter. Pearl's ability to trust anyone was negligible; she looked for support but escalated anxiety instead of being able to seek containment. When unsupported she retreated into a world where fear was dominant; this was quickly followed by dissociation. It seemed uncertain that she was conscious of her threats and retreats from Peter when she reconnected with therapy as she reported incidents that confused her and seemed to have no memory of what she had done.

I continued seeing Pearl throughout Peter's therapy. She spoke of her own life and through her therapeutic relationship, she was able to modify her experience of attachment, and through this, of Peter's attachment. She understood her relationship with Peter in ways appropriate to their current experience rather than as a repeated experience of her own past. Pearl's story was described intermittently, alongside her attempts to understand Peter's behaviour; Peter's therapy continued simultaneously and he developed a stronger sense of his own agency. Knowing that I saw his grandmother seemed to give him added safety, and continuing to work deeply with both helped to stabilise their relationship.

Transgenerational transmission of disorganised attachment patterns

When there is a family history of insecure disorganised/disoriented attachment patterns, dissociation can become a way of coping for both adult and child. The ability to think when aroused emotionally is lost, with consequent difficulty in regulating or repairing disrupted relationships. Disorganised attachment, like all attachment patterns, continues through the generations, leading to each new mother finding it hard to attach to her baby. Consequently the baby has difficulty with all future attachments, including her own babies when the time comes. Knox (2003) tells us that the parent's internal world is the formative influence affecting the child's pattern of attachment; Brisch (2002) concurs, stating that the mental structure of parents, their state of mind, effects the attachment quality of their children. Steele and Steele (1994) examined the transgenerational transmission of attachment patterns and found that while infants construct separate attachment relationships with each parent, if either parent had dismissing, preoccupied or unresolved attachment patterns, the infant displayed insecure-avoidant, insecure-ambivalent or disorganised attachment patterns. This evidence points towards the benefit of teams supporting work with parents to address their own early life trauma in order to address the attachment difficulties of their children.

Internal changes found and expressed through relating

Alongside the building of Peter's house other activities took place over equally long periods of time. These had the quality of unbearable disconnectedness but, when reflected on as a whole, it can be seen that they were important factors in Peter's development. We played games of football and 'ice' hockey. Peter made rules which were seldom kept and played out his fantasy of being a great sportsman, making extravagant saves and throwing himself across the room as he dived for the ball. The hard contact with the floor seemed to give an added sense of his own body being real and of his skin containing and holding him together. It evoked a feeling of father in me, the father who could experience him as fun, physical and male.

Pretend cooking during sessions happened with ovens made from drawers and clay used to make loaves. Peter made such a convincing play that we had to take care not to get burnt and I could almost smell the bread! My countertransference brought to mind my own grandmother's kitchen and the delicious cakes she made and the feelings of belonging invoked in helping.

The temptation to shorten the games, to find ways to talk about what I experienced was great, but Peter rejected this most of the time. He used the process deeply, using many ways to symbolise experience and to communicate this to me. He seemed to feel understood but I was never certain whether he understood what I knew through my attempts to relate to him. Perhaps this did not matter; his experience was of relational, emotional holding, experienced implicitly. As with an infant, the right-brain relational communication was active, and we can surmise that neural pathways were active, deepening Peter's experience of connecting with another person's mind.

Peter's house took on a greater sense of order and space. He crushed walls and straightened and painted them; new furniture for the kitchen, bathroom and toilet was made and a safe was inserted into the wall to hold precious things, hidden with an ornate glass button. The wild animals and reptiles were removed. There was only a tiny space for domestic animals, and flowers were added. The space now belonged to the inhabitants of the house and, for the first time, people were added. Carpets and wall hangings were glued into place. A fantasy that it was made for both of us was alluded to as he put two beds into the bedroom. It began to feel as though integration was taking place. His wildness took on the form of a child with parents and his unconscious world was less unrelated to his consciousness.

Evidence of change in Peter

In place of the angry child who spread water, clay and paint over the room, who bit pieces of wire, wood, plastic and polystyrene, and who took no time to find scissors or ask for help, grew a teenager, whose chaos became creative. Peter became able to take in what I offered and could experience his own feelings safely. Peter's use of art psychotherapy demonstrates how the attachment process developed and how, after several years of consistent and safe relating, he was able to make a final image through the goodbye process. This speaks to me of his having reached a stage of knowing that he can take what he has experienced on his journey to independence.

Peter knew his time in art psychotherapy was finishing and he was going to a residential agricultural college. He was proud to be going, but apprehensive about leaving therapy. He made a lorry-home during the ending period. The front wheel was constructed first; it was made carefully so that it pivoted and turned in every direction. The cab had several materialisations, ending up with four felt figures placed inside. There was a door in the ceiling to reach a sleeping room above made for Peter and his internal image of a loving partner; it had a mattress, duvet and pillow made from felt and stitched with warm wadding inside. The large area behind the driver was left open to carry what he needed, a potential space for life.

This image was full of hope. Hope that Peter would be able to embark on his journey through life in a vehicle that had been given good construction and that his journey might include a family where good attachments were established. Peter showed care and concern for Pearl, asking me to continue her therapy after he went to college. Pearl continued in her care for him when he returned after college. She supported his move to a local farm where he worked as an odd-job help. His ambition was to become a lorry driver when he was old enough.

Working with images helped Peter organise the unconsciously remembered, disorganised and traumatic early relationship into a more attached conscious narrative. Initially this involved considerable attention to affect regulation as he was unable to adjust when emotionally aroused. Peter's initial way of relating was with dissociation and motor activity. He left therapy able to have conscious memory, to decide whether to talk about painful relationships and to gradually change those relationships so that he re-established contact with his mother and sisters. Peter managed to return to mainstream education and acquire skills to support an adult life.

Changes in Pearl through psychotherapy

There is evidence that Pearl's psychotherapy made it possible for her to make sense of her childhood, to unravel her memories and to reflect on the psychological experiences taking place within her. Although she found it difficult to change her expectations, her unconscious memories moved towards conscious memory and she began to talk about things that she thought were long forgotten, enabling her to make sense of experiences that had had no meaning and had made her feel mad. Her physical pain was reduced as the unbearable contents of her mind, known only in her body, were able to come to mind in the safe holding of the therapeutic relationship. Working with Pearl reduced her inner chaos and helped her to resist dissociating when she was psychologically stimulated. She experienced feeling understood for the first time; she became happier and more confident in her relationships because of her therapy. Through her therapeutic experience, she was able to continue to parent Peter so that he did not become separated and lost into the care system, and later drawn towards the streets and drugs, or turning to criminality for survival.

Pearl had previously regulated her own arousal by dissociating, and this accentuated Peter's feeling of abandonment. He responded by escalating his disorganised behaviour in an attempt to bring her back into awareness. Simultaneous working aided stability for both as I was able to contain and regulate their arousal in relation to each other. Both became able to talk about the difficult experiences each had of the other. The benefits of working with both parts of the family came to outweigh the anxieties. Both Peter and Pearl were confident that no leaking of the inner world of one to the other occurred.

When I spoke with Pearl about writing this chapter, she told me shyly that she thought I had been the mother she had never had, both for herself and for Peter, and that this had helped her continue to look after him. I experienced myself being a father to them both. The boisterous games with Peter and the placing of fair and attainable boundaries for him were paternal. I was also the person who could contain the difficulties of caring for Peter. Similar to a 'good-enough' father, I would consistently support that care, and not escalate it into the frightening see-saw of punitive violence or rejection of her early life. Peter evoked early trauma memories in Pearl but she became able to gradually find the stability to think about it before responding. Although change continues throughout life, the patterns of behaviour are embedded very deeply and Pearl had no support until middle age.

Early intervention facilitates change

Peter's earlier treatment gave him greater ability to change. He used the art process to bring unconscious bodily-held memory to thoughts that could be held in mind. He used images to explore relationships and to process his sadness and anger at how bereft his early life was. The art process was essential to his progress. I believe he could not have used a verbal psychotherapy, but he found what he needed in the relationship with me and through his art works.

Some may consider it a luxury to offer this level of support to a family or may be disconcerted by one clinician working simultaneously with two members of the same family. Early insecure attachments give an unpromising start but Pearl benefited greatly from psychotherapy that focused on her own attachment so that she could foster a more secure attachment for Peter. Working practice did not prioritise working deeply with parents or carers and funding was not available. Nevertheless, my workplace gave support to this unofficial use of psychotherapy for a carer, which gave sufficient containment to enable Pearl to support change which otherwise may have proved too threatening for her. Through this Peter accessed education and stayed out of the care system. Although difficulties continued throughout Peter's childhood, the outcome has been beneficial. It has proved cost effective as there has been minimal intervention from social services; further, Peter's future is probably as a working man, someone not dependent on mental health services. Without art psychotherapy this could not have been the anticipated outcome for this troubled pair.

At the point of completing this chapter, Peter arrived unexpectedly to see me. He has grown into a healthy young man. He is living independently and has been interviewed for a career with the police as a traffic officer. He talked to me about his art psychotherapy and his childhood, telling me, 'I couldn't have grown up without you'. This was an unexpected confirmation of the value of the work that was so full of uncertainty. At 19 Peter is able to reflect on his past, mourn its losses and perceive a useful future.

Acknowledgements

I am indebted to Joy Schaverien whose supervision and support throughout the work enabled me to contain and understand so much that was projected and outside of my understanding while the work was progressing, and also to Andrea Gilroy who generously helped me find words to describe it.

References

Alvarez, A. (1992) *Live Company Psychoanalytic Psychotherapy with Autistic, Borderline, Deprived and Abused Children*. London: Routledge.

Brisch, K.H. (2002) *Treating Attachment Disorders: from Theory to Therapy*. New York: Guilford Press.

Carter, R. (1998) *Mapping the Mind*. London: Phoenix.

Case, C. (2005) *Imagining Animals: Art, Psychotherapy and Primitive States of Mind*. Hove: Routledge.

Chazan, S.E. (2003) *Simultaneous Treatment of Parent and Child*, 2nd edn. London: Jessica Kingsley.

Gerhardt, S. (2004) *Why Love Matters: How Affection Shapes a Baby's Brain*. Hove: Brunner-Routledge.

Knox, J. (2003) *Archetype, Attachment, Analysis: Jungian Psychology and the Emergent Mind*. Hove: Brunner-Routledge.

Mollon, P. (2001) *Releasing the Self: The Healing Legacy of Heinz Kohut*. London: Whurr.

O'Brien, F. (2004) The making of mess in art therapy: attachment, trauma and the brain, *The Journal of the British Association of Art Therapists: Inscape*, 9(1): 2–13.

Pynoos, R.S., Steinberg A.M. and Goenjian, A. (1996) Traumatic stress in childhood and adolescence, in B.A. van der Kolk, C. McFarlane and L. Weisaeth (eds) *Traumatic Stress: The Effects of Overwhelming Experience on Mind, Body and Society*. London: Guilford Press.

Schaverien J. (1992) *The Revealing Image: Analytical Art Psychotherapy in Theory and Practice*. London: Routledge.

Schore, A.N. (1994) *Affect Regulation and the Origin of the Self: The Neurobiology of Emotional Development*. Mahwah, NJ: Lawrence Erlbaum.

Schore A.N. (2003) *Affect Dysregulation & Disorders of the Self*. New York: W.W. Norton.

Steele, H. and Steele, M. (1994) *Intergenerational Patterns of Attachmen, Advances in Personal Relationships*, 5: 93–120.

Teicher, M. (2000) Wounds time won't heal, *Cerebrum*, 2: 4.

Terr, L.C. (1996) True memories of childhood trauma: flaws, absences and returns, in K. Pesdek and W.P. Banks (eds) *The Recovered Memory/False Memory Debate*. Burlington, MA: Academic Press.

Trevarthen, C. (1995) Mother and baby – seeing artfully eye to eye, in R. Gregory, J. Harris, P. Heard and D. Rose (eds) *The Artful Eye*. Oxford: Oxford University Press.

Turnbull, O. and Solms, M. (2003) Memory, amnesia and intuition: a neuro-psychoanalytic perspective, in V. Green (ed.) *Emotional Development in Psychoanalysis, Attachment Theory and Neuroscience*. Hove: Brunner-Routledge.

Wilkinson, M. (2005) Undoing dissociation – affective neuroscience: a contemporary Jungian clinical perspective, *Journal of Analytical Psychology*, 50(4): 483–501.

Wilkinson, M. (2006) *Coming into Mind, the Mind-brain Relationship: A Jungian Clinical Perspective*. London: Routledge.

Chapter 3

'I'm the king of the castle': the sibling bond – art therapy groups with siblings in care

Teresa Boronska

'I'm the king of the castle' was a game often played out by siblings in an art therapy group where rivalry dominated. An example of this was an elder brother, who over several sessions created a costume of a 'bear', stitching the furry brown material into shape so that there was enough bearskin to cover his face and body. This gave him the look of a big scary 'Grisly'. Satisfied with the result he went on to act out: 'I'm the king of the castle and you're the dirty rascal', taking the tabletop as his domain. The game evolved as the siblings attempted to topple and kill him. The significance of the play was not lost on them, as he would come back to life and the game would be replayed over again, as each child wanted the position of king.

Introduction: the sibling bond

Since writing this chapter I have become alert to the many references made by people to their siblings. On the radio I heard Jimmy Osmond praise his elder brothers, who had put their own careers on hold as they gave him support in making him a child star. I read an article in the *New York Times* in December 2005 about children born from the same sperm donor; many of these adults were now seeking out their half-siblings, as the need to have a connection with someone with a similar gene pool was a strong emotional pull, even though they had never lived together. These people talked of the comfort they found in sharing similar looks or shared mannerisms. This gave them a sense of belonging. So what then is the significance of sibling kinship?

Once a baby is born, the concept of family exists. With the birth of another sibling there is the possibility of the micro world within a family unit creating the ingredients for community. Siblings are important figures, contributing to development of the psyche and having a powerful and sustaining influence. They act as companions and attachment figures, confidantes, playmates and rivals.

If for any reason family life is disrupted and the children suffer continued neglect and deficit in parental care, then these children may resort to pseudo-parenting of each other and in extreme cases sibling-sibling abuse. Normal stages of child development may be affected as their internal psyche will have developed defence mechanisms to cope with the uncertainty of day-to-day living.

It is normal for there to be rivalry, but should children from disrupted childhoods not have learnt to negotiate these powerful feelings, this will add yet another burden to an already fraught existence.

Coles (2003) gives a succinct description of the origins of sibling rivalry highlighting the reoccurring history in the myths that prevail in many cultures. In the myths of ancient Egypt there was the marriage of Osiris and Isis, brother and sister, king and queen of Egypt (their parents had also been brother and sister). Osiris is killed by his jealous brother Seth, who resents his kingship. In the Old Testament, Abel was murdered by his brother Cain. Oedipus, in Greek mythology, kills his father unknowingly, marries his mother and becomes both father and sibling to his four children. These stories have complex and disturbing consequences that touch on the most profound parts of our psyche relating to kinship.

Having compared two art therapy sibling groups with children in care, using an attachment framework (Boronska 2000), I wish to explore further the use of art therapy groups for siblings, with particular emphasis on the sibling bond. The context of this study takes place within a child protection setting, in which one or more of the categories of neglect, sexual abuse or violence will have necessitated the children coming into care. By extending the appreciation and meaning of inter-family connections, the aim is to broaden the scope of art therapy practice, thereby giving consideration to the possibility for brothers and sisters to be seen together in art therapy.

I begin by exploring the concept of sibling attachment, and the impact that the birth of a sibling might have on the older child. I look at how research informs the legal framework for 'children in need' when removal from home is required. Central to this theme is the literature available from social work findings, psychoanalysis, attachment research and clinical practice, which I explore as an aid to extending understanding of a broader and more global approach to working with children.

There is no writing on sibling art therapy groups other than that of my own experience (Boronska 2000), yet I believe that this approach provides an effective and appropriate intervention that can benefit siblings who are at a point of some stability in their lives, yet in some emotional crisis due to loss and transition. The setting for sibling groups takes place within 'the assessment and therapy services'. Developing the idea for the sibling art therapy group came about as children from same-family groups were being referred for individual therapy. I regarded the art therapy group as both an expedient and appropriate response to managing these referrals, to better effect where appropriate.

The sibling groups that were referred were all white British. I co-worked one group with a family therapist and the other with a senior social worker from the team. Both groups took place over a two-year period. Sibling group B were three middle children (of a group of six) aged between 6 and 11. The elder brother and sister lived with their eldest brother of 15 within the same foster home, while the younger brother lived separately with different carers. During the life of the group he discovered that he had a different father. The social worker had referred each of them for individual art therapy to consider their attachment to each other with a view to their long-term placement plans. All the siblings had been removed from their mother, due to her repeated pattern of ending up with violent and abusive partners. Although she had removed herself repeatedly from these partners, the accumulated disruption in the children's lives resulted in them becoming highly disoriented and insecure. Group S had five siblings, aged 7–13, which included twins. Their mother had been unable to protect them from the father of the youngest child. There was the added dynamic in that their mother had refused to see the two siblings who had disclosed sexual abuse, as she had sided with her partner. This caused rivalry between those siblings who were favoured over the two who were rejected as they had not disclosed. I will use these group cases to demonstrate sibling interrelatedness as seen through blood ties, bringing together issues of rivalry, sexuality, loss and the need for acceptance where there is conflict.

Our understanding of child development in relation to emotional trauma is highly significant within child protection as children only come to the attention of social services when things go wrong. Additionally, children may have experienced multiple moves, creating a deep sense of loss which in turn can be as damaging as the reason for being in care in the first place.

Sibling interaction

Freud (1921) explored child interaction within a nursery setting, where rivalries and jealousies were observed, but he did not develop any theoretical frame concerning the sibling bond. Instead he placed the role of patriarchy as central to the child. Coles (2003) attributes this omission to Freud's own complex family life, where his stepbrother was old enough to be his father and his nephew John his closest friend. Klein (1932) shifts this balance, placing particular emphasis on the sibling bond and the developing psyche, maintaining that heterosexuality is achieved through identification with our siblings. A positive relationship with her older brother no doubt gave Klein an understanding of the role of the sibling as supporting emotional development and assisting in the task of distancing the child from its parents. Klein believed that the impulse of hate, that initiates the Oedipus conflict, is counterbalanced with sibling love. Her premise is that children need to love and it is through the companionship between siblings and peers that envy and jealousy of the maternal breast can be repaired and the unbearable exclusion from the parental bed managed better.

Since the Second World War a broader awareness of child attachments has become prominent. Levy (1934, 1937) focused specifically on the sibling bond, seen as the place where our first meaningful relationships originate. Minuchin (1974), Stillwell and Dunn (1985), and Dunn *et al.* (1994) all see sibling groups as part of a family sub-system in which children learn to relate; where they negotiate support, experiment with conflict, isolate or scapegoat, fight each other, cooperate and compete with each other.

Minuchin and Bronfenbrenner (1979) use the 'mesosystem' (a social ecology model of human development) to demonstrate the compound ways in which families interconnect, beginning with the parents' own relationship, and how these will impact on their children. These inter-family dynamics become ever more complex as more children are born. Most children manage this transition well enough, but in the few families where parents are unable to manage a stable family life, due to risk factors such as economic or marital problems, substance misuse, illness or poor interfamilial communication, the consequences can result in siblings seeking comfort from each other. In extreme cases this can result in sexual and violent abuse. Research now available shows that sibling-to-sibling sexual abuse is far higher than parent-to-child sexual abuse (NSPCC 2000). Sexual play may well be a feature between siblings, and as Klein observed is more common than we realise.

Mitchell (2003) believes that the birth of a sibling will have a profound impact on all members of a family and can be seen as a trauma for the elder child as their position is taken away. In cases where siblings receive little or no adequate care or attention, the ability to manage sibling rivalry of love and hate may be exacerbated by a sense of confusion and despair. In normal development the theory relating to Freud's Oedipus complex will operate and does so at the phallic phase in childhood, where reproduction is not possible. It is this negotiation that allows for the 'non-realization of sibling incest' Mitchell (2003: 76). In cases where children suffer from extreme neglect, then the playing out of the parental roles may lead to the elder sibling abusing the younger.

In Britain today there are legal requirements that recognise the needs of the child. In the government paper *Every Child Matters* (DoH 2003) the first objective for children's social services is to ensure that all children are securely attached to carers who are capable of providing safe and effective care for the duration of their childhood (p. 44, 3.14). Where there are concerns, the aim is to support families in staying together.

Since the 1970s the acknowledgment of sexual abuse and its consequence on the mental health of children has resulted in an increased number of children being taken into care. Finklehor's (1984) research findings did much to open up better understanding of sexual abuse within families, which in the late 1970s became a national concern both in the USA and Britain.

Since then, the number of reported cases has increased, resulting in far higher numbers of children being separated from home and their siblings.

In supporting the concept of the child in relation to a brother or sister, we will need to consider the position of each child within the family, even if we do not go on to work with them as a group.

Clinical material

In my experience, art therapy groups with siblings can help to shift destructive patterns of behaviour relating to pain and hurt, caused by fear of intimacy and early trauma. The group brings them together and in doing so they are confronted with the predicament of how to manage their relationships within the confines of the group. Even when there is agreement for therapy to take place, siblings will initially take cues from each other as to what is permitted for open discussion. Over time the process of the unconscious at work gradually arises and the opportunity to function at a symbolic level allows for a ventilation of emotions. It is this possibility that offers siblings the chance to become observers of their own interaction.

As conscious connections begin to be made with their past we see children begin to have a greater sense of control over their emotional responses. This can bring some relief and satisfaction to a life that has had little stability.

It is usual for the early life of the group to be the most challenging part of therapy, as siblings act out similar ways of relating as they did before coming into care. Behaviour such as irritability, inability to manage moments of concentrated focus on a piece of art work, talking over each other, rivalry and hysteria are all common features that alert the therapist to the level of functioning that exists between them. In both B and S groups the effort of the therapist to be of any significant influence had to be earned.

The use of transference was an essential indicator to the pacing of our interventions: not to be reactive to their attacks on us, or each other, but to question what other ways they might respond that would elicit a reaction they might wish for. Each of the groups was curious as to our dealing with heightened emotions in the group. Alertness to our interjections was noted. Over time we would see from them different ways of relating that conveyed their ability to think through a reaction rather than responding out of habitual fear and attack. When opportunities were missed we were soon alerted to this by the escalation of the emotional pitch. The group needed an experience of relating to each other that was not based on fear but on accumulated interactions that were a calm and safe exchange.

An example of difficult sibling interaction as seen in both S group and B group centred on the use of the art materials, each child wanting what the other had. We would comment on what we saw, asking the group for their understanding of what had just taken place. The case of ownership was seen in context of survival, relating to past deprivation, and to never feeling that they had had enough. In the case of group B, the siblings had suffered hunger before coming into care. They were found wandering the streets looking into dustbins, as well as asking neighbours for food. The school had alerted social services to this, as it also found the children needed feeding at the start of the day. Once in foster care, the carers had to regulate the children's intake of food, as they had little concept of knowing if they were full and so would overeat, not yet trusting that regular meals would be available.

Another example pertaining to both groups related to the children's social deficit: a piece of art work would be fought over, one child taking away another's work and making it their own. They seemed unaware of the importance of personal investment and belonging, which in turn thwarted their ability to gain satisfaction from their own achievements. By drawing attention to these forms of behaviour the siblings were able to grasp the importance of something they themselves had created, and would stand up to the brother or sister who took it away, thereby developing the possibility for active negotiation. These situations alerted us to concerns of neglect and transgression over personal boundaries, which gave both therapist and children much to work with. In all the above cases sexual abuse and violence had been a feature of the children's earlier lives, which resulted in overt sexual play within the group.

Should the level of disturbance within a sibling group be such that there is a high degree of conflict and violence, then co-facilitation is essential. An occasion arose when the permanent removal of the eldest brother in group S became a necessity. He finally attacked his sisters, throwing a pair of scissors at them, with intent to hurt. This coincided with his wish to see his mother and her consistent refusal to see him. Rivalry was rife at this time. Clearly-set limits on non-violence in the group created safety for his sisters, resulting in the development of trust and the possibility for more open discussion on how to express emotions without resorting to emotionally charged and violent behaviour.

Their art work in turn became ever more productive. The containers that they had previously made were reworked, decorated and then placed in boxes to keep them safe. Working in pairs or as a group became a possibility as they negotiated assistance from each other. One sister was better at decorating, the other at construction. A level of aestheticism began to feature in the finished pieces, which they had previously been unable to consider. Confidence in their achievements prompted them to seek individual attention for the pieces they had made.

Sibling sexuality

I use Mitchell's writing (2003) to assess the difference between normal sexual play and sibling behaviour which is abusive. In her presentation given on 'Siblings and Sexuality' (2005), she asked: 'How do we place sibling sex?'

Before coming to present her paper, Mitchell consulted Estella Weldon (an expert in working with clients who have been sexually abused), about what her definition of sibling sex might be, to which she replied: 'a complete lack of parental control'. Klein's and Mitchell's emphasis on the normalcy of sexual play, where siblings act out scenes of 'doctors', 'mummies and daddies', can be seen as 'a continuum from caring and loving, towards or away from incest' (Mitchell 2003: 76).

Mitchell distinguishes sexuality relating to play from that which leads to reproduction, defining sexual abuse at the point at which violence, rape or attack occurs. She points out that the universal taboo of incest is always related to reproduction, a point often missed out in gender-related literature. The child does not at this stage have a full comprehension of reproduction when they play at 'making babies'. The reason for such play can be seen a means of identifying with the parents, mother or father, which lays the foundation for later life as a parent. In sibling group S, it was common for birth issues to be played out, especially at times when there was knowledge that new foster families were being sought. The children would make dens or enact scenes of returning to the womb, enjoying the comfort of being enveloped by the soft cushions, which at times prompted them to stay in that position for some time.

Their concept of parenting was confused as they felt more adult than the parent. At one stage, parent-child play was enacted by the eldest, more dominant twin in S group. She played the mother and I was invited to play the daughter, who was asked to go shopping. I was given a list of things to buy from the chemist, but I was not given enough money for all the things on the list. My attempt at clarifying the situation was ignored and I became ever more frustrated by the dilemma. I was eventually asked to steal from the chemist. This role-play communicated to me the predicament of the child. Coming out of role-play, I was able to discuss my experience and the confusion that she must have felt as the daughter. Role reversal situations would often occur and were a useful way for the siblings to enact what their earlier lives had been like on a day-to-day basis. The eldest siblings had been given too much responsibility for their young years. The residential staff often discussed the fact that the siblings worried for their mother and their belief was that she was more the child than they were.

It was reassuring to see the younger twin, who at the start of the group had significant bouts of disassociation, especially at times of conflict, begin to take a more active role in intervening to keep the peace. She saw how progress was being made in this area and felt that she could heard. The defences used by her to cope no longer took precedent. She began to make progress at the special school she attended and within six months was reassessed educationally and was able to return to secondary education. It is interesting to note that it might well have been this change in her, which allowed her dominant twin to begin to express her confusions more fully, that enabled her to take a less dominant role in the group, leaving space for her siblings to thrive and feel recognised without having to fight for attention.

In sibling group B, other positions were taken, for example that of the unwanted child within a family, where the fairytale of Cinderella would suddenly arise. The children would ask for this story to be told and re-told, taking great interest in the happy ending, as they wished to be placed within families who would care for them. At this stage emotions would swing from hope to despair, leaving us as therapists concerned and sad for their future. Discussion with their social worker kept us aware of the progress of family-finding, so that we did not resort to responses where we might want to make things better than they really were for them. The importance of the siblings experiencing their full feelings allowed them the opportunity to be in touch with the reality of their situation, so that this could be expressed.

A co-working approach appears to be the preferred treatment model in that it helps to reduce the intensity of transference on one facilitator. This establishes a more supportive atmosphere, where the therapists can think together and manage attacks without retaliation, as in the role of supportive parental pairing. The capacity to work with difficult interaction can be sustained for longer and role-modelling to the group helped to reduce tensions. It is at these times that countertransference feelings arise most strongly and these feelings can be discussed directly after the group.

Prokofiev (1998) and Murphy *et al.* (2004) stress the need for structure at the beginning and ending of each group, as chaos and confusion can easily descend. This acts as a regulating function for children who can easily become volatile and chaotic. However, in groups where this is not possible, it is better to allow a flexible approach, yet keep to boundaries which stress the relevance of safety. Stopping the group at such times is a useful intervention, reducing ongoing chain reactions that escalate tensions.

Sub-grouping and pairing were common. At one point this was highlighted in the group when the social worker of group B drew attention to the need to change the surname of the youngest, who had a different father. This caused a considerable amount of angst and working through, as the father of the elder two children had hardly been a presence in their lives. There was an ongoing argument as to who had the better father, who was favoured and who not, and a painful realisation for the older girl who felt rejected by her father, while her brother was favoured.

I remember a situation in group S where the siblings had fantasies about us as co-workers. At one stage we were seen as 'a married couple who had sex', and would therefore be able to adopt them as they saw us as potential parents. The wish for a settled family life was a constant preoccupation, always there in the forefront of their minds, with whoever showed them positive regard. Constant sexual play was a feature as their need for physical contact was strong. They confused intimacy and warmth with sexuality, resorting to sexual play when needing comfort. The myriad of possibilities of being loved and cherished was limited, due to a lack of early nurture, love and holding. This offered us the chance to talk about ways of caring and loving that were not based on sex, but on other types of close and caring relationships.

Sibling attachment

Our understanding of the attachment needs of children continues to develop, since Bowlby's (1980) findings on the difficulties of the poorly-attached child. Erikson (1968), Howe (1995, 2005), Howe *et al.* (1999), Mason *et al.* (1999), Fonagy *et al.* (1991) and Schore (2001a) all stress the importance of a secure and positive identity as an aspect of emotional health, likewise the United Nations Convention (1990) recognises the rights of the child in aiding psychological development and well-being.

In Britain today there are approximately 7750 children in residential schools or other types of setting living away from their families. About 80 per cent of these have a sibling. Ward (1984) states that separating siblings will arouse a strong emotional response; they may display challenging and complex behaviour with the added burden of not being placed together.

Jaffe *et al.* (1986), and Peled *et al.* (1994) concluded that group work is best suited to children with mild to moderate behaviour problems, whereas those with more severe difficulties would benefit from individual therapy. Within art therapy the use of image making acts as a safety net for powerful emotions to arise, thereby allowing for the more disturbed child to function within the group. Each child will have been assessed beforehand and monitored during the life of the group. It is important therefore that the failure of the group due to one individual should be avoided. If for any reason a child leaves a group either from choice or is asked to leave, for the good of group, then this should be managed with sensitivity, so that the child does not feel rejected and their needs are still met.

Over time, weekly art therapy sessions give children some sense of acquired confidence in their own ability to use art materials. This helps to encourage a sense of achievement and mastery, which in turn can affect other areas of the child's life in a positive way. These skills are often a first step in the process to changing their sense of self-worth. Once this step has been negotiated the siblings can undertake the next stage of therapy, which is to have some awareness of their internal world through the images created. This awareness does not necessarily need to be voiced, but a growing understanding that choices are possible in the way they respond to their emotions offers a less chaotic and hopefully calmer level of interaction.

In 1984 Arnon Bentovim (a child psychiatrist and family therapist) led a seminal workshop in which he reviewed the practice of placement of siblings in care. He considered the ways siblings matter to each other, and what priority should be given to preserving or disrupting sibling groups. These same questions need to asked by art therapists when conducting sibling groups in care.

Maluccio and Sinanoglu (1981) remind us that the 'ecology of child rearing should be considered' when placing children away from home. Research has found that there are fewer psychological problems for children in placement if kinship is sustained. In situations where there is little contact with siblings, these children asked for more contact.

We know that siblings are influenced by each other even before another is born (Lamb 1978; Mitchell 2003). This will have implications on the strength of the sibling bond for better or worse, which will last far beyond childhood as it withstands the separation of time and space, providing important emotional security for most people in the later stages of life.

Dunn (1988) found that children as young as 18 months onwards have some notion of how to influence the feelings of a sibling. This can be the start of recognising certain social rules and can be used when one's own interest is threatened. Dunn sees children as motivated to understand the social rules and relationships of their cultural world because they need to get things done in their family relationships. This helps them learn to function as social beings.

Rowe et al (1984), Berridge & Cleaver (1987), the Department of Health (1991), Berridge (1997) all advocate siblings being placed together wherever possible, and if not, contact between them should be maintained.

It appears that the significance to a young person of a sibling does not necessarily relate to the amount of time they have lived together or the fact they are a full or half-sibling, providing contact is maintained. Siblings are known to have a continuing sense of responsibility for each other and therefore it makes sense to see siblings within a therapy group, so as to assess them for future placement.

Gender differences will also play a part in how siblings develop their relationships. Sutton-Smith and Rosenberg (1970) reported that boys are more likely to employ 'attack offence' while girls use 'reasoning defence' in making their siblings feel obligated. First-born children are more likely to boss, attack, interfere and ignore, paradoxically being offensive by bribing their siblings, while second-born children tend to attack property, plead or reason with siblings. Koch (1960) found that a pair of brothers seemed to produce more quarrelling than any other combination. Bank and Khan (1992) however found positive aspects in childhood fighting: 'Aggressiveness is a major vehicle for sibling interaction and as such has a broad utility for human beings. Aggression even when painful represents contact, warmth and another presence.' Greenbaum (1965) found that first-born children took on high-power roles with non-peers, while later-born children took low-power roles with older siblings but higher roles with their friends. This suggests that younger siblings modelled their behaviour on older siblings. These positions can help us better understand the roles of family positions and the impact that positive change can have when there has been little enough care to go round.

Rivalry and loss

Further case material that was highlighted in both groups related to siblings displaying a need for individual attention, exasperated by numbers of siblings within each family. This is of significance when conducting art therapy groups as the seriality in numbers alerts us to the fact that there may be issues for each of the children relating to a lack of uniqueness. The older child may feel ousted from their position and have no place to go, as they still want to be the baby. In their mind the new baby must be got rid of and when it does not vanish then it must be relegated to another place, the place of the 'other'. As in the example given at the beginning, 'I must be the king of the castle, the new baby is the dirty rascal.' If the child has never experienced having been king of the castle in the first place, due to emotional neglect, then the consequence can be such that violence and aggression is played out on the younger sibling(s). The struggle for recognition and the different roles taken by each of the brothers and sisters was enacted, such as the hysterical child in S group who shouted and cried until she had all her siblings telling her to 'shut up' as they were so exasperated by her demands and would not listen to her. This accelerated her situation to the point of attack.

The role of the therapist is to demonstrate that they are able to understand that action needs to be taken when siblings cannot manage on their own. Over time the group comes to realise that the therapist is there in a holding capacity and that their role is effective as an adult. In the countertransference, however, it is common to feel inadequate and insignificant, which the child feels you are, because of their earlier life experience. In managing hysteria, attention needs to be given to the child in finding some cause for the frustration. In the above case the cause often referred back to not being heard when she had something to say. Responses that deny the possibility for the child to be understood only exasperate the situation, causing earlier patterns of relating to be enacted. If the therapist is alert to each individual in the group then this can help to alleviate fears of annihilation.

All babies need to have experienced some sense of omnipotence in the first few months of life, so that the acceptance of another sibling can be more easily managed. Should this not be the case, then problems can occur later in life leading to mental illness such as severe depressive states, affect regulation, disassociation, hysteria, and physical illness such as somatization.

Even though aggression might be rife at the start of a group, the necessity of seeing these roles in the context of the family situation needs to be worked with so that these behaviours can be adapted to more acceptable ways of relating, such as in the case when the oldest child goes on to rule by fear.

The possibility of 'enacting' the death of a sibling in a group, whereby murderous feelings can be directed in lawful channels, reduces the tension of holding such powerful fantasies. If the original trauma of annihilation can become conscious, then hopefully such fears can be minimised.

In the case of B group, the materials cupboard would often spark off a range of different themes. One of the youngest, a 7-year-old boy, who mourned the loss of his mother, dressed up as a woman, using balls for breasts, a dress and a long wig. It was his mother's birthday that week. His sense of separation anxiety and the need to identify with her through female dressing up prevented his mother from being lost to him. He made a concerted effort to remember her, wanting her memory kept alive. The paradox was that she was not yet dead, although he experienced her as having died.

This same boy had settled well in foster care, but his position as the youngest in the family was soon taken away as his foster carer had just had a baby. This had the effect of making him ill: he lost his appetite and would arrive to the group looking pale, sore-mouthed and depressed. We worried about him and in our interventions gave him more attention at this time. He resented the birth of the baby and consciously mourned the loss of his position as the youngest for so short a time. Having the opportunity to play at dressing up as 'mummy' helped him in the grieving process. This gave us hope for his capacity for emotional health as he was able to convey coherently what was upsetting him.

A situation occurred one session towards the end of the life of group B, where the eldest brother who had been fostered separately arrived by taxi, but his siblings did not. He waited silently for them and when they did not arrive, put his feet up on the table. After some time I commented that 'his action spoke louder than words' and 'that I could see that he seemed unhappy'. If he had been in school his teacher might tell him to put his feet down, I was not going to do that as I wanted to understand what this action meant. This gave him the opportunity to verbalise his anger to me and social services. He said that I 'did not see it as important to make sure the cab would bring his brother and sister'. By this stage in the life of the group he wanted his siblings present in the group, not to be singled out, but to share with them the last weeks of the group's life. There had been a significant shift in his behaviour: whereas at the start of therapy he had wanted all the attention for himself, he now wanted to share and enjoy his siblings' company. We did not have to make any observation as therapists; he was more than capable of telling us this himself.

Discussion

To sum up, siblings working together in art therapy groups offers many opportunities for a shared focus on early family life. Older siblings may fill in gaps which otherwise might have been lost to younger ones; each child holding their own family history. These different roles give value to each individual, encouraging family ties and a sense of belonging.

In the engagement of art therapy I have found that siblings can be helped to self-regulate their emotions, and establish more fulfilling and easier ways of relating to each to other, while dealing with the pain and loss caused by the break-up of family life. Issues of hierarchy are central to the notion that younger siblings are affected by their older brothers and sisters, yet that is not to say that the younger siblings do not also mould their older brothers or sisters. These struggles tell us how alive and attuned they are to each other in their struggle to improve their relationships.

The sense of loss experienced by children in care can be minimised by the professional desensitisation of working solely with this client group. Close links with foster carers and social workers in the sharing of information is essential. Updated information keeps the therapist aware of the many changes that can occur in the lives of the children and supports active rather than reactive facilitation caused by countertransference feelings.

The setting up of any sibling group takes time and should only be undertaken where there is full support from the system. Discussion with colleagues will be necessary in seeking the opportunity for such a group to take place. This can broaden the way we think about our referrals assessments and thereby extend our practice, bridging the gap towards supporting siblings who may benefit from art therapy intervention.

Conclusion

The aim of this chapter has been to share my experience of art therapy group practice with siblings in care. Issues of rivalry and conflict may dominate, attachment may be disorganised, yet the art therapy group offers one of the few opportunities for siblings to come together for the purpose of enhancing communication. Shifting old patterns of relating requires effort and commitment so that, where entrenched behaviour dominates, new ways of relating can develop. As new experiences evolve, comfort and pride may become a part of the repertoire that siblings can experience when they are together.

Although I have only discussed social service settings, schools are an ideal place for such groups, as brothers and sisters of a certain age range can come together within a school setting, where no individual child is signalled out. There have been times when individual children have asked for their siblings to be seen in therapy too. How often do we respond to these requests? If we see children as part of a family group, should we not ask ourselves: in what circumstance might there be a situation where it would be effective to see siblings together within a group?

Placing emphasis on the sibling bond in art therapy can bring about some ease in the lives of children 'in need'. Children do not have the same power as adults to speak coherently about what they require; this places the role on the therapist as advocate for the child so that we are attentive to their ideas about what might work best for them.

In my work with individual young people, many in care would speak about their siblings, especially if they had not seen them for some time. They would worry about them and wonder what each of them was doing 'right now'. One 16-year-old girl I saw in individual art therapy actually initiated contact with her younger disabled brother in care, after recognising how important he was to her. Even in worst-case scenarios, where an elder brother had abused his siblings, the bond existed, and the siblings requested contact with him. I worked together separately with him and his group therapist towards initiating their first meeting since his removal from home. In recognising the value that siblings hold for each other, we can help put the sibling bond into our consciousness, bringing another dimension to our practice.

Acknowledgement

I wish to dedicate this chaper to my own siblings.

References

Bank, S.P. and Khan, M.D. (1992) Remembering and reinterpreting sibling bonds, in F. Boer and J. Dunn (eds) *Children's Sibling Relationships: Development & Clinical Issues*. Hillsdale, NJ: Lawrence Erlbaum.

Berridge, D. (1997) *Foster Care a Research Review*. London: The Stationery Office.

Berridge, D. and Cleaver, H. (1987) *Foster Home Breakdown*. Oxford: Blackwell.

Boronska, T. (2000) Art therapy with two sibling groups using an attachment framework, *The Journal of the British Association of Art Therapists: Inscape*, 5(1).

Bowlby, J. (1980) *Attachment & Loss, Volume 3: Loss, Sadness & Depression*. London: Hogarth.

Bronfenbrenner U. (1979) *The Ecology of Human Development*. Cambridge, MA: Harvard University Press.

Coles, P. (2003) *The Importance of Sibling Relationships in Psychoanalysis*. London: Karnac.

DoH (Department of Health) (1991) *Patterns & Outcomes in Child Placement*. London: HMSO.

DoH (Department of Health) (2003) *Every Child Matters*. London: DoH.

Dunn, J. (1988) Annotation: sibling influences on childhood & development, *Journal of Child Psychology & Psychiatry*, 29(2): 119–27.

Dunn, J., Slomowski, C., Beardsall, L. and Rende, R. (1994) Adjustment in middle childhood & early adolescence: links with earlier & contemporary sibling relationships, *Journal of Child Psychology & Psychiatry*, 35(3): 491–504.

Erikson, E.K. (1968) *Identity, Youth & Crisis*. New York: Rorton & Company.

Finklehor, D. (1984) *Child Sexual Abuse New theory & Research*. New York: Free Press.

Fonagy, P., Steele, H.G., Steele, M. and & Higgit, A. (1991) The capacity for understanding mental states: the reflective self in parent & child & its significance for security of attachment, *Infant Mental Health Journal*, 13: 200–17.

Freud, S. (1921) Group psychology and analysis of the ego, in J. Starchey *The Standard Edition of The Complete Psychologica lWorks of Sigmund Freud, vol. 18*. London: Hogarth & Institute of Psychoanalysis.

Greenbaum, M. (1965) Joint sibling interview as a diagnostic procedure, *Journal of Child Psychology*, 7(6): 227–32.

Howe, D. (1995) *Attachment Theory for Social Work Practice*. Basingstoke: Macmillan.

Howe D. (2005) *Child Abuse & Neglect Attachment, Development & Intervention*. Basingstoke: Palgrave Macmillan.

Howe, D., Brandon, M., Hinnigs, D. and Schofield, G. (1999) *Attachment Theory, Child Maltreatment & Family Support: a practice assessment model*. Basingstoke: Macmillan.

Jaffe, P., Nolfe, D.A. and Wilson, S.V. (1986) *Effectiveness of Children's Groups in Canada*. Kerlinger FN.

Klein, M. (1932) *The Psychoanalysis of Children*. New York: Dell.

Koch, H.L. (1960) *The Relation of Certain Formal Attributes of Siblings to Attitudes Held Towards Each Other & Towards their Parents*. Monographs of the Society for Research in Child Development, no. 25(4).

Lamb, M.E. (1978) The development of sibling relationships in infancy: a short-term longitudinal study, *Child Development*, 49: 1189–96.

Levy, D.M. (1934) Rivalry between children of the same family, *Child Study*, 11.

Levy, D.M. (1937) Studies in sibling rivalry, American Orthopsychiatry Research Monograph, no. 2.

Maluccio, A. and Sinanoglu, P. (eds) (1981) *The Challenge of Partnership: Working with Parents*. Arlington, VA: Child Welfare league America.

Mason, C. A., Chapman D. A. and Scott, K. G. (1999) The Identification of Early Risk Factors for Severe Emotional Handicaps: An Epistemological Approach. *American Journal of Community Psychology*, 27: 357–381.

Minuchin, S. (1974) *Families and Family Therapy*. London: Tavistock.

Mitchell, J. (2003) *Siblings Sex and Violence*. Oxford: Polity.

Mitchell, J. (2005) Siblings and sexuality, November presentation at the Tavistock Clinic, London.

Murphy, J., Paisley, D. and Pardoe, L. (2004) An art therapy group for impulsive children, *The Journal of the British Association of Art Therapists: Inscape*, 9(2).

NSPCC (National Society for the Prevention of Cruelty to Children) (2000) *Child Maltreatment in the United Kingdom*. Child Protection Research Findings: Messages from Research HMSO.

Peled, E., Jaffe, P. and Edleson, J. (1994) *Ending the Cycle of Violence: Community Responses to Children of Battered Women*. Newbury Park, CA: Sage.

Prokofiev, F. (1998) Adapting the art therapy group for children, in S. Skaife and V. Huet (eds) *Art Psychotherapy Groups*. London: Routledge.

Rowe, J., Cain, H., Hundlebury, M. and Keane, A. (1984) *Long term Foster-Care*. London: Batsford.

Schove, A. (2001a) Effects of Early Relational Trauma on Right Brain Development, Affect Regulation and Infant Mental Health. *Infant Mental Health Journal*, 22.

Stillwell, R. and Dunn, J. (1985) Continuities in sibling relationships: patterns of aggression and friendliness, *Journal of Child Psychology & Psychiatry & Allied Disciplines*, 23(4): 627–37.

Sutton-Smith, B. and Rosenberg, B.G. (1970) *The Sibling*. New York: Holt, Rinehart and Winsten.

United Nations (1990) *Rights of the Child. A Commentary on the United Nations Convention P113 Article 19*.

Ward, M. (1984) Sibling ties in foster care and adoption placing, *Child Welfare*, 63.

The use of clay as a medium for working through loss and separation in the case of two latency boys

Tessa Dalley

Introduction

When Peter attended his first individual assessment session, he brought with him a hamster that he had made out of clay at home. Clutching it tightly, he stood extremely close to the therapist, pushing the animal anxiously into her face. The therapist wondered about this way of introducing himself. During the course of the two years of his therapy, she came to understand the meaning of his communication.

The focus of this chapter will be to explore the use of clay in working through separation and loss for two 6-year-old boys. In particular, how the process of making objects out of clay enabled them to put words to their pre-verbal experience or 'unknown thought' which enabled thinking to take place and meaning to develop. Peter and Steven were very different children who both expressed their conflicts through preoccupation with bodily products, soiling and fear of vomiting. They struggled to progress developmentally due to the difficult task of separating from an enmeshed relationship with their mothers, who themselves had suffered significant loss. Issues of separation and loss were more complex with twinship relationships, especially in the case of one of the boys, whose twin died at birth. These issues were addressed in the ongoing work through the developing relationship with the therapist. Particular attention will be paid to moments in the therapeutic process when the clay was used to symbolise experience, bringing about understanding and progressive moves into latency.

Attachment, separation and loss

Bowlby (1971) outlined the importance of attachment due to the human need for protection which creates the necessity for the infant to be safely 'attached' to a 'caretaker'. Attachment with the first carer, generally the mother, sets the pattern for the development of all subsequent relationships. When he becomes conscious of his own separate sense of identity, the child develops a secure and valued sense of self, which enables development of himself in relation to others.

Bowlby defined attachment as: 'Instinctive behaviour, built in to all of us as human beings, provides the protection and security we must have to survive. When this is unwittingly broken or threatened, it leads to virtually all the emotional disturbances that humans suffer from (1971: 127). His major work (1971, 1973, 1980) came from direct observations of infants' interaction with their parents and was also influenced by the work of Anna Freud and Dorothy Burlingham (1944) who observed children separated from their parents due to evacuation during the Second World War. The later work of Robertson and Ainsworth observed hospitalised children also separated from their parents. The film *A Two Year Old Goes to Hospital* (Robertson 1953) highlighted the emotional impact of this separation which, subsequently, has played a significant part in bringing about changes in practice for children in hospital that are now taken for granted (Ainsworth 1962, 1977).

Failure of attachment, that is, lack of affectional bonding between a baby and its caretaker, or the loss of a primary attachment, leads to separation anxiety. Judd (1995) describes how all infants and children inevitably experience loss (through weaning, separation and frustration). Some of this loss is in the child's external life and some in fantasy. When faced with a separation, the child may imagine that his mother is dead or will never return. These feelings may also be in response to the child's aggressive impulses. When faced with loss, the child's inner world feels in grave danger of disintegrating. Gradually he realises that his destructive fantasies have not succeeded in destroying the 'breast' or the mother and his despair at the apparent damage is mitigated by loving impulses and attempts to repair: 'Thus a gradual distinction between the vicissitudes of the infant's internal world and the external world emerge' (Judd 1995: 12).

Klein (1940) suggests that the essential part of the work of mourning is the testing of reality and that there is a close connection between the testing of reality in normal mourning and early processes of the mind in the development of the infantile depressive position. The baby experiences depressive feelings during the weaning process. The object being mourned is the mother's breast which is felt by the baby to be lost due to his own uncontrollable and destructive fantasies and impulses. Failure in mourning occurs when the child has been unable in early childhood to establish an internal 'good' object and to feel secure in his inner world. He has never really overcome the depressive position: 'It is by reinstating inside himself the "good" parents as well as the recently lost person and by rebuilding his inner world which was disintegrated and in danger, [that] he overcomes his grief, regains security and achieves true harmony and peace' (Klein 1940: 369).

Klein's views were developed from Freud's earlier work in *Mourning and Melancholia* (1915). He described mourning as a conscious response to loss, whereas melancholia relates to the unconscious loss of a love object: 'Time is needed for the command of reality-testing to be carried out in detail, and . . . when this work has been accomplished the ego will have succeeded in freeing its libido from the lost object' (1915: 252). He continues: 'Each single one of the memories and situations of expectancy which demonstrate the libido's attachment to the lost object is met by the verdict of reality that the object no longer exists' (p. 255). The melancholic, however, who becomes highly self-critical with self-loathing and loss of self-respect, establishes an identification with the abandoned object: 'The shadow of the object fell upon the ego' (p. 249). Identifying himself with the lost object, the melancholic takes it into himself and more specifically feels himself to have devoured it. In this way, Freud added the notion of incorporation or introjection to that of identification.

Maternal responsiveness

With the subtle exchanges between mother and baby, the infant senses the quality of the mother's personality and emotions (Brazelton and Cramer 1991; Trevarthen and Aitken 2001). Bion (1963) suggested that the mother needs to contain the infant's earliest anxieties and in a similar way Winnicott (1945) described the mother's need to 'hold' and 'handle' her otherwise unintegrated baby. While the baby seeks out maternal contact that is open to primitive states, the mother is at the receiving end of these painful and fragile emotions for her infant and needs to be sufficiently strong to accommodate these. Liekerman (2003) suggests that where the mother struggles with her own internal objects and primitive states, she may become overwhelmed by the infant's additional projections, but even more pressures can come to bear on the new mother: 'As well as demands induced by the infant's primitive projections there is a separate sense of stress induced by timeless atavistic conflicts that are stirred in the mother as a result of childbirth' (2003: 303).

Before their birth, both Peter and Steven's mothers had suffered significant loss through miscarriage. In addition to this, Peter was born a twin, delivered by emergency Caesarian section, at which time his twin sister died. This experience of loss impacted on the early relationship between mother and baby. Infants are intensely sensitive to their mother's state of mind where there is maternal preoccupation not directly related to the baby. André Green (1986) describes the situation which he named the 'dead mother complex'. This emerges in the transference relationship in analytic work with adult patients but originates from the experience of the infant whose mother has been absorbed by a bereavement. Green suggests the child experiences impotence if he cannot repair the mother who is absorbed in her bereavement. As a consequence there is 'decathexis' of the maternal object and an unconscious identification with the 'dead mother'. Where there is a death of a child or miscarriage which remains hidden and secret, what comes about is a 'brutal change' of the 'maternal imago, which is truly mutative': 'The transformation in the psychical life, at the moment of the mother's sudden bereavement when she has become abruptly detached from her infant, is experienced by the child as a catastrophe; because without any warning signal, love has been lost at one blow. Premature disillusionment carries in its wake loss of meaning' (Green 1986: 165).

Green suggests this is especially serious if the complex of the dead mother occurs at the moment when the child discovers the existence of the third person, the father. The infant experiences the new attachment as the reason for the mother's detachment. The child also experiences a loss of meaning as he finds it necessary to divert his destructive aggression because of the mother's vulnerability. He therefore turns to his father. This leads to 'an early triangular situation because child, mother and the unknown object of the mother's bereavement are present at the same time. The unknown object of the bereavement and the father are then condensed for the infant, creating a precocious Oedipus complex' (Green 1986: 165). There is a premature and unstable triangulation.

Twinship and loss

These complex ideas are helpful when thinking about Peter's experience in early infancy. Attachment issues connected with separation and loss are complicated by twinships. As infants, they have been together from the beginning and the twins interact from early on in the pregnancy (Piontelli 1992, 2002). It is unclear when the foetus becomes conscious of the other twin but the pattern of relating between twins has been observed by Piontelli to persist after birth. A deep paradox exists in every twin relationship due to the fact that the sense of self is built on the concept of being a pair. To have a sense of a single identity means a denial or loss of the sense of twinship. Anna Freud (1958) suggested that the enduring tie to a twin is a bond on the level of early parental relationships and that breaking that tie is of the same libidinal order as breaking a tie with a mother. The attachment to the twin 'is rooted in the same deep layer of the personality as the early attachment to the mother' (Freud 1958: 266).

The impact of the loss of his twin sister created a confusing infantile experience for Peter. His mother struggled with her grief in having one baby to care for and simultaneously another to mourn. To lose a twin at birth raises complex issues both for the parents and the surviving twin who has a particularly difficult developmental task. The surviving newborn baby will experience not just separation from, but an absence of, the other twin, as well as a grieving mother and father. The survivor guilt of the lone twin and his confusion of identity with the dead twin is likely to affect the personality development of the infant (Lewis and Bryan 1988).

In one of the earliest studies of identical twins, Burlingham (1952) points out that when a twin dies at birth 'this dead twin may have a lasting influence on the live twin, direct his fantasy life and pattern of future relationships' (p. 88). Woodward (1998) notes in her survey of lone twins that the loss of a twin has a profound effect on the life of the surviving twin. When a pre-verbal child experiences the death of a twin the child's ability to share the loss and make sense of it through verbal understanding is severely limited. This will affect the child's ability to grieve. He is not able to resolve this conflict created by the triumph of his survival and the death of his twin, nor can he mourn the loss. The surviving twin can only deal with these issues in the most rudimentary way and is dependent on his parents to enable him to emerge from the complex situation without feeling persecuted and perhaps fragmented. The missing twin is always present in the reflection of the surviving twin.

Woodward (1998: 11) also described some interesting accounts from twins who were told later in their childhood that they had been born a twin. Without exception they said that they had known about it at some level of consciousness and when told felt 'everything fitted into place':

> How far this knowing is due to memories that begin in utero or from many clues picked up from parents including overheard conversations, is impossible at this stage of knowledge to ascertain. Just as these twins knew of the existence of their twin at birth, there were many descriptions from twins of knowing of their twin's death before this was officially told to them.

Woodward points out that when the truth about being a twin has been withheld, the lone twin then feels devalued. Parents struggling to manage their own grief or monopolising it within the family tend to leave the surviving twin suffering a deep sense of isolation. In addition, the surviving twin may feel in some way responsible for the death of his twin, perhaps by kicking it *in utero*, developing a deep sense of guilt. This denies the surviving twin the opportunity to experience ambivalence about his twinship. When a subsequent child is born this may become a 'replacement' for the lost twin who then becomes an adored, wanted child and the surviving twin has deep feelings of being cast aside.

Peter

When Peter brought his clay hamster to his first session, he looked lost and perplexed. The way he clutched his precious object suggested an urgency as if he was letting the therapist know about something very important. Although she came to understand that this was about his loss, the hamster represented part of himself which he experienced as being very much alive. It was important for the therapist to be available to this painful communication as Peter's mother was still struggling with her feelings of loss. As she had not worked through her own grief, his mother had chosen not to tell Peter that he had been born a twin and that his twin sister died, as she thought that this would further add to his distress. This served to continue his confusion.

Peter was referred to a Child and Adolescent Mental Health Service (CAMHS) clinic at the age of 6 for persistent soiling. Although toilet trained by the age of 2 and an half, and consistently dry for over a year, at nursery he started having a few accidents. On starting school, his soiling became more frequent and soon occurred on a daily basis. As an infant, Peter fed well but his milestones were mild to moderately delayed. He did not speak until he was 3. At referral, his problems with expressive and receptive language had already been thoroughly assessed by educational psychologists, speech and language therapists and occupational therapists.

Peter lived at home with his mother, two older brothers and a step-sister, who was two years younger. His mother had suffered a miscarriage before he was conceived and his father left home shortly after Peter's birth and the death of his twin sister. His mother's new partner lived at home but travelled a lot for his work. Peter's older brothers teased him. His younger sister was rapidly catching him up in terms of educational and emotional development. His mother was understandably protective of Peter and increasingly concerned about his lack of educational progress. Peter was becoming more aware of the gap between himself and his peers, particularly in the acquisition of his literacy skills. He was clumsy with poor impulse control. His fear of failure meant that he would avoid tasks that he found difficult to manage.

Assessment

Peter's mother had specifically asked for art therapy as she felt this would not 'mark him out as different'. Peter was of average height with an open face, gentle eyes and shy manner. His clothes were usually messy and muddy. Peter was a creative child and enjoyed drawing, painting and making things at home. On assessment, his complex emotional difficulties and his internal sense of fragmentation became evident. He presented as an isolated and sad child, with low self-esteem, who was anxious and appeared 'lost' in a dream world, and would at times not answer as if he was deaf. There was a question whether his tendency to retreat into his own world, fend off questions and avoid interactions was an inability to process simple communications or an expression of undifferentiated anxiety and aggression in his confused sense of self.

However, during the assessment, his capacity to communicate non-verbally through his art-making was a striking aspect of his relatedness. When he chose to use the clay he totally immersed himself in this activity as if taken over, lost in his own world of thoughts, fantasies and feelings. He made a tortoise and then a hamster, putting them away with great care to keep them safe. At this stage, he seldom spoke about his work and most of his comments seemed rhetorical as if he was not expecting a response. He was disoriented by the breaks, finding the end of the sessions very difficult and surprised to find his things again the following week.

In the third assessment session he asked for the therapist's help to make a telephone. While they were involved in this activity, Peter commented that he always seemed to make two of everything: 'Last week I made two things and this week I am making two telephones.' When the therapist wondered why that might be he said, 'I don't know – sometimes I do things and I don't understand why.' The joining up in the activity with the therapist created an illusion of the twinship. The experience of his sense of self as a pair came into consciousness but had not been named.

In the following session he made 24 baby gerbils out of yellow Plasticine and placed them in a ring, not touching at all, but surrounding the hamster and tortoise. He said he could not mix the yellow gerbils with the pink ones he was making at home. This seemed to be some expression of his need to be separate or defined, a fear of fusion or intimacy again relating to his early twinship experience. The way he placed the gerbils around the two animals was suggestive of a womb or container.

As Peter was continually confused and in an unspecified anxiety state it was difficult to maintain links in his thinking. He denied knowing that it was the last assessment session and in this session he made a machine that fed the gerbils with peas, mashed potatoes and orange juice. He spoke under his breath that his sister was a sneak as she was always chucking his things out. The therapist wondered aloud if he thought that she was like his sister – a sneak that might be chucking his things out; or him out. He did not reply in his characteristic way, as if he seemed unable to hear. Perhaps this resonated with a painful early memory of chucking his twin sister out and damaging her. He had mentioned that he went to 'Castaway Kids' after school as he had few friends, but perhaps also felt identified with this feeling of being cast aside by his sister and the therapist, as at this stage it was not clear whether he would continue into treatment.

Treatment

Peter attended individual art psychotherapy for two years. Parent work with his mother continued at the same time At the beginning of his treatment, Peter was anxious and worried about 'what he would do'. To manage this anxiety he tended to bring objects from home. His therapist understood this to be a manifestation of his separation anxiety and an attempt to make a concrete link with his mother and home. The 'doing' – that is, drawing, painting and using modelling clay that he chose to do in his sessions – was a chaotic, confused and messy process. Peter would smear, drop and spill, jumping from idea to idea. He tried to make models but they tended to fall apart. There was no sequencing to his thoughts and the room would end up with mess and fragments of objects everywhere, which seemed to represent Peter's internal world.

After a few weeks into his therapy, his soiling stopped. There was a sense that Peter was already beginning to feel internally gathered up and contained. However, he found it difficult to talk and think about his art work and respond to any of the therapist's thoughts, leaving her feeling very shut out. She was also aware of her experience of the 'deadness' in his responses but did not verbalise these thoughts at the time. The communication was a powerful one and led to the therapist herself feeling deadened. This counter-transference response may have resonated with Peter's fantasy of his dead twin as well as his relationship with a mother deadened to his needs.

In the emerging transference, the therapist became aware that the internal twin relationship was expressed as if she was the dead twin (Lewin 2004). Peter had become immersed in his disorganisation, he did not have to think. It seemed the dead twin remained a potent object relationship for him as a developmental refuge to protect him from his painful experience of loss. The therapist remained available to all aspects of his communication, in particular Peter's deep sense of sadness. Over time Peter was able to enter into more dialogue with his therapist. He began to articulate his concern for his mother, feeling responsible for her upset, which became a central aspect of the transference. He began to 'understand' the beginning and ending of the session and to internally experience the rhythm of the regular weekly session. Slowly he became increasingly able to think for himself and reflect on his own thoughts and feelings. He was discovering an experience of being held in mind by someone who was emotionally available just to him. The individual relationship with the therapist was starting to have meaning.

Clinical vignette after six months

Peter was covered in clay but managed to complete his object which he said was a tortoise. He said, 'The tortoise is grumpy as he has to eat salad.' I wondered aloud after some thought, 'How do you know he is grumpy?' Peter did not answer and continued to fiddle with the tortoise. It was as if he ignored my question. After some time, I asked him how we knew when Peter was grumpy. Again he seemed completely unable to answer. After some time of thinking about this he then said, 'You know when I am grumpy by my face don't you?'

The above event marked an important shift in Peter's capacity to express his predicament verbally using his clay models. There were many aspects to this communication. Firstly there was an acknowledgement of two people alive in the room talking and communicating together. The therapist wondered to herself how much he identified with the tortoise. Was he like an animal that hibernates for long periods with a tough shell and a vulnerable soft inside that only comes out when he is feeling brave enough? She thought with Peter about this and what the tortoise might be feeling. Through the process of displacement, he was also bringing his 'grumpy' feelings. For Peter it was safer for the tortoise to be grumpy than for him to think about his own grumpy feelings. He was beginning to bring his aggression directly into the room.

Interpretation of cross feelings about himself and towards the therapist, in particular his sense of being intruded upon by her thoughts and words, began a process of acknowledging the problems he had with his own aggression. Peter always denied he felt cross as he feared his aggression would become out of control. He thought it was 'bad' to be angry. He started to use the clay to express his aggression which was now conscious, by taking great lumps of it, banging, hitting and stamping on it. The therapist reflected on her sense that she was witnessing Peter use his physical body that was alive and kicking in the womb-therapy room without fear of destruction.

While Peter began to explore his relationship with his mother, it was more difficult for him to think about his absent father. In the parent work, his mother came to understand how important it was to tell Peter about his twin sister. After this he became more relaxed and thinking was possible. He claimed that he had always known. Peter began to speak about his experience of being in the womb. While banging a piece of clay on the table, feeling angry and frustrated, he said he remembered kicking his mother (and sister). He added that he worried that he had hurt her. He was struggling with unconscious guilt that he may have damaged them both. His sister and his mother were interlinked in his mind as the object of his aggression which he experienced as so destructive. As these initial conflicts about survivor guilt surfaced, the therapy room became like the womb. The therapist was able to process and reflect on Peter's experience of being in the womb with a live twin who then dies. This helped them to understand together why bringing his aggression directly into the room was so complex for Peter.

The use of clay

The inherent properties of clay create a particularly helpful medium for those children struggling to symbolise their experience. The smallest of gestures with a lump of clay makes a mark or indentation. The tactile sensation makes the child feel instantly in control, sensually aroused, compelled to continue the exploration, usually at a deeply unconscious level. The nature of clay is suggestive of aspects of body products and those children who soil can express and work through the relationship with their faeces. Clay work offers many opportunities for making and destroying, bashing, smearing and cutting without losing its qualities. The sense of clay having a 'body' that can survive punishment is useful as the pliability of the clay encourages aggression to be overtly expressed. Giving shape to pent up feelings develops a sense of mastery, potency and self-esteem.

The therapeutic use of clay has been well documented over the years (Case and Dalley 2006). Henley (2002) gives a broad overview of the uses of clay with children both individually and in groups. Other writers have contributed to the discussion when working with particular client groups. Case (2005) writes about three different children in therapy who came to symbolise their internal experience using clay. She describes how the three-dimensional aspect of clay produced a separate object which created a triangular interaction, the third perspective of the Oedipal triangle: 'Creating this separate third object with an internal dialogue with the self enables many aspects of unconscious processes to emerge which can then be put into words and meaning takes place' (p. 182).

In describing her work with severely disabled children, Rabiger (1990) cites further properties of clay in the development of self and other with an awareness of 'inside' and 'outside' and the beginnings of symbolic awareness: 'Clay can be used as a substance to be manipulated, to help acknowledge just *something* outside of the self . . . the child may be helped towards autonomy' (p. 26). The clay can be changed, broken, fragmented into tiny pieces, put together, moulded, put back in the bag. As playfulness and spontaneity develops in the creative moment, deeper issues such as fear of fragmentation, annihilation and loss of control can be addressed.

Sagar (1990) suggests that clay helps those children who have been sexually abused to establish clearer body boundaries. When frequent masturbation or preoccupation with the child's own genitals – whether in private or public – occurs, clay objects can provide the means for reworking the trauma. Clay is often used in conjunction with other materials such as paint, sand, string, paper and plastic containers. It can be shaped to mirror the internal experience of the child and also come to represent aspects of the self the child wants to externalise – 'an operation to remove the bad stuff' (Sagar 1990: 110). Lillitos (1990) describes how a child referred to her for intestinal motility problems spent two full sessions working silently on a clay model which she painted red and green and then proclaimed it was a 'throne surrounded by precious jewels'. 'Being on the throne' is a recognised euphemism for going to the lavatory. Lillitos describes how she came to understand the 'precious jewels' were the child's idealised faeces that she used unconsciously as a bargaining point for the love and attention of which she felt deprived.

Clay was a medium through which Peter could search for the lost object which slowly emerged into consciousness. In the making of something concrete, which he undertook in a careful and thoughtful way, he began the gradual process of working through. When he was told about his twin he could think about and understand his sense of loss, which had become part of who he was. His loneliness was central in the establishment of a relationship with the therapist, a live mind who was available to him without distress. He found his 'live' twin in the transference, and by thinking about the therapist's interpretations in a meaningful way he could take them in and think about them for himself.

These internal shifts helped Peter's development into latency with symbolic play that had a narrative. He made considerable progress in understanding his frustration and communicating his thoughts and feelings. In developing a capacity to think, he began to channel his aggression, master his anxieties and develop the capacity to think, to speak and to learn. He could take pride in the growing collection of carefully constructed clay objects which included houses, animals and weapons. There was a growing sense of a peer group. He began to play with cars, build strong towers, talk about scary monsters and play fighting games with 'good and bad' in which conflict was resolved. As this phallic material emerged, he became more assertive, potent and began to say what he wanted rather than feel so helpless and hopeless. He was becoming a strong masculine boy rather than a messy, pooey baby. Talking about his feelings and thoughts was helpful in bringing more clarity to his world. In particular, he began to ask questions and be curious rather than just accept that he did not understand and remain in a unknowing confused state of mind as if identified with the unknown loss of the mother.

Steven

The separation process for twins is therefore problematic. Twinship relationships pervaded the dynamics of both of these families. In Steven's case, his mother was a twin. She had considerable difficulty in separating from her own mother and her twin sister, and since adolescence had developed a chronic eating disorder. In turn, she was unable to let Steven separate from her. On referral at the age of 6, Steven presented with obsessive behaviours, panic attacks, fear of vomiting and eating. He was particularly anxious about separating from his mother on going to school for fear of being sick. He sought constant reassurance from her that he would not be sick, which in turn escalated his mother's anxiety on leaving him. When in school he had panic attacks at lunchtimes and he would not eat or use the toilets.

Steven's mother suffered a late miscarriage of a daughter before Steven was born. The impact of this loss pervaded the early relationship with her baby son. Steven was a healthy baby but prematurely weaned from the breast at 3 weeks as his mother felt unable to manage the demands of his brother, three years older. His experience of loss of the breast and a mother who was emotionally unavailable, due to her own bereavement, was compounded by the birth of his younger sister three years later. Steven met all his developmental milestones and there were no separation problems when he began nursery at 2 and a half. The onset of his phobic symptoms began when he was 3, soon after the birth of his sister. Steven had been out with his father and older brother and on returning home to his mother he was sick all over her. Since then Steven had been intensely anxious about separating from his mother for fear of being sick. By the time of the referral it was difficult to get him into school or indeed any activity that would involve parting from his mother.

Steven's situation will be considered in less clinical detail but it is helpful to think about him in relation to Peter because they were such different children who came to use the clay at different points in their therapy to symbolise and bring meaning to deeply buried experiences – that is, to put words to an experience that was not yet consciously known. While Peter used the clay throughout his treatment to slowly build up a language to put words to feelings, shifting from a state of internal disorganisation to a more integrated sense of self, Steven, on the other hand, used the clay to express internal 'mess' and fragmentation that had been deeply buried. He was a highly verbal and articulate child, who presented as overtly capable but internally vulnerable. Over the two years of his treatment he used art-making to explore and understand his predicament. However, at a particular point in his therapy, in the termination phase, there was an experience of getting 'stuck' as he became lost for words, overwhelmed by his feelings, and had no way of explaining or understanding his confused and angry state of mind.

Assessment

When Steven was offered an individual assessment, there was a question whether he would be able to separate from his mother to work on his own. In the event, he separated easily from her. Over the course of the assessment, Steven engaged quickly, establishing his chatty manner with the therapist. He was an endearing little boy. His small stature elicited a positive but protective response from friends, teachers and the therapist. He spoke anxiously of the sick feeling in his tummy when he was away from his mother and how it was only her that made the feeling go away. He presented the conflict of wanting to be the big independent schoolboy who could manage on his own without his mother, but at the same time a regressive wish to be the baby with a fear of growing up, becoming separate from his mother.

Treatment

At the beginning of his therapy, Steven chose structured activities such as drawing, painting and model-making, working with purpose as if he had already decided what he might bring to his weekly sessions. He readily engaged in the therapeutic process. His articulate speech and superficial cheerfulness hid underlying anxiety and an undifferentiated internal world. It became clear that when there was no structure to his activities he began to feel anxious and then sick. This psychic emptiness that was filled up with the 'sick tummy feeling' disappeared when he found his mother. He had no sense of a mother who held him in mind when they were apart. Steven feared his aggressive impulses towards his mother as, in fantasy, he might destroy her. It was hard to differentiate Steven's anxieties from those of his mother. She was equally gratified by his continual dependence on her.

Slowly Steven's anxiety about separation shifted into confusion about himself generally. He began to realise that if he was worried about his mother then he did not worry about himself. Through making models and painting, he created structures and activities that defended against his deeper feelings of helplessness, emptiness and loss. He came to understand that his 'sickness' was related to his worries, and in particular his worries about leaving his mother. Steven was beginning to recognise the part of himself that wanted to remain a regressed infant staying continuously attached to his mother with no anxiety and no feelings of conflict at all.

As Steven made progress in understanding his emotional difficulties, his symptoms significantly diminished. He seldom spoke of his sick feeling. He became more assertive, able to leave his mother without needing persistent reassurance and go to school without complaint. He tentatively began to join his father and brother in their activities and stay away from home. His mother felt more able to let him go and be with them. As this progress became consolidated, an ending to his therapy was agreed.

While this termination phase was underway he witnessed his younger sister being sick in the car on the way to the clinic. On arrival, his mother, herself in some distress, described the situation in graphic detail to the therapist. Although Steven was able to process feelings of disgust and fury in the session that followed, this incident precipitated the recurrence of extreme separation anxiety and phobias about being sick. Vomit still represented the undigestible anxieties of his mother which he could not process on his own. Once again he began to complain of stomach-aches and his mother sought further medical solutions to Steven's emotional distress. She told him that he had a phobia.

In the context of this termination phase, Steven was struggling to work through issues in relation to separation and loss of the relationship with the therapist. The therapist had in mind his premature loss of the breast and wondered about the timing of the ending and whether patterns were being repeated. However, she did not want to collude with Steven's symptomatology by extending the therapeutic timeframe. During this phase of treatment it was possible to work with Steven's deeper feelings that he had defended against until now. Hostility and rage towards the therapist surfaced. In the transference, she became a paternal figure, coming in between Steven and his mother in his pre-Oedipal rage. In his mind she was going to abandon him (end the therapy) and leave him feeling vulnerable with unresolved Oedipal conflicts. Battling with her in his resistance to attend his sessions, he became silent, defiant and withdrawn over several weeks. In order to break the impasse and also as an attempt to re-establish play together, the therapist silently passed Steven a blank piece of paper. This initiated a series of notes that passed between them. Words were exchanged in written form.

Here is an example of the dialogue:

I Want
mummy
now

How will it help you?

Because Ill
Be with
her.

😊
It
will
help
me

Can you say a bit more about
why you need mummy when you
feel cross and upset.

Because I didn't feel well
one and I Sat with mumm
and I felt Beter

For several weeks this dialogue continued on paper. Steven remained defiant, sitting with his back to the therapist, but gradually he became curious. They read together what had been written the week before.

Following the half-term break, Steven returned, still angry and silent. He looked around the room and found the clay. There was a sense that this was an act of defiance and self-determination. He had never used clay before. Silently, turning his back, he made what came to be called his 'man'. He could find no words for his confusion and rage. The therapist also felt bewildered but remained in the confusion. She felt excluded and totally shut out by his silent rage but had the strong feeling that Steven, 'twinned' with his mother, was in touch with a 'deadness' that could not be reached or named. The clay offered him an alternative way to give shape to these infantile conflicts. The figure of the 'man' led on to a series of clay work in which Steven came to play with the clay, make pools of vomit with different colours and shapes and master his fears in this way. In one session he courageously announced that if he was sick in the session 'this is what it would look like'. He tentatively made a pool shape with the clay, added water and then mixed together paint to make what he called 'a disgusting yukky mess'. The therapist was able to reflect on how this was like 'his disgusting yukky messy feelings'. He was able to say with a grimace on his face what his sister's vomit looked like.

This process was a potent agency for change. He experienced the therapist receive and contain his 'disgusting feelings' in a meaningful way. They were not as destructive as he had feared. Symbolising the experience helped him to put this into words. The important thing was that the feelings were exclusively his own and, by externalising them he could begin to understand them. The clay had provided a means to express this part of himself, his disintegrated state of mind, that was so frightening, messy and chaotic and had no words. He could, at the same time, be a 'man' and face up to his difficulties in a more 'ego-syntonic' way.

Subsequently he was able to work towards the end of his therapy, think about the impending loss of the therapist and also about separation from his mother. He was building a separate sense of self as a strong young boy. He needed this in order to withstand his mother's anxieties and projections, and her own problems of separating from him. Steven's fear of loss of a significant object had created his need to control his world and that of his mother. There was a sense that he had never really found her and he had been struggling with an 'unknown thought'. When he was able to experience her as a separate maternal object, he could move on in his development.

Conclusion

Peter and Steven were very different children linked by the experience of loss. Peter lost his twin sister and both children 'lost' an available maternal function at birth. Alvarez (1992) describes how the 'synchronised responsiveness' in the mother-baby relationship provides the necessary conditions for the infant to develop a sense of 'potency' as distinct from the creation of omnipotent illusions. The absence of real emotional availability on the part of the mother presented Peter and Steven with an experience of 'failed potency'. Both turned to their own body products, faeces and vomit, having failed to establish a satisfactory relationship to the breast. Their symptoms appeared at significant points of separation. The twinship in both families had a direct impact on this problem.

Peter, whose language was delayed, used the clay to help him to put his experience into words, develop ego strength and symbolic functioning. As the surviving twin, his loss created a situation of endlessly seeking an attachment that could not be found and a sense of deep disturbing loneliness. His mother's postnatal depression compounded this confusing infantile experience. On leaving his therapy, he was able to name his feelings of sadness and loss. Peter had begun to take control of his world, to learn and understand.

Steven attempted to control his world through structure and activity. To defend against the emptiness, 'the unknown thought' he obsessively worried about being sick. His difficulties were connected to the loss of an emotionally available mother and premature separation which developed into severe separation anxiety and phobic symptoms. When facing the loss of his therapy, and a relationship with a maternal figure that did listen and understand, profound feelings were stirred up for which he had no words. The clay 'man' began a process of coming to terms with the experience in his early infancy and separation from his mother and the therapist. This led on to a series of clay works that consolidated this developmental shift. Steven found a masculine assertiveness leading to improved sense of self. The 'man' had a similar function to Peter's hamster in the concrete representation of his experience.

The clay forms gave shape and meaning to the pre-verbal experience of both boys. Peter found what he had lost – his twin. Steven came to understand what he never really had – an emotionally available mother. Parent work enabled both mothers to work through their grief and understand their responses to their children. This helped to free a space within their minds so that Peter and Steven could be seen as separate and viable sons. Working through the loss, Peter and Steven made the necessary moves into latency.

References

Ainsworth, M. (1962) The effects of maternal deprivation: a review of findings and controversy in the context of research strategy, *WHO Public Health Papers*, no. 14. Geneva: WHO.

Ainsworth, M. (1977) Social development in the first year of life: maternal influences on infant-mother attachment, in J.M Tanner (ed.) *Developments in Psychiatric Research*. London: Tavistock.

Alvarez, A. (1992) *Live Company*. London: Routledge.

Bion, W. (1963) *Learning from Experience*. London: Karnac.

Bowlby, J. (1971) *Attachment*. London: Penguin.

Bowlby, J. (1973) *Separation*. London: Penguin.

Bowlby, J. (1980) *Loss*. London: Penguin.

Brazelton,T.B. and Cramer, B.G. (1991) The Earliest Relationship. London: Karnac.

Burlingham, D. (1952) *Twins: A Study of Three Pairs of Identical Twins*. London: Imago.

Case, C. (2005) *Imagining Animals: Art, Psychotherapy and Primitive States of Mind*. London: Routledge.

Case, C. and Dalley,T. (2006) *Handbook of Art Therapy*, 2nd edn. London: Routledge.

Freud, A. (1958) Adolescence, P*sychoanalytic Study of the Child*, 13: 255–78.

Freud, A. and Burlingham, D. (1944) *Infants Without Families*. New York: International Universities Press.

Freud, S. (1915) *Mourning and Melancholia*, SE 14. London: Hogarth.

Green, A. (1986) *On Private Madness*. London: Hogarth.

Henley, D. (2002) *Clayworks in Art Therapy*. London: Jessica Kingsley.

Judd, D. (1995) *Give Sorrow Words: Working with a Dying Child*. London: Whurr.

Klein, M. (1940) Mourning and its relation to manic depressive states, in *Love, Guilt and Reparation*. London: Hogarth.

Lewin, V. (2004) *The Twin in the Transference*. London: Whurr.

Lewis, E. and Bryan, E.M. (1988) Management of perinatal loss of a twin, *British Medical Journal*, 297: 1321–3.

Liekerman, M. (2003) Depression and the mother's conflict, *Journal of Child Psychotherapy*, 29(3): 301–15.

Lillitos, A. (1990) Control, uncontrol, order and chaos: working with children with intestinal motility problems, in C. Case and T. Dalley (eds) *Working with Children in Art Therapy*. London: Routledge.

Piontelli, A. (1992) *From Fetus to Child: An Observational and Psychoanalytic Study*. London: Routledge.

Piontelli, A. (2002) *Twins from Fetus to Child*. London: Routledge.

Rabiger, S. (1990) Art therapy as a container, in C. Case and T. Dalley (eds) *Working with Children in Art Therapy*. London: Routledge.

Sagar, C. (1990) Working with cases of child sexual abuse in C. Case and T. Dalley (eds) *Working with Children in Art Therapy*. London: Routledge.

Trevarthen, C. and Aitken, K. (2001) Infant subjectivity: research, theory and clinical applications, *Journal of Child Psychology and Psychiatry*, 42(1): 3–48.

Winnicott, D.W. (1945) Primitive emotional development, in *Through Paediatrics to Psychoanalysis*. London: Hogarth, 1977.

Woodward, J. (1998) *The Lone Twin: Understanding Twin Bereavement and Loss*. London: Free Association Books.

Chapter 5

Working with the whole class in primary schools

Dean Reddick

Introduction

Pupils, aged between 8 and 9 in a Year 4 class, had been asked to draw themselves as an animal and then to join together in groups of like animals to make a piece of work to present to the whole class (Plate 2). One of the animal groups provided the following narrative:

> The mum monkey asked the dad monkey to get a banana for the baby. The dad monkey refused. The mum monkey stabbed herself. The monkey children argued amongst themselves about who is the oldest child and ignored their parents and the baby. The baby monkey called one of his siblings stupid and fat. She replied that she is not fat. The fat monkey cried. The three older monkey children described the baby monkey as smelly and explained that the mum monkey does not wash the baby. The narrators look worried as they told us this and the story ended here.

There was quiet at the end of this presentation. I reflected that this was a story about a baby who is not looked after. I invited the class to comment. The task was made more difficult as the baby monkey in the story was identified as a child who I believed to have been neglected in reality and who I had worked with in individual therapy. This child had no friends in the class and behaved in bizarre and challenging ways (such as being an animal). One of the children said 'the dad does not help the mum'. Another said 'the mum is depressed'. I encouraged the class to describe what this meant and they came up with the idea of a mum who cries and is sad. I said that the depressed mum in the story does not look after the baby who is smelly and the dad does not help feed the baby. The monkeys in the story were described as fighting and arguing but it was the older monkey children who noticed that the monkey baby was smelly. I commented that I thought the monkey children were worried about the baby, that this was a sad and unhappy family of monkeys and that maybe some children in the class do not always get looked after properly. The presentation acted as symbol for the class's anxiety about the neglected child in their midst and touched on shared experiences of depressed parents and familial conflict.

This chapter focuses on therapeutic work with whole school classes, including the teachers and support staff. This innovative model is described through the case material of work with two classes, a Year 1 class and a Year 6 class, which covers the ages and spectrum of the latency period. The setting is a primary school in an inner-city area with high poverty and an ethnically diverse population. While I was working as an art therapist, the headteacher asked if I would develop this model of working as we both understood that learning depends on the emotional state of the learner and that emotional pain associated with knowing can lead to attempts to avoid pain by modification or evasion, a failure to 'learn from experience' (Bion 1962). The school had a learning-centred ethos which included an understanding that 'learning is a social and emotional relationship' (West Burnham 2004).

My initial reaction was to decline this request, for several reasons. I feared that working with 30 children would provide too much material (Skaife and Huet 1998). A school class is not a therapy group. It has its own agendas, beliefs and dynamics and the pupils have formed relationships. I could not treat it as a small art therapy group on a larger scale. I was anxious about watering down my practice and losing my professional identity by moving away from usual models of art therapy. This anxiety was exacerbated by working in an educational rather than a clinical setting.

Despite my initial reticence, the idea of working in the class did appeal to me. I had previous good experiences of co-designing and co-conducting multi-family groups of over 30 people at a Child and Adolescent Mental Health Service (CAMHS). Co-working with other mental health professionals gave me confidence to expand and develop my practice. Working in the classroom would present staff with 'a knowledge of group dynamics [which] would seem to be invaluable for all teachers' (Waller 1993: 90).

Developing the model

The development of the educational curriculum in personal, health and social education (PHSE) and citizenship alongside other government policies such as *Every Child Matters* (DoH 2003) and The Children's Act 2004 have raised the profile of emotional issues and relationships in primary schools and provided an educational context for the development of whole-class work. 'Circle Time', and in particular, 'Quality Circle Time' (Mosley 1998) provide educational models for understanding the impact of emotional well-being on children's ability to learn. Quality Circle Time employs a whole-school approach: 'a highly structured group listening system ... [which enables children] to practise and participate in relationship education' (Mosley, 1998: 15). The model uses experiential learning, stresses the importance of developing empathy and links academic achievement to self-esteem.

Mosley emphasises the importance of the school staff feeling emotionally safe for the model to be effective, and states that PHSE is too often falsely divided from behaviour: 'Only if people understand and care about other people's inner worlds will they modify their behaviour' (1998: 4).

In developing the whole-class work, I wanted to preserve aspects of small art therapy groups while bearing in mind the importance of large group dynamics. Dalley (1990: 169) states that 'There is an argument against withdrawing children from the classroom, but in most cases, the value of removing one child and working individually far outweighs continuing the experience of the competition and battlegrounds within the classroom.' I wondered if it was possible to work in 'the battlegrounds' of the classroom as opposed to a separate art therapy group which provides a safe and contained space and 'gives ... children an opportunity to explore aspects of competition, leadership and dominance ... and also their feelings of anger, envy, rivalry' (Dalley 1993: 137). The classroom might be safe and containing but might also 'set up the worst areas of conflict' for children (Dalley 1993: 169). Working with children's experience of their class from within the class is different to working with these experiences in an art therapy group.

Yalom (1995) conceived a heterogeneous group as a microcosm of society where maladaptive forms of relating can be 'seen' in the group, experienced, thought about and changed through understanding of the emotional experience in the 'here-and-now'. 'Here-and-now' relating is a feature of the whole-class approach; it shows group dynamics in action. Prokofiev (1998) reminds us that the resolution of disturbances aroused by difference is a crucial therapeutic factor and one that is available when working in a class. Dalley (1993: 138) offers a description of the small group 'as a reconstruction of the family'. How far the class as a group was understood as a family as opposed to a society became an important issue in the work.

Primary-school children and latency

As a stage of development, latency comes after infancy and before puberty and adolescence. During this period the interests and struggles of infantile sexuality give way to sexual latency: 'The sexual impulses cannot be utilised during these years of childhood, since the reproductive functions have been deferred' (Freud [1905] 2001: 178). There is a move away from the intensity of the family and toward society. Freud understood the move to latency as coming from the resolution of the Oedipus complex, and at the cost of infantile sexual impulses. Sexual energy is sublimated by the latency child through the mechanism of reaction formation, a process that allows the child to build up the mental dams of disgust, shame and morality. Freud understood that manifestations of sexuality which are not sublimated make a child ineducable. He wrote that educators knew the importance of the moral defensive forces of latency but were unable to do much about interruptions to latency ([1905] 2001: 179).

Edwards (1999) sees Freud's original formulation of the latency child as emphasising a defensive and disappointed turning away, a giving up of Oedipal love objects through the internalisation of the Oedipal prohibition and the development of the superego (and the child's interest in rules). Edwards emphasises how the resolution of the Oedipus complex leads towards growth as the child identifies with and introjects the parental couple rather than repudiating them, leading to the desire to make friends. Meltzer (1973) described the latency-aged child's craving to develop areas of strength and skill, a hungering for facts and for collecting, which can lead to learning without meaning.

Latency ends with the onset of puberty and with the reawakening of infantile sexuality. The period of latency coincides fairly accurately with primary school ages (5 to 11). The primary school class with up to 30 children is the most constant social group for children and is the arena where many latency concerns are appropriately placed. Many of the problems in primary school classes arise from children's failure to achieve latency.

The model

The aim of the model was to:

- develop understanding of how the class operates dynamically;
- lessen the impact of defensive group dynamics in order to allow the class to function socially, emotionally and educationally;
- increase class cohesion;
- introduce to staff a way of working with the class at an emotional level which extended the concepts of Circle Time.

The model is based on my experiences of children's art therapy groups (see Prokofiev 1998 for a thorough review of art therapy groups for children), of multi-family groups (Behr 1996; Asen and Scholz 2001), and my understanding of large group therapy and its focus on culture (de Mare *et al.* 1991). Transference is present but is not the primary therapeutic factor. Art is central but art-making is not. I looked for and focused on group-wide events (Whitaker 1985) and 'here-and-now' (Yalom 1995) interactions.

When I first used this approach I asked the class to draw themselves as an animal. Case (2005) explores in detail the occurrence and meanings of animal images in children's art therapy and states that 'our likeness and difference from other animals allow an interplay in our minds with parts of the self through anthropomorphic animal images' (p. 44).

I had never set themes before, having been concerned that it would interfere with the transference and the group dynamics (McNeilly 1984, 1987;

Liebmann 1986; Greenwood and Layton 1987). I chose to use a task as part of a structured approach because structure contains children's and therapists' anxiety (Prokofiev 1998: 52). Multi-family groups also rely on structures to contain anxiety and chaos (Laquer 1972, 1980; Behr 1996; Asen and Scholz 2001).

As I grew more confident with the model the children were invited to draw what they wanted. When using a task every child had a turn to present their image. Without the task we were able to move away from turn-taking into a more fluid, group orientated way of working.

Each session lasted between one and one and a half hours and for between 6 and 14 sessions. Sessions were held in the classroom, weekly, and at the same time each week. They began and ended by meeting in a large inward facing circle with any art-making happening in the middle of the session.

Whole-class work with a Year 6 class

This Year 6 class, aged 10–11, were in the final term of their primary school and facing transition to secondary school. Many members of the class had been together since they entered the school. The class had 30 children and was ethnically diverse. I met the class for six sessions with the class teacher present.

When I first entered the classroom, two boys immediately spoke to me. The first boy, Paul, said 'Alright mate', and the second boy, Hamza, echoed him. This was repeated several times. Both boys were grinning, and I felt that I was being challenged. I said 'Hello' and added that I was not their 'mate' and asked them to wait until I had been introduced. This quietened the two boys. Initially my response seemed unfriendly and terse.

The class came together in a circle. Pupils were allowed to sit wherever they wanted and without exception the class arranged themselves into a boy/girl divide. The teacher introduced me and I explained that we would be working together to think about feelings and relationships. I described the format of the sessions and answered some initial questions.

I asked the class to draw themselves as an animal, to work on their own and not to ask for help from each other. During the art-making the majority of the class worked independently and there was a sense that pupils were enjoying the activity. A handful of pupils found the task difficult, complaining that they were unable to think of an animal or that they were unable to draw. These pupils were given some individual attention by the class teacher and myself. We did not suggest an animal and instead encouraged the pupils to think about their difficulty with the task. Paul and Hamza found the task difficult and diverted each other by deriding each other's drawings. They managed to make drawings, with adult support and supervision. Another boy, Jack, was anxious about attempting the task but finally made a small drawing of a rhinoceros.

We returned to the circle. Several pupils had not completed their drawings so we decided to finish them next week. Instead of looking at the drawings, we talked about how people had experienced the activity. Several pupils described feeling embarrassed, shy and worried about their drawings being laughed at.

During this part of the session it became clear that the girls found talking about their experiences easier than the boys. The girls seemed animated, engaged and confident while the majority of the boys seemed uncomfortable, uncertain and unwilling to talk. I commented on this to the class and asked if they had any ideas why. Several girls who sat together were particularly vocal and answered that boys were not confident in speaking about themselves but were confident about doing sports. They enjoyed fighting rather than doing their work. One girl accused the boys of being naughty and lazy. As none of the boys challenged this view, I asked the boys if they agreed with this. One boy answered angrily that he did not agree with the girls and that not all boys were as they described. I asked the class if they understood why only one boy had disputed the claim that they were lazy and naughty. Again it was several of the girls who wanted to reply. I asked them to wait and I challenged the boys to speak. They declined to respond and one of the girls said that the boys wouldn't speak because there were three boys in the class who were very powerful.

There was a general murmuring of agreement from the class. Paul and Hamza were identified as two-thirds of the triumvirate (the third member never attended a session, he was refusing to attend school). I restated the contention that some of the girls were saying that three powerful boys were somehow responsible for the rest of the boys being silent. I asked Paul and Hamza if they had anything to say. Paul said that talking about themselves was not something that boys did, that talking about feelings was for girls. He had some support from both boys and girls for this opinion. I wondered aloud if the class had organised themselves along a boy/girl split, with the girls being responsible for thinking about feelings and the boys being responsible for being disruptive and uncooperative, for being naughty. As we were coming to the end of the session, I told the class that they had identified a powerful dynamic, something we would continue to think about in future sessions. I thanked the class for their hard work and collected all the drawings in order to keep them safe.

The class teacher told me the class nearly always organised themselves according to the boy/girl division and that it was a problem as the boys missed out on their learning. I noticed that many of the girls seemed more mature than the boys. This was in part due to the unequal development of boys and girls at this age. Several of the girls in the class were already pubescent and therefore moving out of the latency period. The boys, in general, seemed smaller and younger. This session also demonstrated the importance of attending to the 'here and now' (the discomfort about talking, fear of ridicule) and of allowing a dialogue to develop (between the girls' words and the boys' silence).

In the second meeting we finished our drawings, reformed the circle and took it in turns to show our work. I went first and showed my drawing of a dog fox. I explained that I had been a bit nervous about meeting everybody for the first time and that I had felt challenged by Paul's and Hamza's greeting to me. I said that my fox looks like it is on guard and I asked the class what they thought about my picture. Several pupils made associations to the drawing, saying it looked like a cat, and that foxes are sneaky; they hunt other animals. I agreed that foxes are often thought of as sly and cunning and wondered to the class whether my sneaky fox could be trusted. There was some relieved laughing at this and I suggested that we did not know each other very well and that maybe it was hard to trust a fox.

Going first and speaking openly about my work was a way of modelling for the class to think and speak about their animals, a technique from multi-family groups. It gave the class a chance to talk about how they felt about my arrival in their classroom and also addressed fear of ridicule, a common latency fear of being seen to get it wrong.

We continued around the circle with each pupil speaking about their image and with the class being invited to comment. This way of working allowed for comments to be made to the picture rather than directly to the person, making it easier to say potentially difficult things. Paul showed his scorpion (Figure 5.1). He wrote, 'Its sneaky'; 'People is scared of it' and 'It hurts people'. When he spoke about its poisonous sting, he seemed both proud and ashamed of his scorpion. The class were attentive and thought a scorpion was a good choice for him. Paul's drawing allowed him to show that he knew he could be poisonous and hurtful and the class were able to acknowledge this. I drew the class's attention to the scorpion's thick armour which, along with its sting, was a way for it to protect itself. Paul was able to allow himself (and others) to hear these ideas without protest and the class supported him with their seriousness and attention. Hamza represented himself as a tortoise, another animal with a hard shell.

As noted, Paul and Hamza were two-thirds of a triumvirate which was actually a pair with the third member absent. This suggests an unresolved Oedipal constellation: the three could not survive and had regressed further to a pair. My sense of being challenged as I entered the room and representing myself as a dog fox were transference manifestations which related to the two boys feeling threatened by the arrival of the Oedipal father. The boys' power, their use of aggression and derision, and their defiant attitude to authority, were linked to a need to protect their unresolved infantile needs. They had not achieved sexual latency and yet were on the point of entering adolescence, and their infantile needs impacted on the whole class. The whole-class approach gave both boys an opportunity to represent their dilemma and the class a chance to acknowledge it. A more detailed working through of their difficulties would be the remit of individual or small-group therapy.

After this, five girls each presented a butterfly drawing. Samira presented

It's sneaky

People is scared of it

It hurts people.

Figure 5.1 Scorpion.

first, describing her butterfly as pretty and colourful. The class responded to this and quickly came up with the belief that the boys would not draw butterflies as they are girlish. Neeta said the colour of her butterfly was important (Plate 3). The striking orange and black reminded me that colour in nature can be used by prey animals to startle, threaten and intimidate predators. Sadie showed her butterfly and said she liked to be well presented, colourful, tidy and smart. Jade was quiet when invited to speak about her butterfly. The class spoke for her, as though the butterfly image belonged to them, and decided that the antennae were how the butterfly sensed its environment. Roxanna described her butterfly as pretty, clever, colourful and good at making friends. The shared themes seemed appropriate to these girls who were in the process of leaving the school and latency behind them. The reference to colour also related to the girls' ethnicity (black, asian and white), an acknowledgement of the importance of racial difference among similarity. The butterfly girls and several other girls talked about how they were a 'crew' and how this was a way to protect themselves from the boys (both literally, in terms of some of the boys' physical aggression, but also in terms of keeping latency in place).

In the third session the class teacher was absent and the covering teacher, Ms Jones, had been the class teacher in a previous year. Paul and Hamza were defiant and distracting while the class, in a circle, reviewed the work. The 'mood' (Whitaker 1985) of the class became lethargic and unresponsive despite the first four presentations being eloquent and interesting. I asked why this was. Roxanna said they were tired and had been working hard. The ennui continued for the next two presentations and I raised the issue again. Various suggestions came forward that Ms Jones was like a shark for setting difficult work (the 27-times table), like a tiger or lion, sly like a snake, or like a fox. Ms Jones responded playfully: it was clear that there was a lot of trust between this teacher and the class and this allowed for the expression of anger and loss about the forthcoming end (leaving the school). The class were able to move out of their repressed, bored state once they acknowledged their angry and sad feelings about leaving their teachers and the school.

Unable to stay with this mood of the class, Paul and Hamza acted out their angry feelings, becoming defiant and delinquent. This brought to mind Case's description of the stereotypical boy who is, 'outwardly defended . . . who, if touched by feeling would erupt into aggressive defences of physical and verbal abuse.' (1990: 136).

In the next session I asked the class to group themselves according to their animals, and produce a piece of art or writing, a play, song or drama about the 'family' of animals. This task took up most of the session. In the last two sessions we sat in a circle and the groups presented their work. The first group consisted of two boys and three girls who had drawn sea creatures. They produced a poem called, 'We'll Never Get Along'. The girls in this group blamed the boys for being uncooperative. The boys refuted this. Many in the class thought that working together was difficult and someone said it would be easier if there was a leader.

One of the difficulties of the task was that by introducing family-sized sub-groups I was moving the class away from class-wide thinking. The above group demonstrated this difficulty by remaining firmly in latency and choosing not to descend into the intensity of the family (nominally pre-latency) context.

The butterfly family presented a poem by reciting it in unison as follows:

> Butterflies are all related like us, beautiful, colourful and pretty
> Usually they all start of [*sic*] as caterpillars
> Today they rest
> Tomorrow they fly
> Every time they make a flight, they see their families flying high
> Roses and flowers are mostly what butterflies are attracted to
> Fluttering and flapping their wings
> Lovely colours make them stand out
> Yes they are a beautiful and colourful family.

The group told us that the family are all female and one girl said it would have been gay to pretend to be male. I commented on the derogatory use of the term gay and wondered if the class was worried about playing with gender roles in relation to their developing sexuality. Roxanna said that if they had drawn a mum and a dad they would have been called lesbians. I commented that a mum and dad could represent a creative way of male and female being together. I wondered to the class if their anxiety was in part about sex. This group had also come up against a latency prohibition of thinking of each other as a family, with sexual partners in the form of parents being omitted. The butterflies remained a latency-aged, single-gender peer group. The idea of pretending to be the opposite gender was designated as homosexual, a latency fear of identifying with (rather than relating to) the opposite gender. The idea that butterflies 'usually' come from caterpillars seems to cast doubt that girls come from babies (with its implication of sexual intercourse). The family is present but remote. However, the colourful butterflies are attracted to flowers (possibly a reference to sex as flowers are sexual organs) and they flutter and flap their wings, which can be interpreted as representing flirting. The poem and the discussion were concerned with resisting a regressive pull back into the family and infantile sexuality, while alluding to the coming teenage years and the development of sexuality in adolescence.

The gender split in the class had its roots in the latency tendency for boys and girls to form same gender peer groups, a tendency 'based on identification rather than object love' (Edwards, 1999: 81). The boys' triumvirate was overly defensive, as normal latency mechanisms could not keep a lid on infantile needs. The butterfly girls' 'crew' had a more normal defensive latency function and allowed some sexual symbols to emerge as the girls moved into adolescence. It was an 'enabling solution', in terms of a group focal conflict (Whitaker, 1985): it dealt with both the wish (to explore developing sexuality) and the fear (that developing sexuality was prohibited or homosexual).

Whole-class work with a Year I class

In the work with a Year 1 class, the children aged between 6 and 7, the gender issue emerged but in a different way. There was a similar ethnic mix to these 30 children and the teacher was also present in the group. No theme was set in these sessions and we looked together at the images and discussed what we could see.

During the first two sessions the children were polite and the dialogue was stilted. The class was reluctant to talk about strong feelings. One girl mentioned she had an argument but would not elaborate. The class suggested her reluctance was due to being frightened of being 'told off' and told me that arguing was 'rude' (impolite). This deadening latency atmosphere dissipated when the class used the drawing materials and we noticed a reoccurrence of superhero images in the boys' drawings and a large number of rainbows and flowers in the girls' drawings. Several boys excitedly said that superheroes were fast, powerful and tough. At the same time most of the boys took part in denigrating the girls, saying that boys are cleverer, faster and more powerful.

Superheroes occur frequently in latency children's play and art, mostly among boys. Many latency concerns can be discerned in superheroes: issues of morality, strength, skill and often a stereotyped and split attitude to gender (e.g. Man of Steel). Superheroes therefore provide powerful representations for male latency children to identify with.

In the fifth session a girl drew a picture of a Power Ranger in and out of costume. This drawing reminded us of the fantastic nature of the superhero: beneath the façade is a human being, often with a traumatic past including loss and separation, such as Batman and Superman. (Haen and Brannon 2002). The link between loss and separation and the defensive formulation of a fantastic persona resonates with some latency boys' struggle to negotiate the move away from the mother as an Oedipal partner and as an object to identify with. In this formulation the superhero is a symbol of the rescuing father who helps the mother and child to separate (Gerrard 1992). This need for a stereotyped male figure is demonstrated by Fred's drawing of the 'Hulk' (Figure 5.2). He described the Hulk as a monster not a man, perhaps alluding to the monstrous, extreme masculinity that the Hulk represents, but also that he was 'farting'. Although the Hulk and many other superheroes demonstrate a paternal urge to protect, care for and rescue the vulnerable, the 'farting' might refer to the expulsion of this felt-to-be-dangerous quality and had an attacking quality to it. During this session Fred and another boy accused me of being 'girly' for having long hair and wearing a pink shirt, as

Figure 5.2 Hulk

though the dangerous and denigrated feminine feelings were split off and placed in me.

Several boys, including Fred, described their peer Jonathon as the leader and the class, in general, agreed with this. Jonathon was described as fast, strong and clever. Fred said that Jonathon was faster than anyone including me, which prompted his suggestion that Jonathon should race me in the playground. I resisted the challenge and asked who the class thought would win. It was mostly boys who answered and they all favoured Jonathon. I had been disposed of as a leader and Jonathon had been elected in my place, as a sort of superboy.

The next session began with the girls being less passive and more talkative, with several girls not doing as they were asked. I commented on the difference in the class and one girl said the boys and girls had 'swapped brains'. When the class went to draw at the tables I noticed that without exception boys and girls sat opposite each other. Previously the class had arranged itself into blocks of same-gender groups. The seating, arranged without discussion by the class, suggested that boys and girls, while on opposite sides of the table, were in relation to each other, rather than separated from each other.

The drawings from this session showed several images of trees, all drawn by girls. The trees were similar – all solitary or drawn with a figure, strong-looking and bearing fruit. As a group-level representation I thought they symbolised the position of the girls who refuted the group belief that girls are less strong, fast and clever than boys. The active (vertical) tree trunk bearing fruit seemed to suggest a less split view of male and female attributes. Two boys had copied Jonathon's drawing of a fight scene, a third boy had given up on his copy and was annoyed and disappointed by his failure. The class said the copying showed that the boys were trying to be friends. This 'friendship through copying' was based on identification with Jonathon as a stereotyped male figure. The friendship functioned to keep latency in place by bolstering the boys' male identity and repressing worries about sexuality left over from infancy, a repudiation of the Oedipal mother. This process, based on normal latency defences, left little room for the development of real friendships between these boys. Fred's next drawing of a Hulk and Superman was suggestive of intercourse and could herald the arrival of a sexual, parental couple, coinciding with Fred moving away from Jonathon (both physically in the circle and in respect of Fred supporting and idealising Jonathon in the session's work). This move represented a lessening of Fred's over-identification with Jonathon and enabled Fred to be more in the group.

Several girls developed a discussion about friendships, describing how some girls get excluded. We thought about how the boys avoided these problems by making Jonathon the leader: as long as the boys followed him they were all friends. Farzanah asked if I was saying that the girls should have a leader. I said no, the girls' problems with friendship were more honest than the boys, who tried to hide worries about friendship.

In our penultimate meeting the class teacher said the class had decided during a Circle Time that there would be no leaders among the children. I wondered if this was a decree from the adults, a top-down system change which I felt uncomfortable with. I thought the intervention by the adults related to the imminent end of the work, an attempt to get rid of the issues and problems that had become visible during the work. I asked Jonathon how he found the change and he said it was hard. However, I sensed that other members of the class were relieved at the new ruling.

The final session began by looking at the images from the previous week. I reminded the class that this was our last session and that we would review our work together. We looked at a drawing of a football match of boys versus girls. The score showed the girls losing 4 to 0. I asked the girls to comment and several girls said it was rude. Keshisha said sometimes she wins against the boys. Although this image shows boys beating girls it is different to the earlier grandiosity of the boys and the denigration of the girls. There are no super-heroes on the pitch and the game is a play arena where boys and girls can compete. The score line is not unrealistic and the girls in the class were able to express their feelings about the image freely. It felt like the powerful dynamics between boys and girls (which were clearly about these latency children trying to find safe de-sexualised gender identities) could now be played with.

Summary

Working in the classroom allowed powerful group dynamics to become more visible. Normal Circle Time activities and didactic approaches to emotional working are unable to achieve this because of the lack of a consistent experiential component (see Dudley *et al.* 1998). Art works were used to either represent a group self (as in the 'draw oneself as an animal' exercise) or to make visible 'shared themes [which] can build up in groups' (Whitaker, 1985: 35).

Pupils in both the classes were having difficulty learning due to either 'interruptions of latency' (Freud [1905] 2001) or strong defences such as repression, identification and splitting. Unsurprisingly, these interruptions and defences became expressed through gender issues with the most vulner-able children (e.g. Jonathon, Paul and Hamza) taking on specific roles for the group. The younger children used superheroes to express this, the older children were more explicit about their fear of sexuality, sometimes expressed as their fear of homosexuality. In the work the children's fear of sexuality was based on the power of identification as a way of relating. Identifying with the same gender was safe (nominally de-sexualised). To identify with the other gender threatened the latency child's carefully defended sexual identity; for the younger children this threatened to throw them back into infancy and an Oedipal maelstrom. For the older children, identification with the opposite sex reminded them of the closeness of adolescence and of the imminent reawakening of sexual relating.

In terms of assessing the impact of the whole-class work on the educational functioning of the class, broad conclusions can be drawn (see Reddick 2005).

In the Year 1 class, working with the group dynamics produced a noticeable shift in the functioning of the class. The class moved from being overly polite (based in a latency fear of breaking the rules), to recognising the gender split, to a more open and dynamic latency atmosphere. The politeness inhibited dialogue and expression which in turn deadened the learning atmosphere and risked splitting off emotion from learning. This gave way to a gender split which also had a negative impact on the class's ability to learn. The boys' preoccupation with getting close to Jonathon and the powerful fantasies, 'which denied reality and [were] irrational, even magical in quality' (Waller 1993: 33) allowed the boys to dispose of adults and deny their dependency needs. The girls became passive in the face of this and gave up their aggression. This impacted negatively on their learning as they became less curious and more inhibited.

Woods (1993: 73) writes that in mixed gender groups 'girls . . . can benefit from withdrawing some of their projections of badness and aggression on to the boys' and this process was relevant to this class. As some of the girls became less passive and as some of the boys moved away from Jonathon, new forms of relating (and therefore learning) emerged. Boys and girls came into relation with each other and the class teacher was able to impose a class rule banning child leaders. This top-down ruling is at odds with a psychodynamic group therapy approach but is of course not unusual in the normal context of the classroom. It demonstrated the regaining of authority by the class teacher which was met with relief by most of the class. The class teacher was not naturally given to working emotionally but tolerated the confusion and chaos generated in the middle part of the work and chose to use a strategic intervention towards the end to help the class move away from a restrictive group solution (Whitaker 1985). The whole-class model gave the teachers an insight into the power of group dynamics based on the emotional needs of individuals and the group, and allowed teaching staff to recognise how these dynamics impact on the class's ability to learn.

With the Year 6 class I was able to develop a less structured approach where I could move between addressing the group as a whole, the various subgroups and the individual; a fluid way of working which promotes a cohesive large-group system (Behr 1996). It was harder to assess the impact of the work on the educational functioning of this class as the group only ran for six sessions. The children were preparing to leave the school and appropriately used the space to think about this transition. This was in itself a valuable opportunity. The transition from primary to secondary school is hugely important for children. It involves a transition from latency to adolescence and these themes ran through the work with this class. From the work I was able to report some of the vulnerabilities of individual children, such as Paul, and support referrals for further therapeutic interventions.

Generally this model has developed using a framework of containment already provided by the teaching staff and the institution of the school. Its success is due to the average class being made up of a majority of emotionally-well members, some of whose latency has been temporarily interrupted. This whole-class approach can re-establish children's learning, social and emotional development as well as providing teachers with a clearer understanding of the dynamics operating in their classrooms.

References

Asen, E. and Scholz, M. (2001) Multiple family therapy with eating disordered adolescents: concepts and preliminary results, *European Eating Disorders Review*, 9(1): 33–42.

Behr, H. (1996) Multiple family group therapy: A group analytic perspective, *Group Analysis*, 29: 9–22.

Bion, W. (1962) *Learning from Experience*. London: Heinemann.

Case, C. (1990) Reflections and shadows: an exploration of the world of the rejected girl, in C. Case and T. Dalley (eds) *Working with Children in Art Therapy*, London: Routledge.

Case, C. (2005) *Imaging Animals: Art, Psychotherapy and Primitive States of Mind*. London: Routledge.

Dalley, T. (1990) Images and integration: art therapy in a multi-cultural school, in C. Case and T. Dalley (eds) *Working with Children in Art Therapy*, London: Routledge.

Dalley, T. (1993) Art psychotherapy groups, in K.N. Dwivedi (ed.) *Group Work with Children and Adolescents*, London: Jessica Kingsley.

De Mare, P., Piper, R. and Thompson, S. (1991) *Koinonia: From Hate, through Dialogue to Culture in the Large Group*. London: Karnac.

DoH (Department of Health) (2003) *Every Child Matters*. London: DoH.

Dudley, A., Gilroy, A. and Skaife, S. (1998) Learning from experience in introductory art therapy groups, in S. Skaife and V. Huet (eds) *Art Psychotherapy Groups: Between Pictures and Words*. London: Routledge.

Edwards, J. (1999) Kings, queens and factors: the latency period revisited, in D. Hindle and M.V. Smith (eds) *Personality Development: A Psychoanalytic Perspective*. London: Routledge.

Freud, S. ([1905] 2001) Three essays on the theory of sexuality, in J. Strachey (ed. and trans.) *The Standard Edition of the Complete Psychological Works of Sigmund Freud* (vol. 7). London: Vintage.

Gerrard, J. (1992) Rescuers and containers, fathers and mothers, *British Journal of Psychotherapy*, 9(1).

Greenwood, H. and Layton, G. (1987) *An out-patient art therapy group*, Inscape, Summer, pp. 12–19.

Haen, C. and Brannon, K.H. (2002) Superheroes, monsters, and babies: roles of strength, destruction and vulnerability for emotionally disturbed boys, *The Arts in Psychotherapy*, (29): 31–40.

Laquer, H.P. (1972) Mechanisms of change in multiple family therapy, in C.J. Sagar and H.S. Kaplan (eds) *Progress in Group and Family Therapy*. New York: Brunner/Mazel.

Laquer, H.P. (1980) The theory and practice of multiple family therapy, in L.R. Woldberg and M.L. Aronson (eds) *Group and Family Therapy*. New York: Brunner/Mazel.

Liebmann, M. (1986) *Art Therapy for Groups: A Handbook of Themes, Games and Exercises*. London: Routledge.

McNeilly, G. (1984) Directive and non approaches in art therapy, *Inscape Journal of Art Therapy*, December: 7–12.

McNeilly, G. (1987) Further contributions to group analytic art therapy, *Inscape Journal of Art Therapy*, summer: 8–11.

Meltzer, D. (1973) *Sexual States of Mind*, Strath Tay: Clunie Press.

Mosley, J. (1998) *More Quality Circle Time*. Cambridge: LDA.

Prokofiev, F. (1998) Adapting the art therapy group for children, in S. Skaife and V. Huet (eds) *Art Psychotherapy Groups Between Pictures and Words*. London: Routledge.

Reddick, D. (2005) What can children's drawings of themselves as animals from a year four class produced in a therapeutic group context tell us about the dynamics in the class? Unpublished MA thesis, Goldsmiths College, University of London.

Skaife, S. and Huet, V. (1998) Dissonance and harmony: theoretical issues in art psychotherapy groups, in S. Skaife and V. Huet (eds) *Art Psychotherapy Groups Between Pictures and Words*. London: Routledge.

Waller, D. (1993) *Group Interactive Art Therapy: Its use in Training and Treatment*. London: Routledge.

West Burnham, J. (2004) Creating the learning centred school, paper presented at an educational conference, White Hart Lane, London, 2 September.

Whitaker, D.S. (1985) *Using Groups to Help People*. London: Routledge & Kegan Paul.

Woods, J. (1993) Limits and structure in child group psychotherapy, *Journal of Child Psychotherapy*, 19(1): 63–78.

Yalom, I. (1995) *The Theory and Practice of Group Psychotherapy*, 4th edn. New York: Basic Books.

Chapter 6

Playing ball: oscillations within the potential space

Caroline Case

> Psychotherapy of a deep going kind may be done without interpretative work . . . the significant moment is that at which *the child surprises himself or herself*.
>
> (Winnicott 1971: 50–1)

Introduction

This chapter will address core therapeutic work in the development of play and creative work with materials within the relationship with the therapist. In Dorothy's (a child of 10 with dyspraxia) therapy, working with transference interpretations and moving the relationship onto a verbal level were not as significant as the 'doing together'. We literally 'played ball games'. The ball games could also serve as a metaphor for the need to meet those children who are hard to reach half way, in order to get them started in their own creative process, as a precursor to being able to live creatively. This needs a careful movement forward and back, something like playing ball, in order to take into account the child's ability to meet the therapist, and the hope and despair when they are very stuck in depression. Play can be self-healing when preoccupations are played out and a solution found.

Winnicott (1971: 38) wrote on play:

> Psychotherapy takes place in the overlap of two areas of playing, that of the patient and that of the therapist. Psychotherapy has to do with two people playing together. The corollary of this is that where playing is not possible then the work done by the therapist is directed towards bringing the patient from a state of not being able to play into a state of being able to play.

Ball-playing and playing the squiggle game allowed the development of varying intersubjective states. Some quality of a ball in play allowed experiments in relationship, including humour, flexibility and a new enjoyment of 'surprises': a response to the moment. Ball-playing gave her a state of readiness for contact with her own imagination. It would also be possible to think of Dorothy and me playing with her infant self, hard on the outside but soft and vulnerable inside, like the soft ball. In this way the two of us as parents could toss her infant self around and play with her.

Dali and the surrealists

Significant in Dorothy's therapy was the work of the surrealists. In previous papers, the influence of other artists, such as Monet (Case 1987) and Holbein (Case 1996, 2000), on children's work in therapy has been discussed. Dorothy was particularly entranced by images from the work of Salvador Dali, which I felt gave her permission to imagine and also served as a liberating model for thoughts, feelings and impressions for which there was no name. Dali was associated with the surrealists in the late 1920s and 1930s. In the 1920s the surrealists experimented with automatism, that is, writing or drawing without any conscious control. They were attempting to free themselves from the 'constraints of reason': 'The surrealist technic has something remarkable about it, at least in theory: it strives towards an unconscious exploitation of the unconscious, something like the automatic writing of mediums' (Ozenfant 1952: 132).

An attraction to a particular artist's pictures may represent an unconscious investment related to the matching of an inner experience as well as the unconscious beginnings of one's own image-making. (see Case and Dalley 2006 for further discussion on aesthetics). Dali seems to have had an ambivalent relationship with the surrealist movement and eventually was excommunicated because of his commercial success by the 1940s. However, earlier, he was greatly admired for the power of his imagination: 'It is perhaps with Dali that for the first time the windows of the mind are opened fully wide' (Breton quoted in Masters 1995: 5). The intention of the surrealists was to liberate the mind, in a form of cultural revolution: 'Surrealism is not a poetic form. It is a cry of the mind turning back on itself, and it is determined to break apart its fetters' (Breton quoted in Harrison and Wood 1992).

Dyspraxia

Dyspraxia can hinder and inhibit a child's ordinary and educational progress since it involves all those aspects of functioning which we describe as relating to 'doing'. Dyspraxic children may have fine and gross motor problems, difficulties with sequencing, with tenses and with time. They have memory impairment, are unable to remember where they left things or recall what they have learnt, they forget instructions and become disoriented. They have difficulty in playing creatively with others, but dislike playing alone. In the past, children with dyspraxia were often described as clumsy and did not receive appropriate help. They may have great difficulty both in writing mechanically and in organising ideas, and may, for example, only write on one side of an exercise book. They are usually treated with occupational therapy, perceptual and physiotherapy, as well as having specialist support at school.

Dorothy

Dorothy was almost 10 when she was referred to a Child and Adolescent Mental Health Service (CAMHS). She was a blonde, well-built child physically in the world, but she communicated very little, just saying 'don't know' or 'don't mind'. In family meetings she had a lethargic, empty feeling, and seemed very far back in herself, in a depressed way. She had been diagnosed with dyspraxia when she was younger. She had short-term memory impairment, poor coordination, and 'developmental verbal dyspraxia' – that is, oral difficulties affecting the movements necessary for speech. She found swallowing difficult which meant that she was a very slow eater. Her difficulty in making speech sounds and in making her language clear indicated an immaturity in expressive language development. She was in receipt of special learning support at school because of the resultant learning difficulties. She also presented with Asperger-related symptoms relating to change and lack of imagination. She was not able to visualise.

Damasio (1994) describes how our primary emotions that are innate and pre-organised are used as scaffolding for our secondary emotions that are learnt from experience. Awareness of body changes is linked to the feelings which he calls 'somatic markers'. When we reason or make a decision, we call on past knowledge that is stored in the mind in the form of images. These are retrieved and translated into language and are used together with our response in the immediate situation. In this way, recalled images, present images, body changes and feelings are all interconnected in a process of thinking.

This may help us understand the everyday difficulties for those with dyspraxia. One example would be getting dressed in the morning. If we have no difficulty with them, we take dressing skills for granted. However, as they involve fine motor skills, perceptual motor and organisational skills, many dyspraxic children struggle. Dorothy had been given advice by an occupational therapist about the order of getting dressed. She still had great difficulty and needed constant supervision. She refused to go swimming at school because she could not get dressed and undressed by herself.

During the initial family meeting with parents and the three siblings, it became clear that Dorothy's mother suffered from depression which was incapacitating and meant that she did not work outside the home. There had been domestic violence in her childhood. Dorothy was referred for tantrums connected with change. Dorothy would often come home from school and have a huge tantrum and scene over something that had gone wrong during the day. Dorothy's disability affected the whole family in different ways. The endless tantrums and arguments between the siblings, and the effect of this on the parents' relationship added to the mother's depression and reduced her ability to cope. Dorothy's siblings resented the extra attention that she needed for everyday tasks and disliked playing with her because she had difficulty in amusing herself or playing creatively with others. In turn, she would have huge tantrums because they refused to play with her. The father, who worked in middle management, had become the main source of energy within the family unit. However, he could also become incapacitated, constantly battling with the children, and his wife's depression.

Maternal depression

Balbernie (2001: 249) writes: 'A baby's developing brain is damaged when exposed to neglect, trauma, and abuse, and *prolonged maternal depression*' (emphasis added). An infant's brain is shaped by emotional interactions with the mature brain of the caregiver (Seigal 1999), so that 'for the developing infant the mother essentially *is* the environment' (Schore 1994: 78). The brain starts life with multi-potentialities in development. The early use of the brain within the co-created environment between mother and child and the wider circle about them will foster the growth of use-dependent pathways (Perry *et al.* 1995). Reflections and understandings of the baby's emotional life by the mother will be mirrored in mind development in the baby. In this way the orbital cortex, which is the site of reflective thought, will develop. The orbitofrontal cortex mediates empathic and emotional relatedness, or attuned communication. It contributes to generating self-awareness, personal identity, episodic memory and the ability to imagine oneself in the future or to remember oneself in the past (Balbernie 2001). Particularly in the right hemisphere, functions develop which control emotion, and appraise incoming stimuli and interpersonal communication: in fact it is here that the emotions are managed: 'The orbitofrontal cortex is known to play an essential role in the processing of interpersonal signals necessary for the initiation of social interactions between individuals' (Schore 2001: 36).

Maternal depression is a form of unintended neglect (Zeanah *et al.* 1997). It is thought that babies exposed to short-term depression may recover but prolonged depression is damaging to the left frontal region of the cortex associated with outwardly directed emotions (Nelson and Bosquet 2000). Depressed mothers find it difficult to respond to the baby. Having a depressed mother between the ages of 6 and 18 months of age can lead to persisting emotional and cognitive difficulties (Murray 1997; Sinclair and Murray 1998; Balbernie 2001). Maternal depression affects mother-infant communication which plays a crucial role in protecting the child against mental or emotional disorders: 'this position of communication is based on the specific adaptive relevance of communication in human evolution' (Papousek and Papousek 1997: 38).

The mother supports the child's development of symbolic capacities and acquisition of language, and this is adversely affected by maternal depression. Tronick and Weinberg (1997: 73) posit the toxic effect of maternal depression on a child's social and emotional functioning and development: '. . . the human brain is inherently dyadic and is created through interactive exchanges'. A healthy mother and infant develop a model of mutual regulation which if successful allows the creation of dyadic states of consciousness, allowing disruption and repair. Infants become aware of their mother's depression and become hyper-vigilant of the mother's emotional state in order to protect themselves, causing them to become emotionally restricted. In the dyadic mother-infant system, during maternal depression the infant is deprived of the experience of expanding his state of consciousness in collaboration with the mother. Instead they may take on elements of the mother's depressed state – sadness, hostility, withdrawnness and disengagement – in order to form a larger dyadic system. In the service of growth the infant incorporates the mother's depressed states of consciousness.

There is a difficulty in knowing how the child's symptoms have arisen when there is depression in a parent which has clearly been quite incapacitating. The child's symptoms may be a result of the known dyspraxia or the parent's depression may have been internalised by the child who then has a deathly inhibition in responding to what life may offer. It is likely that the two conditions intertwined to produce the picture presented at Dorothy's assessment. She stated that she had no friends, although there were children that she liked. Life in the family could fall into two extremes, of arguments and aggression barely contained, or a giving up and passivity with the mother taking to her bed. There was a question as to whether it would be possible to support the family in finding new solutions and an emotional middle ground where ordinary life could carry on.

Assessment sessions

In the first assessment session Dorothy sat in a lumpen way, unable to speak, engage with me or the materials, and only able to say 'dunno' in response to attempts to engage her in conversation. After some long silences, I remembered a brief animation in a family meeting around the subject of her pets, so I asked her if she would like to draw a picture of one of her pets, trying to find a way in, to begin to meet her. She drew her rabbit and her guinea pig, but they had no faces or features and were tiny, barely half an inch long, almost hidden at the edge of the page. She began to talk about her birthday party, which was terribly sad. She had invited two friends at school but one child could not come, and the other had said she would come, and then had gone to another girl's party. When I tried to talk about this devastating disappointment, she said that she did not mind. In the assessment sessions she brought her Game Boy and her mobile phone. I thought that these were being used as concrete objects to relate to, instead of human interaction, much as she apparently immersed herself in TV in her bedroom at home. There did not seem to be the expectation that I would be interesting enough on my own or that the materials or toys would provide a catalyst for a meeting to bring us into contact with each other. Any communication was like a brief spark flaring which then flickered and died. There was no feeling of animation, unless it was within a loop between her and the Game Boy.

I noticed that she had a Winnie the Pooh mobile phone cover and asked her if she knew the stories, which she did from video. I asked about her favourite character. She said that she liked Pooh Bear but also Eeyore. She seemed identified with Rabbit, who was 'sensible'. In the session, it felt so deadly that after acknowledging the lost birthday party I decided to try to bring some life to her and suggested that we play the squiggle game. In this game we took turns to make a squiggle and pass it to the other to make into something. Playing this she surprised me with her capacity to see a shape in a line and respond.

While we were doing this, she was much more animated and smiling, and talked of kite-flying and things at school. In response to a shape I drew she made it into two figures in a basket with a balloon above, but the balloon has collapsed. The image brought Eeyore's birthday into my mind. If you remember, Pooh Bear and Piglet take Eeyore a jar of honey and a balloon for his present. Pooh Bear eats the honey and Piglet falls and the balloon bursts, but Eeyore puts the balloon in and out of the jar with his teeth, and Winnie the Pooh and Piglet say 'it can go in and it can go out' as the balloon is put inside and taken out of the jar. It is an image of a container and the contained, a fitting together, in that Winnie the Pooh and Piglet have responded to Eeyore's original gloom and resignation in thinking that no one has remembered his birthday. Earlier in the story Pooh Bear and Eeyore had this conversation:

> 'Good morning, Pooh Bear,' said Eeyore gloomily. 'If it is a good morning,' he said. 'Which I doubt,' said he.
> 'Why what's the matter?'
> 'Nothing, Pooh Bear, nothing. We can't all. And some of us don't. That's all there is to it.'
> 'Can't all what ?' said Pooh, rubbing his nose.
> 'Gaiety. Song-and-dance. Here we go round the mulberry bush.'
> 'Oh!' said Pooh. He thought for a long time, and then asked, 'What mulberry bush is that?'
> 'Bon-hommy', went on Eeyore gloomily. 'French word meaning bon-hommy,' he explained. 'I'm not complaining, but There It Is.'
>
> (Milne [1926] 1973: 60)

We talked a little about this and Dorothy's failed birthday party, which produced a deadening quality. I felt that her state of mind was a mixture of Eeyore's melancholy, Rabbit's sensible getting on with what was in front of him, and Winnie the Pooh's concrete thinking as in 'What mulberry bush is that?' We talked together about the collapse of Eyeore's balloon and how he was able to make something out of it, out of very little, and how he responded to the giving rather than the gift. On a different level I was thinking about the experience of the collapse of the life-giving breast for Dorothy as an infant when her mother had been depressed. Although she seemed to have internalised a sensible father, they all could be swamped with a deadening feeling that was quite incapacitating. At this time, she told me that, in her classroom, her seat by a girl that she liked (the one whom she had invited to her party) had been taken by another girl. It felt quite hopeless, and as if nothing could be done.

I decided to offer a term of sessions to see if I could reach her through this deadening feeling that came into play. I asked a colleague to work fortnightly with her parents and we decided to review after a term. In fact the work continued for a year.

Making contact

In the individual sessions Dorothy could not choose what to do or make and said 'nothing' if I asked her what she was thinking of, or 'dunno', or 'don't mind'. She did want to play the squiggle game again. Generally these first images were made quite faintly and tentatively using coloured pencils. However, their importance was firstly in the quality of time spent together in the making of them and secondly in that, like the surrealists, we were experimenting with directly contacting the unconscious, drawing without thought or conscious control, which was unknowingly preparing the ground for her contact with Dali's images. Making strange and weird images together enables children to tell you of other odd things; it becomes acceptable, for instance, that later I would be interested in Dali.

In the second month Dorothy was able to take a risk and use clay, making the letters for her initials, a confirmation of her identity. She used Plasticine to make a figure, which she named 'Fred'. This figure was passed between us, each adding something. This was followed by Mrs Snowman in the next session (Figure 6.1) and a request to play the squiggle game again. One of the images was of a 'speedy snail'. She liked the snail, saying that everyone thought she did things slowly but this snail was fast; as indeed she was able to rapidly respond to my squiggle with an idea of her own. If I suggested that she now choose something to do it was terribly hard for her to choose even a material, let alone what to do with it. I found that if I just stayed with this, talking about how hard it was, she did eventually choose and get started, but she wanted me to be making something too. There was a wish not to be

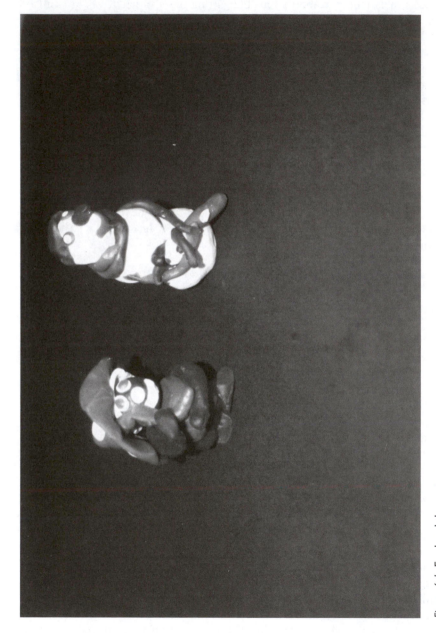

Figure 6.1 Fred and the snowman.

separated out from me, with more awareness of our different roles in the therapy. Equally, she seemed to have no capacity or base from which to choose. I felt she needed drawing out through a playful mother/child interaction, to reach the younger child within. My aim was to facilitate the child becoming confident enough to choose a material and get started without me, so that I gradually phased myself out.

Dali and the melting clocks

In the third month there was the start of a new phase. Dorothy began to volunteer information about school and began asking me, 'What do you do that is fun?' There was a curiosity for the first time about me, and some curiosity about the other people that I saw at the clinic. She also wanted to know what I did out of the session.

In talking about school she told me that they were doing a project on surrealism. She began to talk about Dali's paintings which had been shown to the class by Dorothy's teacher. She liked one with elephants that she had chosen to work from for her school project (*The Temptation of Saint Anthony*, 1946). She told me about the 'melting clocks' (*The Persistence of Memory (Soft Watches)*, 1931), and that she would like us both to make one out of clay (Plate 4). We both worked with clay to make a 'clock' and then when we got to the hands I asked what time it should be. She wanted mine to be at 11.00 when we started the session and hers to be at 12.00 when we ended. I asked what she thought that the artist had been trying to tell us, and she said, 'It goes slow when you're bored and fast when it's fun'. She persevered with using the clay, reminding me to put mine hanging over the edge of the table so that it looked like it was melting. Time had gone extraordinarily fast while we made these. I thought that Dorothy was responding to the different quality of time that she experienced in the sessions as we worked together. In the experience of the intersubjective relationship with me, her perception of her experience was altered.

Simon Wilson in the Tate Catalogue for the 1980 Dali exhibition writes about *The Persistence of Memory*: 'The soft watches are an unconscious symbol of the reality of space and time (Camembert of time and space, Dali described them), a surrealist meditation on the collapse of our notions of a fixed cosmic order' (Wilson 1980: 16). The soft watches were inspired by Dali contemplating some soft Camembert cheese. They were important as a sexual metaphor, of limpness, but also for the psychological aspect. Christopher Masters (1995: 68) writes:

> in his account of the creation of the work Dali described his inner state as characterized by 'super-softness', in contrast to his public image, which was, thanks to Gala's influence, as hard as a 'hermit-crab's shell'. Dali's highly personal interpretation of the painting even extended to

claiming that it represented 'the horrible traumatisation of birth by which we are expunged from paradise'. Certainly the watches, all stopped at different times, create a sensation of timelessness which is associated with life in the womb.

This linked with my experience of Dorothy and my uncertainty about her condition and its causes. There was a way in which she felt 'not yet born', in the sense of 'coming into being' as an individual with tastes, choices and her own volition. There was also the impermeable exterior that she presented to the world and other possible feelings hidden beneath. Children with dyspraxia have significant problems with time as the ordinary person understands and relates to it. They have problems with sequencing and the understanding of past, present and future. They have poor memory and difficulty recalling information. Time of day, seasons and routine have no meaning. In trying to feel oneself into this state of mind it would be like living in an unconscious dream-like state with no markers to give structure. Possibly Dali's images gave Dorothy a sense of recognition, a form for her own experience. The images that she had chosen depicted an internal world experience and her re-creation of them helped her to begin a process of developing emotional literacy.

Playing ball

In the next session Dorothy noticed, apparently for the first time, that there was a ball in the box of toys. She began to play with it, throwing it up and down the room. She then threw it to me experimentally. I threw it back. A game gradually developed where we had to copy the other person's actions, so that we threw the ball to each other in lots of strange ways. We did not know what each intended so we had to observe very closely each other's expressions and actions. For instance, I bounced it twice, threw it up in the air and then threw it to her but it bounced on the floor before reaching her and she had to do exactly the same back. This was very tense for her when she copied me because she had to remember a short sequence of actions, which is one of the difficulties of dyspraxia. Playing this game meant that her difficulty could be played with, and in our intense interaction of close observation she was able to do it. I was amazed when we stopped. What had been so lively and animated and involved could go so flat and dead in an instant. She stopped as we had to end the session and went quite 'dead'. This made me wonder if as an infant she had dropped in and out of animation, as she had dropped in and out of her mother's mind, her presence and absence. Her mother's depression left her with nothing to sustain her in the absences. Ball-playing can lead to a kind of recharging, with a more vital quickening of the body, which can be energising. It is part of ordinary mother/child interaction to mirror each other's responses and for a baby to need such close attention and lively response with a live mind in order for their own mental development to take place, as we saw earlier in the chapter. The rhythm of trying something new with materials, some talk about it, and then more silent ball-playing allowed Dorothy to just 'be' with me in play with no other demands, a necessary regression where she did not have to think or try to articulate.

Dali and *Fried Eggs on the Plate without the Plate*

We painted the clocks when the clay had dried. Dorothy mixed a big variety of colours, wanting them to be 'all colours'. She said again that time went fast when you were having fun but ticked slowly when you were bored. She had more to sustain her in this session so that I managed not to make something with her but to step back slightly. She chose to make the Dali egg on a piece of string in the desert (*Fried Eggs on the Plate without the Plate*, 1932). She said that her teacher could not show them all the pictures at school, as some were rude. It is possible that the surreal images gave her permission to play, as I did. They challenged her usual way of looking at the world and offered an image of a different internal experience. While waiting for the paint to dry, we played 'copy-cat' with the ball which was a mixture of being funny and tense, and very involved with each other. At the end of the session, this time, it did not feel so flat.

The following session she decided to paint the egg and did this carefully, not asking for my help. She got stuck choosing what colour to paint the string. She wanted me to choose and do it for her. Rather than make more of an interpretation, I reminded her of all the colours she had created when she had painted the melting clocks last week and suggested that she start mixing and see what happened. She was then able to make the light mauve and painted the string (Figure 6.2).

Neret (2002: 29) writes of the *Fried Eggs* picture: 'a favourite motif which Dali connected with pre-natal images and the universe of the womb'. Both soft images suggest melting and vulnerability. The eggs are vulnerable to the dry desert landscapes and feel exposed, with no shell or dish or frying pan to sustain them. Wilson writes of Dali's landscapes that they are in the tradition of European Romantic paintings in the early nineteenth century, 'in which the central theme is man's awed contemplation of the immensity of nature, of the infinity of time and space, and his realization of his appalling isolation in it' (1980: 16). Both the eggs she had made and those in the Dali painting were surprising and fun for Dorothy but also had an appeal on a different register of deeper feeling, resonating with her own infancy. I talked about the egg in terms of the picture, 'the egg is feeling lost, out of the shell with just a piece of string attached, it slides about on the surface, it hasn't got a plate to keep it safe'. This way of working, within the metaphor, can be responded to by the child or not. I sensed that relating it to her directly would thrust something indigestible into a flow of work, possibly interrupting the process.

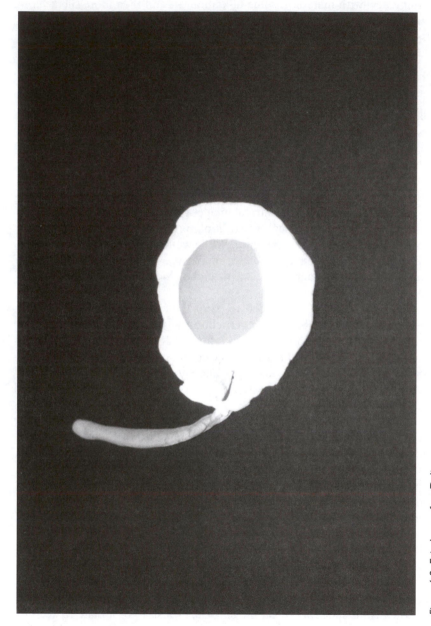

Figure 6.2 Fried egg, after Dali.

Over time and as her sessions progressed I was able to be less actively involved in making, just occasionally joining Dorothy in modelling play to create some characters together, and to encourage her to take the risk of choosing what to make and doing it alone. I had been told that she was slow and rarely finished things at school, but in fact found that this could be positively framed as being quite careful and meticulous, for example, in mixing the exact shade of colour that she wanted.

Having fun

Subsequently, each week, there were a lot of questions, for example, 'Have I been having fun, what do I do that is fun?' There was curiosity about me, my life and family, but also a new wondering about different ways of being and quality of life. In this way I was acting as a transitional person between Dorothy, her family and the outside world. The copy-cat game seemed to be a way of making close contact that was fun, and also served to 'bring her to life' when she arrived low and deadened, after arguments at home, or when things were going wrong at school. Later it was possible to play with 'things out of order', in the ball-play, with the unpredictable and unexpected, but in a way that was not too overwhelming. Because she found it funny, it was bearable for things to go wrong.

The ball games widened from copy-cat, to throwing to each other, to trying to trick the other as to where and when you were going to throw, and then to football. In all these the ball was the third element, often having a life of its own, hitting off things, rolling under things. She liked this unpredictable element and the comments we made about the throws and the ball. There was something about having a ball in play that could lead to laughter, whether it was because it bounced off the wall and hit you on the head, or you failed to catch it, or there was a fantastic catch, against all the odds.

The following week there was mention of a new friend she had made. It seemed that her school life was beginning to be more social as she mentioned a friend coming to stay the night, and the boys making her laugh by singing silly songs. She brought in a sherbert dab that fizzed in her mouth, wanting me to listen to it, to put my ear to her cheek. 'It sounded alive' – as her internal world was also becoming fun and accessible to being communicated to others.

Move to secondary school

In the parent work, Dorothy's move to secondary school was causing great anxiety for her parents. How would she manage the change, or find her way around with different teachers and subjects? Her parents were also anxious that Dorothy was not going to get enough help. The extra support that she had been given at school was to be withdrawn as the school felt she no longer needed it.

After the Easter holiday she was very low and lacking in energy; everything felt dull and lifeless. She said she liked to play with her rabbit but that she had to limit this because 'his chin gets sunk on his breast' when she was at school. This felt very sad; better not to experience fun if it cannot happen all the time. She was able to express these feelings through talking about her rabbit (Case 2005) and I linked this to the Easter break and missing her sessions. She was then able to ask to play ball and became much more animated, laughing at the funny kicks of the ball and how it bounced off objects in the room and landed in unexpected places. We played football, catching, and doing funny throws to make each other laugh. After this she made a white boat out of Plasticine and floated it in the sink of water, pleased it was afloat. I felt that she had become afloat with the interaction through the ball game. She finally made a white picture on black paper of outlines of buildings. She called it 'black picture'; clearly this related to the depression that the rabbit/Dorothy had when there was no one to play with, during the break.

Dorothy and the shrimps

Almost a year into therapy, after a break, Dorothy brought in three hybrid shrimps in a tiny two-inch bottle with a cork in the top. They were 'sea monkeys' and were very lively, in constant movement up, down and around the bottle. They were almost transparent and were entrancing to watch as they fired off in movement, presumably by jets of water. Dorothy showed me that the male was bigger and that the female had egg sacs. She thought the tiny specks in the water might be eggs. The shrimps were bought from a supermarket in a packet and were just added to water. She then told me that she had been clearing out the attic together with her mum the previous week. They had found a tank and had decided to use it again. They had also found bags of baby clothes and some favourite old toys from when she was little. This clearing out and also finding new containers in the attic was a healthy sign that psychic contents in their relatedness were at last in movement. Dorothy and her mother were engaged together in revisiting her babyhood and finding containment for the shrimps, which suggested nurturing and the potential for looking after a lively baby.

In the parent work Dorothy's parents were beginning to understand how the past might be affecting the present relationships in the family. Parent work was enabling Dorothy's mother to try out new ways of relating to the children and also to co-parent rather than leave her husband to struggle with often difficult situations on his own. Dorothy was also engaging with me in a lively way and taking what she learned from this relationship back into family life. For example, Dorothy said that her mum had wanted her to show me the lively shrimps. Her mum had thought that I would want to see them 'because they were strange'. This was an interesting communication from the mother through Dorothy to me. The shrimps suggested the stirring of a lively new part both of the mother, and of Dorothy, in their relationship together. A part of them had been ossified, like the dried shrimps, and had come to life when put into fresh water. The tank in the attic was able to provide a good womb-like environment for the shrimps. It was also more possible for the family to nurture the baby parts of each other. The shrimps, in their rapid movements, were mesmerising and engaged us together in animal-watching. We stirred inside in response (Case 2005).

Bridges and connections

Dorothy looked in her folder and got out a card of a black and red baby chick that she had made the previous week. She had no memory of having made it. This was often the case when she started a session trying to remember what she had made the previous week. She said that the chick looked angry and had funny eyes and decided to put it away. I talked with her about the angry chick that she had forgotten, and linked this to the holiday gap and my absence, but also to how the chick gets angry when there was no response. I talked about the forgetting of things and events and what she had been doing last week, and of her need for a bridge between the sessions to carry her over and keep her in contact, as well as over the holiday gap. Her trait of forgetting had been present throughout the therapy but it was at this stage that it came into our focus.

Damasio (2000: 186) argues that the foundation of consciousness is the presence of a consistent non-verbal, imaged narrative to which we second-arily give words: 'the nonverbal narrative of knowing'. One of Dorothy's difficulties in play and general living was not being able to imagine or have an image in her mind. Dyspraxia is not to do with nerve damage but seems to be a failure to interpret messages from the brain.

Damasio (1994) writes that our mind responds to imagery we imagine in the same way that it responds to imagery that we see. Dorothy could respond to a line on the page but found it difficult to bring an image in her mind to the page. Research findings into left and right hemispheres have shown activity on both sides of the brain when mental images and art-making are taking place, although originally the right brain has been associated with intuition and creativity. Western thinking about the mind and body has been domin-ated by the Descartian split which separated thinking from feeling. Damasio's work with patients with neurological damage to parts of the brain has enabled him to reassess this division. What he has found is that emotion and feeling assist us in 'predicting an uncertain future and planning out actions accordingly' (Damasio 1994: xv). He sees feelings as a continuously updated image of the structure and state of our body. In this way feelings serve as 'internal guides'.

Damasio found a close bond between a collection of brain regions to do with processes of reasoning and decision-making; personal and social decision-making; and the processing of emotions. Emotion and feeling are part of the neural machinery for biological regulation that is to do with survival. He posits that a large part of knowledge is recalled in the form of images, from many sites in the brain. We retrieve images and translate them into language form, holding them in our attention. We need to have them actively in mind and have a high-order working memory. The brain has the capacity to 'display images internally and to order those images in a process called thought' which in turn influences our behaviour in the future. Essentially, we reconstruct memory from dispositional representations which are made up of past experiences. These combine with perceptual images and the recalled images of the past and an imagined future. Damasio suggests that emotions and feelings are a central part of biological regulation and 'provide a bridge between rational and non-rational processes between cortical and non-cortical structures' (1994: 128). In our 'mind landscape', images correspond to myriad options for actions and outcomes. Basically the body provides a ground reference for the mind.

Dorothy responded to my thinking about 'bridges' literally, getting out Plasticine and beginning to make a bridge to go over a river which she drew on paper (Figure 6.3). There are 'gateways' to the river on each side where people can play, or go boating or throw pebbles to see whose goes the furthest. The two gateways seemed to be the passage in and out of the session where she can play. Dorothy made more bridges in the following sessions and then, to both our surprise, started to remember what she had been making the previous week. It was as if actually making a concrete set of bridges enabled the bridge in her mind between events to start being formed. At the next parent review her mother told me that Dorothy had bought a hairy dog cuddly toy (her first soft toy), which was the beginning of a transitional object, allowing more play and development around separation.

Ending

In the summer term Dorothy's parents discussed their worries about her moving to a new school but in fact she was feeling quite confident and pleased that two of her friends would be moving with her. She had done really well in her recent exams, especially science. Just before starting at the new school she decided to make a new melting clock. She experimented with different designs, no numbers, just lines for hands, but eventually did four bees for 12, 9, 6 and 3 o'clock and some melting pieces.

The next session I received a message to say that Dorothy did not want to come any more. Her reason was that she had successfully started at secondary school and did not want to leave the class as this would mean missing double science. We arranged to meet to discuss the situation and I acknowledged how she was feeling and backed her wish to be at school full-time. Her

Figure 6.3 Bridges.

parents did not want her to stop, but I thought that she was more able than they realised and had chosen school because she was engaged with the subjects and fellow pupils. One of the aims of therapy is to re-interest children in the world and then to step back and let it take over. It was not possible to offer her a session after school. When we met to discuss the situation and to think about how to end she told me excitedly about school. It was 'fun' when Stephen hit the bottom of her drink and it went all over her and he called her 'Tropical Smith'. She described how he called for her and they called for Sheila and they walked to school together. For the first time she talked about friends and school for the whole session. I put several possibilities to her as to how to end and she chose to work on until half-term and then to finish. The following session she painted her clock, and we played the squiggle game, but she put out all the colours of crayons, felts and pencils, and for the first time images overlapped.

Birthday party

We had come full circle as it was her birthday. This year she invited her three friends from school and they all came. She designed her own invitations for her sleepover. She wanted to do the Squiggle game with me. She immediately made good, imaginative use of a line. When I talked about this, she said she could do this, but not on her own. For the first time she used lines from one image as part of another. In the imagery was a snowman with a frying pan with eggs inside. This recalled 'Mrs Snowman' and the fried eggs without the plate, but here they were contained safely.

In these last sessions we would play ball at the end and each week the clock was repainted. Each week we also mulled over what we had done over the last year. The way that the clock was repainted each session in all the last weeks seemed to mean that time was standing still: while thinking about ending, nothing new could be made, it was her clock and her sense of time. Each of these sessions she told me tales of having fun at school, of times when something went wrong but it worked out, and of enjoyment of the new lessons, though sometimes it was boring. The last clock was finally set at 9.00, set for school time. In the last session she wanted to take everything with her, rushed out to the toilet when I talked about feelings about finishing, then came back to add more to her last picture. This was of a river with several animals cut from squiggle games. She painted boathouses behind the animals, and a path leading down to the water making a connection with her previous rivers and bridges. The river had come to represent the play and flow within the banks of the session. The bridges had made connections between past and present; between conscious and unconscious; and between what is known and unknown.

Conclusion

In Dorothy's case there was a mixed presentation at assessment of symptoms to do with known dyspraxia and depression. I have described quite a short-term way of working to try and engage a child who feels withdrawn and hard to reach.

Winnicott's squiggle game elicited a lively response and we were able to work together, until Dorothy was able to work spontaneously. The ball-playing together during this seemed to be essential. One aspect of this is the touching base with my liveliness, and the need to be 'in relationship'. This new relationship allowed Dorothy to internalise a liveliness of being together that could transfer to relationships outside the therapy. Another aspect is the natural fun that develops once a ball is in play that can offer surprises. In a concrete way ball-playing can act as a model for the exchange of thoughts and feelings between two people. Alongside this, parent work enabled both parents to talk about their childhoods and the family dynamics in which they could all get caught up.

Dyspraxia is a dysfunction of 'doing' and I have described play and art work where I have engaged very directly with the child and then gradually withdrawn as she was able to take initiative. Winnicott uses his understanding of creativity in terms of one's whole attitude to external reality. When children and adults play together, they both use their whole personality. It allows the discovery of the self, in that the surprising can happen. In a transitional object there is interplay: between originality and acceptance of a tradition as the basis of inventiveness; separateness and union working together (Winnicott 1971: 70). In the Dali images I think there was a good combination of tradition and inventiveness as Dorothy took elements of paintings she had seen, and made them her own. In this way she was able to develop an emotional literacy. The found images helped her to develop a language in finding forms for inner feeling. Her particular difficulties with accessing mental imagery suggested that making two- and three-dimensional images helped her in discovering thoughts and feelings of her own.

References

Balbernie, R. (2001) Circuits and circumstances: the neurobiological consequences of early relationship experiences and how they shape later behaviour, *Journal of Child Psychotherapy*, 27(3): 237–55.

Case, C. (1987) A search for meaning: loss and transition in art therapy, in T. Dalley, C. Case, J. Schaverien, F. Weir, D. Halliday, P. Nowell Hall and D. Waller (eds) *Images of Art Therapy: New Developments in Theory and Practice.* London: Tavistock.

Case, C. (1996) On the aesthetic moment in the transference, *Inscape*, 1(2): 39–45.

Case, C. (2000) Our Lady of the Queen: journeys around the maternal object, in A. Gilroy and G. McNeilly (eds) *The Changing Shape of Art Therapy*. London: Jessica Kingsley.

Case, C. (2005) *Imagining Animals: Art, Psychotherapy and Primitive States of Mind.* London: Routledge.

Case, C. and Dalley, T. (2006) *The Handbook of Art Therapy,* 2nd edn. London: Routledge.

Damasio, A. (1994) *Descartes' Error: Emotion, Reason and the Human Brain.* New York: Putnam.

Damasio, A. (2000) *The Feeling of what Happens: Body, Emotion and the Making of Consciousness.* London: Vintage.

Harrison, C. and Wood, P. (eds) (1992) *Art in Theory 1900–1990.* Oxford: Blackwell.

Masters, C. (1995) *Dali.* London: Phaidon.

Milne, A.A. ([1926] 1973) *The Complete Collection of Stories and Poems.* London: Methuen.

Murray, L. (1997) Post-partum depression and child development, *Psychological Medicine*, 27: 253–60.

Nelson, C.A. and Bosquet, M. (2000) Neurobiology of fetal and infant development: implications for infant mental health, in C.H. Zeanah (ed.) *Handbook of Infant Mental Health*, 2nd edn. New York: Guilford Press.

Neret, G. (2002) *Dali.* Cologne: Taschen.

Ozenfant. A.J. (1952) *Foundations of Modern Art* (trans. John Rodker). New York: Dover.

Papousek, H., and Papousek, M. (1997) Fragile aspects of early social integration, in L. Murray and P. Cooper, (eds) *Postpartum Depression and Child Development.* New York: The Guilford Press.

Perry, B.D., Pollard, A., Blakeley, T., Baker, W. and Vigilante, D. (1995) Child-hood trauma, the neurobiology of adaptation, and 'use-dependent' development of the brain: how 'states' become 'traits', *Infant Mental Health Journal*, 16(4): 271–91.

Schore, A.N. (1994) *Affect Regulation and the Origin of the Self: The Neurobiology of Emotional Development.* Hillsdale, NJ: Erlbaum.

Schore, A.N. (2001) Effects of a secure attachment relationship on right brain development, affect regulation and infant mental health, *Infant Mental Health Journal*, 22(1–2): 7–66.

Seigal, D. J. (1999) *The Developing Mind: Towards a Neurobiology of Interpersonal Experience.* New York: The Guilford Press.

Sinclair, D. and Murray, L. (1998) The effects of post-natal depression on children's adjustment to school, *British Journal of Psychiatry*, 172: 58–63.

Tronick, E. and Weinberg, M.K. (1997) Depressed mothers and infants: failure to form dyadic states of consciousness, in L. Murray and P. Cooper (eds) *Postpartum Depression and Child Development.* New York: The Guilford Press.

Wilson, S. (1980) Tate catalogue: Dali exhibition. London: Tate Gallery.

Winnicott, D.W. (1971) *Playing and Reality.* Harmondsworth: Penguin.

Zeanah, C.H., Boris, N.W. and Larrien, J.A. (1997) Infant development and developmental risk: a review of the past ten years, *American Academy of Child and Adolescent Psychiatry*, 36(2): 165–78.

Chapter 7

From 'beanie' to 'Boy'

Zara Patterson

Introduction

Through working for a countywide Service for Autism over many years, I have had the privilege and opportunity to work with a broad range of young people from primary-aged children to young adults. Although there are obvious similarities in their difficulties, every person with autism spectrum disorder (ASD) presents very differently, each having their own unique personality.

The Service for Autism has autism resource bases attached to host mainstream schools, both primary and secondary. The Service also has an outreach advisory team supporting children maintained in mainstream schools. The students who attend the bases are those who need an individualised timetable and autism-specific teaching and intervention. With specialist staff support, children are able to benefit from spending time with their mainstream peer group for specific curriculum subjects or for social inclusion. Through an eclectic approach and a nurturing environment, the bases provide 'safe havens' for the students.

Working alongside the teaching staff, the Service has a team of therapists comprised of an art therapist, a dance/movement therapist, a music therapist and a psychotherapist. Having a team of therapists working together within an educational setting is rare and all staff have worked hard to develop and maintain this.

All new students are assessed by one of the therapeutic team. This assessment is used as an indicator for prioritising need for therapy as well as to enable the therapists to contribute to case discussion with the teaching staff. The therapists' knowledge and perspective contributes to a comprehensive overview of all aspects of the child's development. Referral for therapy can also be made at any stage of the student's school life and may be initiated for reasons such as behaviour changes, family crisis, and issues concerning adolescence – for example, sexuality, ASD awareness and difficulty with relationships.

In this chapter, I will describe the therapy process with a young boy over a period of four academic years. Specific sessions will be chosen to illustrate key periods in the child's life and development. Starting with the initial therapy session, I will describe my first experience of the child and how he engaged with the therapy process. Consideration will be given to some of the themes that arose over the following two years during his preparation for leaving primary education and his transition to secondary school. The final part of the chapter will describe and reflect on therapy during his first year in secondary school, including the ending of therapy.

ASD

Differing theoretical points of view are discussed in two further chapters on ASD (Chapters 10 and 13). Therefore I will only give brief background information regarding this very complex disorder. I will however offer more specific and detailed description particular to the child in the case study, although he should not be considered typical of all children with the diagnosis.

ASD is a developmental disorder that cannot be cured. It affects the way a person relates to other people and their environment. To receive a diagnosis of ASD a person has to exhibit the 'triad of impairment'. The areas of difficulty are:

- *social interaction*: a profound lack of emotional contact with people;
- *social communication*: difficulties in all areas of communication, verbal and non-verbal including gesture, tone of voice, facial expression and body language;
- *imagination*: lack of imaginative play, interpersonal play and empathy.

Those with ASD may have additional learning difficulties. They can also show a fascination for certain objects, an over-sensitivity to certain stimuli, the need to preserve sameness, a developed ability at performing certain assembly skills and good rote memory.

In 1943, Dr Leo Kanner, an American child psychiatrist, was the first to use the term 'autistic' to describe a particular type of child displaying these specific abnormalities of behaviour. Hans Asperger was another major contributor. Recognising those at the higher functioning end of the spectrum with an average or above average intelligence led to the formulation of Asperger's syndrome (AS).

Many questions remain unanswered about the cause of ASD. In the UK, at present, there are an estimated 535,000 people affected. Genetics may play a large part but with what seems to be an increase in the numbers diagnosed, genetics, it is believed, cannot be the only factor. New brain imaging technologies have allowed researchers to study the structure and function of the brain and there is evidence that there may be a variety of physical factors affecting brain development, resulting in autism. There also continues to be much controversy and debate regarding possible environmental influence.

Without definitive answers, discussion concerning causation and treatment therefore remains open-ended. Different disciplines have alternative perspectives and contribute to the debate. From a child psychotherapist's point of view, Anne Alvarez (1992) considers that 'the opposing camps have moved a little closer' and that 'non-psychoanalytic organicist's theories of autism overlap with the psychoanalytic' (Alvarez 1992: 184).

The Boy

Throughout this chapter I will refer to the student in my case study as 'The Boy'. This was his request when he gave me his permission to write about our work together during his weekly therapy sessions. The Boy did not want to be given an alternative name to maintain confidentiality but was adamant that the reader knew the facts. He requested initially to be called 'The 12-year-old Boy' but through discussion he allowed me to shorten it to The Boy. For The Boy it remains more important for the reader to know *what* he is rather than *who* he is. By others knowing he is a 12-year-old boy he can 'hang onto' that identity. His anxiety is heightened by the possibility of any confusion.

The Boy has an attractive face. He has strawberry-blond hair, blue eyes and a freckly pale complexion. He has a small frame and is not very tall. The Boy lives in the family home with his parents, both working professionals, his brother, two years older and his twin brother, who is non-identical.

Referral

The Boy was referred for art therapy when he was 7 by his teacher because of his anxious behaviour. At the time The Boy was very concerned about the children attending the base whom he perceived as being more autistic than himself. This anxiety exacerbated his need to gather factual information and appear all-knowing. In turn however this defensive response behaviour was blocking any possibility of him learning.

The Boy had a difficult birth as the second-born twin and spent some days in special care while his brother went home with his mother. He was a 'floppy' still baby and did not move his limbs after he was born. He responded well to intensive encouragement to develop his bodily movements and by 6 months was sitting up, and was walking by the age of 1. He was constantly compared to his twin brother whose development was more advanced in every way. At nursery, he had some separation difficulties and since then has experienced a variety of educational settings. Difficulties with poor mouth and tongue control and therefore difficulty in producing speech sounds meant The Boy initially attended a specialist language provision. Following this he had approximately two years of unsettled schooling. In mainstream school as

The Boy's needs were not understood, with non-specialist staff working with him. His behaviours were observed as being impulsive, unpredictable and dangerous, and he was, without natural inhibitions, easily distracted, chaotic, and unable to stay focused and emotionally stable.

His eventual diagnosis, when he was 7, described his behaviours as being on the autistic spectrum with an additional description of difficulties with attention, motor control and perception (DAMP). The Boy was finally placed in the resource base at the age of 7.

The first session

The Boy entered the small room in which I worked and the space was immediately filled with movement and questions. From that very first moment I needed to provide containment. The Boy came in clutching a small soft object that had no recognisable shape. It was only when he dangled it in front of me, to show me that I could see it was actually a bean-filled plush animal, a beanie. From its condition, I could see that this small toy creature was well loved. The Boy, at the same time as showing me his toy, was moving around, spinning and flopping against me and the furniture. His movements had a dance-like quality, although without tone or coordination. Like the beanie toy he held The Boy too appeared to have no internal structure to hold him up or together.

I felt I needed to find a way to anchor The Boy before we could begin anything. I guided him to a chair and he flopped down, the beanie still being held. It was obvious The Boy found it impossible to sit for long. He appeared to spill off the seat as he constantly moved. At the same time the toy was flapped and wrung. Being seated did focus The Boy's attention a little and I was able to establish that the beanie toy was called Bee bee. The Boy would not allow me to hold Bee bee but willingly held him up for me to look at. At other moments Bee bee was securely tucked in The Boy's armpit.

While The Boy was constantly moving he was also asking questions. 'How do you know they are called beanies?', 'Real beanies have labels on them don't they?', 'Did you know this one is called Bee bee?', 'Bee bee is a mountain lion', 'Did you know Bee bee was a mountain lion?', 'How did you know?', 'Did you know because he has black marks on his face?', 'Do all mountain lions have those black marks on their face?', 'How do you know?', 'Do mountain lions come from Asia?', 'Other lions come from Africa don't they?', 'How do you know?'

I had put paper and art materials out on the table and before I could offer any explanation or say why we were meeting for art therapy, The Boy grabbed at the felt pens and began drawing, Bee bee still tucked under his arm. Even while drawing The Boy's whole body was continually moving. He slid on and off the chair, sat on my lap, stood and flopped against me or the table.

It became evident that The Boy was ideas-led and he changed from one picture to another without any sense of order and with no one image being completed. The pens were scattered all over his drawing. Unable to bear the chaos, I had to push them aside and keep clearing a space for him to see to draw.

His imagery mirrored the fragmentation I was experiencing. He drew beanies, very quickly, it seemed without thinking. They appeared isolated and disconnected. They were without any musculature or skeleton and so they were more like amoebas than animals. The beanies were drawn and labelled as if they were a list of facts (Plate 5).

When it was time to finish I had to repeatedly prompt The Boy to stop drawing. Although I had a clock in the room, he showed no ability to reference time and ending seemed impossibly difficult for him. He just could not stop drawing. His difficulty ending and separating was evident when he eventually reached the door but then had to rush back, grab a pen and add another mark to his drawing. After several attempts I managed to get The Boy out of the room. I watched him twirl down the corridor to his classroom with Bee bee dangling from under his arm. I was left feeling exhausted with my mind in a whirl. I began to tidy up the art materials which The Boy had left strewn on and under the table. It had not felt relevant or possible to address tidying up with him this first week.

The chaotic nature of this first session made me feel mindless. I felt a sense of relief once alone and able to regain some thought.

As soon as The Boy had entered the room, I had felt his anxiety about not letting go of his precious toy. It was as if once separated there would be no possibility of being reunited. His handling of Bee bee reminded me of the images seen of the foetus moving, twisting, touching and interacting with its twin in the womb. I wondered about The Boy's traumatic birth and first experience of the split from his twin. Born second, The Boy's cord prolapsed and there were two occasions within the first hour of his birth when he had to be resuscitated. During the first few days The Boy showed little movement and having met The Boy and his toy, I now had an image in my mind of him as a beanie baby.

I began to think about Bee bee as a confusional object as described by Tustin (1992: 127). Thinking of Bee bee as a distraction, to avoid having to experience the raw feelings associated with separateness and non-existence, was something I shared with The Boy's teaching staff. I was concerned that in a school setting toys are often removed from children without thought to the child's emotional world. Understanding the importance of Bee bee for The Boy seemed vital. Bee bee also needed to be thought about as a transitional object (Winnicott 1971). I therefore considered the beanie, at this stage, as an object that might hinder development as well as one that could assist.

I also thought about The Boy's questions as a defence mechanism. They had been fired at me without any apparent pause to allow me to reply. The Boy was filling every space with questions to which he already knew the answer. It felt as though he was testing himself about what he knew and he was also testing me in such a way that he could be sure I knew that he knew. The Boy was desperate to appear knowing and not, as I learned later, 'stupid like a baby'.

Witkin (1974: 1–29) describes the child as having two worlds. One world is the environment that exists whether the child exists or not. This external world is full of objects, facts and other people. The second world, the inner world, is made up of the child's own sensations and feelings. This world exists because the child exists and is a private space that only the child inhabits. It is through the child's behaviour and adaptation that these two worlds mesh together and the child becomes integrated and develops a sense of self.

For The Boy and many other ASD children who are trying desperately to make their world understandable and predictable, holding facts in mind offers some feeling of safety and control but it is important for educators to recognise that a child with ASD who knows a great deal of factual information does not necessarily have insight, knowledge or understanding: 'If his existence in the world disturbs his being in ways that fragment him and render his relationships in the world emotionally confused or even meaningless, then he is ill-adapted, and no amount of intellectual grasp of logical or factual relationships will change that' (Witkin 1974: 1).

The Boy very clearly showed this lack of relatedness to a sense of self. Through his gleaning of facts, he was attempting to adapt to the school and wider environment. Looking at The Boy's drawings from this perspective I became aware of his skill, through adaptation, to con himself and others into believing his ability. In reality his drawings were lists and labels lacking in imagination and symbolic thought. Through ongoing therapy, The Boy was going to have my attention for 45 minutes every week. I was acutely aware that unless I could begin to help him develop a mechanism for thought, he could spend the time confirming to himself his knowing. I was going to have to avoid colluding with him and his agenda and attempt to develop shared and meaningful communication.

The first year

From my first experience of The Boy, I knew I had to offer containment through clear boundaries for such a chaotic youngster. It felt vital to establish a definite beginning and end to the session. This was achieved over several months through a directive approach. The Boy needed constant reminders to begin with but gradually he became able to walk in, close the door and say hello before grabbing the pens and starting his drawing. Although always needing me to count down the last five minutes of a session, with some prompt to stop drawing, The Boy became able to end the session, and with a word of farewell, close the door behind him. On many occasions he would say goodbye and leave the room only to return, open the door a few inches and say goodbye again and confirm 'See you next week'. Actually tidying up, packing away the pens and putting his drawing in his folder took much longer to achieve!

As I got to know The Boy, I learned he had some awareness of his difference from his brothers and mainstream peer group but his understanding of his autism was limited. By attending the base, he knew that he was being treated differently from his brothers who continued to attend their local primary school. Feelings of jealousy and anger were evident in his drawings but he was unable to process these feelings at this time. The Boy wanted, and believed he needed to be, the best at everything. He showed intolerance to those less able than himself, calling them names and rubbishing the work they did. With such a fragile sense of self, The Boy believed that by being with people more autistic than himself, he would become one of them. At the same time his behaviour was too chaotic for him to sit alongside his mainstream peer group for many lessons. It was difficult for him to feel he fitted in anywhere and to have a sense of belonging.

In therapy it felt as though The Boy drew list after list of beanies but his imagery actually developed fairly quickly. By the end of the year the beanies, rather than being drawn with a line around separating them or in list form, were drawn in a landscape and with the hint of a story. The beanies had the possibility of some internal structure, were developing more shape and living within an external environment – they belonged somewhere.

Although brought into sessions, Bee bee was now flopped on the table. He was picked up and twisted around occasionally but was rarely tucked under The Boy's armpit.

All year The Boy had continued to bombard me with questions but I had found that if I did not respond he did not panic as other ASD children might. On the contrary, by not answering I created a chink of space. Allowing this space to remain as a silent pause, I would then speak and express my view that he was asking something he knew the answer to or asking something that he did not really need to know. I also tried on occasions to be very firm when The Boy's questions were relentless and told him to stop. This did create a silence, although fairly intolerable for him at first. Over time the silent space grew. It felt as though this youngster, whose engine had been constantly revving, now idled and even stalled for a few seconds occasionally. By slowing him down, creating tolerable space in his mind, little by little, The Boy was enabled to hear and receive more.

The second year

During the second year Bee bee was only brought into school occasionally but was often talked about and was always drawn. Instead The Boy brought different beanies to his session. Often they were new ones he had bought or been given. Being introduced to these beanies had a very different feel to meeting Bee bee for the first time. They felt separate from The Boy. He would put them down and would be quite happy for me to handle them. He even enjoyed me animating them and pretending to make them talk. Because The Boy enjoyed listening to what the beanie was asking him, I was able to extend our conversations and explore some issues in more depth. This way of working was very positive. It created a more playful aspect to our work and introduced the concept of pretending.

Not all beanies were featured in every drawing but The Boy had favourites and these were the ones that he regularly drew. There was a strong feeling of togetherness developing in The Boy's pictures, with the beanies bonding as a group of friends and embarking on activities and journeys. Rather than the floppy beanies of his early drawings, the beanies were now drawn walking either on four legs or upright like humans. They were no longer helpless blobs but active. The pictures had become very colourful and alive. Beanie Island, the beanie's home, was illustrated as a place of many contrasts, having mountains, volcanoes, rivers, woods, jungle and beaches. The Boy's images depicted the beanies travelling through these different parts of the island. The Boy gave them thoughts and ideas, and strategies for solving problems. Sometimes, for example, if the beanies had a long journey, Pounds, the elephant, would be drawn giving them all a ride.

The sense of camaraderie seen in his images was a reflection of the therapy relationship too. The Boy's therapy sessions had become very important to him. I was prepared to share the beanies' journey and story while at this time he was being asked to keep his beanies in his bag if he brought them to school. I experienced the sense of relief felt by The Boy when he was given permission to free a beanie from his school bag and bring it with him into my room.

Over this year The Boy's sense of humour had developed and he had begun to understand teasing. After asking me one of his 'testing' questions, he would glance at me and with a glimmer of a smile say, 'I don't need to ask that question do I?' He knew this question would not be answered either and would look at my facial expression, which he began to read also. We were actually beginning to share a joke.

Transition to secondary school

At the end of Year 6, students move from primary school to secondary. In the base, students begin a programme of transition visits from Easter so that by the end of the summer term they are as fully prepared as possible for the permanent change in September. The Boy was excited about his move up to the very large school and the base within it. We had discussed the continuation of therapy so he knew I would still see him.

I had seen him for weekly therapy for two academic years by this stage and although still drawing beanies, The Boy was using his drawing of beanie stories more and more to process thought and make sense of his own world.

It felt as though a layer of defence was being peeled away and for the first time there was a feeling of The Boy being able to be honest about himself.

Through having a more robust sense of self he was able to admit to not knowing. I was continually surprised by the words he asked the meaning of as he was so skilled at using them in context. I realised how tenuous and fragile his existence must have felt.

With his ability to be more honest about his not knowing he also became more able to express feelings he had perceived as weakness. The Boy acknowledged his anxieties about the changes that were going to take place, in one particular session during April, when he drew the beanies in what he described as a pub restaurant called The Jolly Boar. This was a place where the beanies could get 'lovely food and drink'. The Boy drew himself serving drinks from behind the bar. There was a sense of being inside somewhere very cosy (Figure 7.1).

The Jolly Boar represented a holding space. It acted as a buffer preventing The Boy sliding backwards. It was also the place from which to move on when ready.

The cloaked beanies, able to be 'disguised', made me think about the ambiguous feelings The Boy held about his past and future.

Although The Boy had included himself in two images previously, drawing himself as the barman in this image seemed very significant. The barman is someone with a specific role to play and in this case is a provider for others. The Boy has a generous personality and serving food and drinks to his friends seemed very appropriate. As he drew he expressed pleasure and a sense of pride. There was a palpable feeling of warmth and generosity.

Once The Jolly Boar had been drawn, The Boy talked about the place where the beanies' enemies eat and drink. Here the food and drink were 'awful', in fact 'poisonous'. The Boy described horrible concoctions and his mood changed. He became over-excited, giggling and moving around the room, reminiscent of his early years. He kept coming to the table to draw more and then moving away again. I felt The Boy's fear and anxiety as he slipped into more chaotic behaviour. I talked to him about the mixed feelings of excitement yet nervousness he might be having about moving schools. He proceeded to complain about the school work he was being asked to do, saying it was too easy for him now. He said he felt he knew everything that primary school could teach him. I felt the only way The Boy could cope with the change was to make his primary years and base the bad objects.

During the last few weeks before the summer holiday The Boy separated the beanies from the cosy and familiar internal world of The Jolly Boar and drew them launching off into space. A favourite few beanies were illustrated inside the space craft, strapped into their seats with Bee bee at the controls. The large window in the space craft was drawn from the perspective of the beanies looking out as well as in some images the beanies being viewed through the window. The depiction of both an inside and outside became a

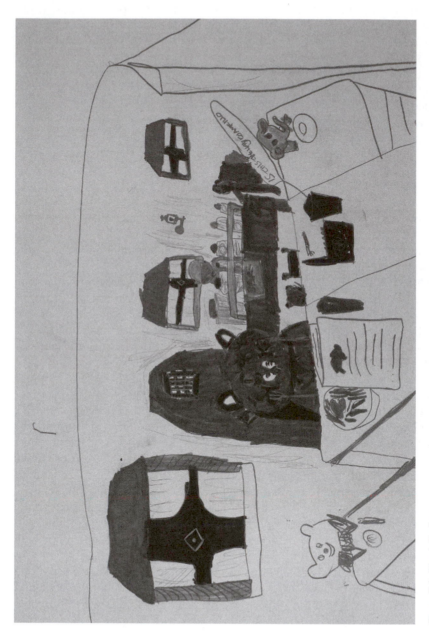

Figure 7.1 The Jolly Boar.

theme in The Boy's drawings. If he drew an interior picture he always had to draw, somewhere on the page, a little image showing the outside. We talked about what the beanies could see if they looked out of the window, as they left Beanie Island, as well as what they could see ahead as they travelled into space. The Boy was able to acknowledge that he felt he was being launched into the unknown. For a while he was lost in space. He dare not think back to his primary years because of his mistaken belief that if he remembered how he once was he would become that boy again and at the same time had no image of himself in the future. He was literally lost in space.

Secondary school

The first time I saw The Boy in his new secondary school environment was when I called into the base to confirm my session times for the students. On seeing me The Boy rushed up and asked when he was going to see me. He looked older, as the children tend to when I haven't seen them for the whole of the six-week summer break. The darker-coloured school uniform he now wore also made him look older. His new school identity became a theme of his work over the next half term.

Having left the beanies up in space before the holiday I was relieved to see they had landed in the first session. I was even more pleased once The Boy explained to me that they were now in a new school. Immediately I was able to share the beanies' story and make connections to The Boy's own life. He seemed very open to listening and enjoyed the comparison between what the beanies were experiencing and what I thought he was.

The same beanie characters were drawn but now rather than cloaks The Boy drew them wearing 'robes'. These robes The Boy thought about as similar to the robes worn by the children who attend Hogwarts in the *Harry Potter* stories. We talked about the different colours and how each colour represented a different house in *Harry Potter*. The Boy was pleased with the thought that when wearing his uniform everyone would recognise he attended the secondary school.

After a few weeks drawing the beanies in their new uniform, in their new school, The Boy became more anxious. He drew his characters without any context. Single beanies were drawn on large pieces of paper looking very isolated and alone. The Boy's world that started so positively began to fall apart. He had experienced the first weeks of 'honeymoon period' and now was experiencing the reality of his new situation. I have experienced other students have a similar reaction to the change from primary to secondary school. There is a desire to leave the past behind but an unrealistic belief that the move will change everything and they will leave their ASD behind as well. Once the reality becomes evident that the move does not make their difficulties go away and in fact school life may become harder, they experience a crisis period. Displacement behaviour becomes evident with some students exhibiting challenging behaviours, others becoming depressed and withdrawn, others rigid and obsessional or, like The Boy, chaotic.

In sessions The Boy's collapse was evident. He could not stay seated and would lean his whole body across the table. He needed to be closer to me physically and on several occasions actually sat himself on my lap. As when The Boy was younger, he became unthinking, his mind full of ideas rather than thoughts. His imagery reverted to unfinished single characters, started and dismissed as soon as the next idea popped into his head. The Boy's insecurity and anxiety was also apparent in the re-emergence of his need to ask questions he knew the answer to. Suddenly he was clinging onto his existence again.

The Christmas holiday facilitated some change for The Boy and he returned in a less chaotic state.

One session in particular generated a great deal of discussion about The Boy being able to remember his past and think about how he once was, without becoming that young child again. The Boy drew the beanies asleep in a dormitory. They had been visited by Father Christmas and all had a gift on the end of their bed. In the room there was an alarm bell because there could be an attack from the 'ertigs' but the door was securely locked. One of the beanies was dreaming of The Jolly Boar (Figure 7.2).

I thought about the locked, womb-like dormitory, full of beanies, as The Boy's wish to retreat into a safe place. The drawing was the first showing any evidence of The Boy's acknowledgement of the existence of an unconscious. He had never talked about his dreams or made any reference to a dream world before. This image enabled us to explore the idea of dreaming. The Boy sought confirmation that a dream was different from real life. I felt his relief at knowing he could dare to dream and that by doing so he would not actually live his dream or become that person in his dreams.

From this time there was real development in The Boy's ability to stay with a thought and think about something that was said. He began to hold a thought in mind long enough to expand on it and seek further explanation. I found I could engage in a very honest, frank conversation with him because thoughts could be processed and resolved. I was able to talk about how I had experienced him in the beginning and how I experienced him now. He enjoyed this confirmation of change and it reassured him enough to allow him to think back and reflect on how he had felt at certain times. The Boy began to be insightful, offering possibilities for his feelings and behaviours, and he became curious. He wanted to hear other opinions asking, 'Zara what do you think?'

The Boy's imagery developed too and, mirroring The Boy's integration, the beanies regrouped and were drawn moving between the inside and outside of their castle. They wore medieval-style tabards that, over several sessions, became chain-mail. Each beanie was given either a sword or bow and arrows.

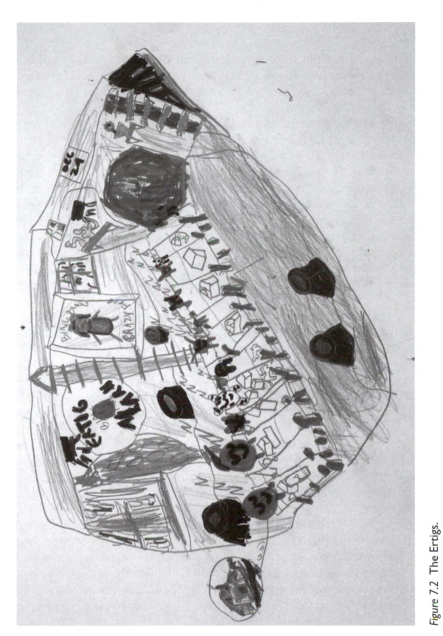

Figure 7.2 The Ertigs.

Some were given a rank but most importantly, it seemed, Teddy, the rabbit, was shown as leader, having been crowned king.

Ending

Having survived a difficult period, settling again and making significant development, I was nervous telling The Boy that I would be leaving in July. This meant we would have to work towards the ending following the Easter holiday.

When I told him my news his immediate reaction was to ask, 'Can I have therapy with that other lady when you've gone?' I did not answer straight away because I recognised this was The Boy's need to make life predictable again as quickly as possible. The Boy continued to draw and after about 15 minutes stopped and looked at me and said, 'I'll miss you Zara.' I believe this illustrates so clearly the autistic anxiety response versus meaningful thought. I was really encouraged that The Boy demonstrated he was able to think and respond in a more meaningful way once the initial feeling of anxiety had passed. The affect caused us both to remain rather subdued for the remainder of the session.

Once The Boy had acknowledged his true thoughts, we were able to think together about ending. He expressed his anxiety that once I had left he would not be able to remember me. His anxiety was that I would drop out of his mind and he would drop out of mine. We planned to take some photos as a practical solution but also discussed memory and how we cannot possibly hold everything in mind. Together we thought about the memories we had of therapy together and this demonstrated to him that he had remembered a great deal and, most significantly, that he had remembered what was important to him. It was not surprising that recognising who was who became a theme in his drawing during the remaining weeks.

Reference was made each week to how many sessions we had left but the sessions changed little otherwise. The beanies were drawn either leaving a place, journeying to the battleground, preparing to go into battle or facing their opponents. On occasions the battle had actually taken place but they were all safe and 'no one had been killed'. This movement between past, present and future felt very fluid and positive. The main difference in The Boy's drawings was that the beanies were now shown wearing full armour with helmets and shields. They appeared very masculine and strong. It was no longer possible to know who was who just by looking at the picture. The Boy would tell me whom he was drawing and once the characters were drawn he would point to each one and test me and himself to check we agreed on who was who behind the armour.

Perhaps to alleviate my own anxiety feelings about not remembering who was who in the picture, I found myself pointing out that in real life there were lots of aspects of a person we use to help us recognise and remember them. I talked about how I would remember him for his friendly personality, the things he had done and said as well as for how he looked.

It was in images following this conversation that The Boy began to draw what became symbolic emblems on the beanies' armour. The Boy thought the lion on Bee bee's armour could stand for courage. This led to further discussion about other emblems representing different things. We had a humorous conversation about how we could wear a different emblem on different days depending on how we felt. The Boy liked this idea and included a new emblem on one of the characters, a red 'Y'. I asked him about this symbol: 'It's for the days when I need to ask lots of questions.'

Last session

The last drawing session started with The Boy saying, 'The beanies are in battle' but once he began drawing, although in armour, they looked more as though they were lined up for a photograph than about to fight (Plate 6).

Although The Boy was keen to establish that all the beanies were in the picture, some being so far back they were stick figures, the usual ones were presented and given emblems. Suddenly, while drawing, The Boy shouted out 'Bye Zara!'. I experienced this as an outburst of both his anger and unhappiness. It shocked me initially and then left me feeling very sad. Following his outburst, The Boy drew the landscape in which the beanies are travelling. The forest was drawn first. The Boy and I talked as he drew:

TB: They have come out from the forest.
Z: So what is ahead of them now?
TB: Who knows, anything could be there, they just can't know.
Z: You're right sometimes we can't know. Do you think they will be all right though?
TB: Yes they will win all the battles.

The Boy's optimism was confirmed I felt in the drawing of a fire. Although the rain is beating down the fire is alight. The Boy said, 'That's unusual isn't it, for a fire to burn when it's raining, how unusual is that?' The fire burning in the rain gave me a positive glow. I felt this illustrated a spark that could not be extinguished, an inner strength that The Boy had developed.

With ten minutes of the session remaining The Boy drew a wizard talking to the beanies. The wizard is greeting them and saying, 'Teddy my friend and king of Beanie Island. You have travelled far and the battle field is over there.' Another speech bubble says, 'There's no questions to ask so bye.' I acknowledged that perhaps he thought I was like the wizard He answered very thoughtfully but with a slight questioning tone, 'Even if wizards disappear they still exist.' I confirmed I would still exist even if he did not see me and he asked me what I would be doing. We talked about me visiting the base and seeing him one day. This prompted a discussion about how one recognises another in the future, The Boy saying, 'We still have the same face even if we change our clothes.'

The Boy drew a small green space ship for the wizard to go off in. He wrote the number 132. I asked him about this number and he replied, 'It is the number of pages in the book.' Although this seemed to be a number plucked out of nowhere it is very close to the total number of sessions we had had together!

The Boy wrote the final words on his image:

> And so our final
> Chapter of the
> Book has reached its
> Final sentence
> On its final
> Page bye

Conclusion

When working with students with ASD it is not unusual to feel paralysed and in a state of autistic stuckness. Working with The Boy, at times, generated such feelings, rendering me unable to think and speak. I felt despair and frustration and, by the power and repetition of some themes, was made to feel they had continued for many more weeks than they actually did. The drawing of beanie lists at the start was an example of this paralysis. In reality this defensive imagery was very short lived. As The Boy began to be able to let go of some of his anxiety, thoughts rather than ideas started to be held in mind and development became possible. His drawings developed into colourful pictures that told a story and illustrated how he risked exploring some previously intolerable thoughts and feelings.

Although there will still be difficult times, The Boy is now more able to be honest with himself and others. He no longer feels he should be all-knowing all of the time but can allow himself to admit to not knowing on occasions and can express genuine curiosity. He has the opportunity now to truly learn.

References

Alvarez, A. (1992) *Live Company: Psychoanalytic Psychotherapy with Autistic, Borderline, Deprived and Abused Children*. London: Routledge.

Tustin, F. (1992) *Autistic States in Children* (revised edn). London: Routledge.

Witkin. R.W. (1974) *The Intelligence of Feeling*. London: Heinemann Educational Books.

Winnicott, D.W. (1971) *Playing and Reality*. London: Tavistock.

Growing up can be so hard to do: the role of art therapy during crucial life transitions and change in the lives of children with learning disabilities

Barrie Damarell and Dot Paisley

Introduction

The aim of this chapter is to explore and illustrate the natural processes of child maturation from the extraordinary perspective of learning disability. The use of case material will show the challenges experienced by such children and discuss aetiology as a combination of psychological, systemic and social construction phenomena.

Our intention is to illustrate how the interrelationship of the child, the art materials and the therapist has the capacity to provide an opportunity for the exploration and understanding of transition and change in the learning-disabled child's life.

In the context of this chapter the relationship of the co-authors is supervisor and therapist, and in this sense there are two voices. A period of therapy with a boy called Jack will be described, interwoven with the supervision process.

The social construction of childhood

It is difficult, from our present twenty-first century orientation, where children are regarded as in need of care and education, to think of childhood as a relatively recent western phenomenon. Yet it is true that, prior to nineteenth-century legislation concerning compulsory education and child labour, children were expected to contribute, by means of their work, to the survival of the family (Swain *et al.* 2003: 143).

Therefore, despite contemporary concerns regarding pressures upon children to grow up before their time, notions of prolonged playfulness, experimentation and learning that delineate childhood are very much of our time and not to be seen as always so. If we needed proof of this peculiarly western concept we only need look towards the developing world where child labour is still part of cultural practice.

The social construction of the child with learning disabilities

Children with learning disabilities, unlike other children but like their adult counterparts, have received a range of imposed and powerful social constructions that have shaped their identities and influenced cultural disconnectedness.

Carter Park and Radford (1999) trace the development of asylums, whose original purpose was to provide education to children away from the influences of social and economic difficulties that were believed to militate against their primary aim. Importantly, they make a link between what happened within the institution and the way children with learning disabilities outside the asylum were regarded. This link underscores the nature of institutional power in establishing the discourse that shapes the social and cultural identity of the individual.

Although this period essentially ended in the 1970s (having begun 150 years earlier) the discourse process continues, an example being The Warnock Report (1978) that recommended the inclusion of learning disabled children in mainstream educational provision and Ofsted's (2004) report concerning the benefits of inclusion. All of this represents the latest incarnation of the inclusion-exclusion discourse that powerfully and, we argue, often unconsciously (mis)shapes the lives of people with learning disabilities from the beginning of their childhoods.

Growing up, life cycles and tasks

From a systems theory perspective, Carter and McGoldrick (1980, 1989), describe a series of events they recognised as being experienced by families in western cultures.

This 'family life cycle' has six stages that require transition:

1. Leaving home: single young adults.
2. The joining of families through marriage: the new couple.
3. Families with young children.
4. Families with adolescents.
5. Launching children and moving on.
6. Families in later life.

Worden (1999) notes that families experience the greatest stress when about to make a transition from one life stage to another and that events that disrupt the cycle exacerbate the tensions already evident in the system.

Dallos and Vetere (2003) point out that in the context of learning disabilities, families have to cope with transitions that happen at unexpected times and often not when usually anticipated. Sometimes transitions do not happen at all and these events require exceptional adjustment for the entire system.

They list transitional difficulties that might be experienced by such families:

1. Educational statementing procedures and the requirement that parents be explicit about their child's abilities.
2. Issues of social comparison and social isolation for the young adolescent in terms of their own developing sense of autonomy.
3. The transition of leaving home for many may be psychologically marked by independent employment and establishing one's own intimate relationships and family life – this is sometimes less possible for young adults with disabilities and sexuality is seen more as a risk than a human need or right.
4. Whether or not to ask for genetic counselling in the light of heritable conditions.
5. Decisions about respite and future placement if the caring adult becomes unable to continue with the task.
6. Changing relationships with siblings over the life cycle; forming relationships with changing professional staff.

It is clear that difficulties are higher than average for the learning disabled child and his family. The survival rate of children born with disabilities has risen in tandem with advances in medical science and intervention. The complications experienced as a learning disabled person in the world seem linked to the evidence that people with learning disabilities experience higher incidents of mental illness than the general population (Dallos and Vetere 2003). Therefore, it is crucial that difficulties are recognised as early as possible and appropriate interventions made.

In the context of this chapter the main interventions are through a multi-disciplinary team of practitioners – namely psychology, speech and language therapists, music therapists and art psychotherapists. The case material will explore the effects of family illness upon the learning disabled child and the anxiety associated with the inextricable approach of adolescence as marked by the child's difficulties at school and home. Before progressing further to look at the art psychotherapy literature it is important to take a moment to consider the relevance of life transition in association with rites of passage.

Rites of passage

As is widely known, rites of passage enable an individual to negotiate a change in their status. The Belgian ethnographer Van Gennep (1977) identified three phases: *separation*, where the individual begins to move between groups or identifications, enabled by a loosening of the ties with the group of origin;

liminality, a state of limbo where the individual has no membership of either group; and *incorporation*, where the individual re-enters society as a member of the group that is congruent with their new status.

In modern societies rites of passage can take the form of 'firsts' such as first words, steps, day at school, boy- or girlfriend, driving licence, beer, job, child and so on.

Rites of passage are linked to life transition in that they require room within the family for their facilitation, but they also have a role in the development of the socio-cultural identity of the individual.

Upon reviewing the list of 'firsts' above it becomes apparent that, for many children with learning disabilities, these rites are frequently delayed, and by implication diluted in their cultural meaning, or evade achievement entirely.

Often children and young adults with learning disabilities seem to move toward Van Gennep's first stage in that they attempt to separate from their group of origin – often other children with learning disabilities with whom they are grouped. Some appear to get 'stuck' in liminality, not wishing to associate with their socio-medico constructed group but not enabled to enter the valued social groups associated with economic contribution and social mobility. Therefore, many children enter and negotiate adulthood in a state of limbo, characterised by phantasy achievements and identifications.

British art therapy literature

In 1984, St Albans College of Art and Design hosted a second conference entitled 'Art Therapy as Psychotherapy in Relation to the Mentally Handicapped?' The questioning tone of the title reflected a change that was taking place in the profession with regard to working with people with learning disabilities. Four papers focused exclusively on work with children (Case 1984; Hiller 1984; Lindsay 1984; Rabiger 1984).

At this time art therapists often employed developmental models in their work; the task being to encourage shifts in the individual's graphic development[1] (Stott and Males 1984). In terms of social construction, this model inadvertently juxtaposed the learning disabled with the children from whom the data for 'normal' development was sourced (Kellogg 1970). Interestingly, this way of working has now vanished from the practice landscape, but at the time of the conference, both coexisted.

It is worth noting the influence of Valerie Sinason (1992) upon the form

---

1   Evans and Dubowski (2001) also write about developmental art therapy. Referring to his work in the 1980s Dubowski describes the use of psychodynamic and psychoanalytic models that underpinned his work on the iconic communication potential of the art object.

and practice of art psychotherapy in the context of learning disabilities. Her landmark book, *Mental Handicap and the Human Condition*, challenged assumptions about the usefulness of psychodynamic work with people with learning disabilities, in particular children. Sinason's further achievement was to propose the existence of 'secondary handicap' beyond the original disability and the result of subsequent trauma associated with having learning disabilities.

Since that time much of the published material has related to work with adults with learning disabilities, with two of the original authors, Rabiger (1998) and Case, (1996, 1998, 2000a, 2000b, 2003; Case and Dalley 1990) continuing to publish about children, and Dubowski and James (1998), Evans and Dubowski (2001), Evans (1998), Evans and Rutten-Saris (1998) and Tipple (2003) commenting on their paediatric work in the context of autism and learning disability. The only British art therapy book focusing solely on the learning disabled (Rees 1998) explores assessment, the nature of art in art therapy and body image in relation to children.

The case material

Context

The following case material began as a joint project between the participating school for children with moderate to severe learning disabilities, and the Child and Adolescent Mental Health and Learning Disability Service. It involved a newly-qualified art therapist who had previously been on placement in National Health Service (NHS) settings. The favourable outcome to the eight-week pilot led to the development of a jointly funded, fixed-term art therapy post within the school.

Jack

Background to the clinical work

During the work with Jack that took place as part of the pilot within the school, two major points of transition in his life were encountered. One concerned Jack's need to negotiate a change in relationships and power dynamics at home, and the other was his mother's diagnosis and treatment for breast cancer when she was, occasionally, both physically and emotionally absent or different in her relationship with Jack.

The referral

Jack was 10 years old when he was referred for art therapy. He was diagnosed as having a communication disorder on the autistic spectrum and a neurodevelopmental delay or learning disability. He struggled with sharing and relating to his peers. He found it difficult to attend to and understand what was being said to him and would react to attempts to stop him from doing something by attacking verbally and physically. He naturally used art materials and drawing to show to others his view of the world in his everyday life. It was therefore hoped that art therapy would build on his positive use of the creative process to begin thinking about his feelings and behaviour towards others.

Developmental history

Jack's mother recognised differences in his interaction, as an infant, to his older brother. She was concerned about his development. At 6 he was diagnosed as being on the autistic spectrum with associated learning disabilities. Jack was described as having a global developmental delay, with rigid, ritualistic behaviour and an obsessive repertoire of interests. However, unusually for those on the autistic spectrum, he was also reported as developing some capacity for imaginative play.

Family history

Jack lived with his mother, step-father, older brother (12) and half-sister (3). Jack's natural father had left the family home when Jack was around 5. He lived far away and had little contact with his sons. The family subsequently moved area to have easier access to education and health services. When Jack's step-father moved in, he became the primary carer for him and his younger half-sister, Susie, as Jack's mother went out to work. As he had not known Jack when he was younger, his step-father had little understanding of his complex needs. They would often clash. The differences in paternity, ability, age and gender between Jack and his younger step-sister became more pronounced, putting additional strain on the step-parent/child relationship. Jack also seemed to struggle to adjust to his step-father becoming mother and mother becoming father.

The setting

Therapist. The therapeutic work was conducted in a cluttered technical room. To access this room, it was necessary to negotiate through the seniors' classroom and to clear an island of space among the piles of donations for the bric-a-brac stand of the PTA fete, the stage props and scenery left to dry and the computers displaying abandoned Playstation games.

This situation, on the one hand, was understandable given that the school had little space and art therapy was new to the context, but at another and less rational level, it was rather irritating. There was a question about what

Jack would make of this obstacle-course-like journey and his subsequent interpretation of the therapy.

Supervisor. My initial thoughts at this early referral stage alighted on Jack's attachments and losses. He had obviously experienced the loss of his father and little contact appeared to remain between them. I reflected with Dot on his possible need to control events in an attempt to avoid the loss of subjects in his life. Jack had also witnessed the arrival of a new male into his household in the form of his mother's new partner. I thought that this expansion-contraction-expansion of the triangular space might complicate Jack's Oedipal experience.

Another factor in the supervision discourse was the length of the pilot. Although there were high hopes for a second, seamless phase, all that was presently certain was eight weekly sessions. Therefore, it was paramount that Jack knew and understood this by introducing a calendar-aide where each session was represented and marked off as it passed.

The early sessions

Therapist. Jack was a lithe, slim, attractive boy with no physical signs of difference or disability. He was a very talkative, animated child, keen to engage in art activities and story-telling. I went to his classroom to introduce myself and the possibility of us doing some drawing together. Once in the art room, I produced a calendar of our sessions and described the limits and boundaries of therapy. I suggested that, when we had got to know each other a little better, we might be able to think about some worries he may have and what that 'felt' like for him.

Jack did not appear anxious or inhibited in any way. He moved straight towards the art materials and began to draw, introducing me to Jack/Aladar, the friendly dinosaur from the Disney film *Dinosaur*.

He tended to use different voices, switching between characters and directing my actions and interactions with him as co-actor. He used these initial sessions to adapt and retell stories of Aladar the dinosaur and of characters from the film *Monsters, Inc.* It seemed important for Jack that someone witnessed his art-making and could tolerate his focused interest in one particular thing. He tended to use one felt-tipped pen and borrowed characters from films and video games which resonated with him in some way. Jack seemed to identify and connect the feelings of these characters to his own and other people's behaviour. However, when I pointed this out, he found it difficult to hear and he would tell me to 'shut up'.

During this early stage of the work, Jack represented himself as a 'monster'. The accompanying narrative and role-playing described a feeling of being scary to others and scared inside him. In our interaction, he would direct the acting out of his stories, switching between being the roaring, terrifying monster and the cowering, frightened little boy. Jack adapted the *Cinderella* story by replacing the original characters with *Monsters Inc.* style figures. He narrated and dramatically acted out the various parts as he drew a depiction of Cinderella locked in her room by her step-mother, being rescued by the hero, 'Aladar' the dinosaur (Figure 8.1). I contemplated whether Jack might be scared of me and that I might lock him in, although he told the story as if I too was at risk of being locked in.

Jack and I had been preparing for the end of art therapy from the beginning of our work together, Jack crossing off one session at a time from the calendar list. The ending of the initial pilot coincided with the school's summer break, creating a natural pause in the work.

Supervisor. Looking at Jack's drawings, I experienced a range of emotional responses. I was, and still am, captured by the aesthetic quality of his line, the inventiveness of his narratives and the quality of urgent communication embodied in his art works.

Jack's use of imagery from popular visual culture is interesting, as is his ability to weave figures such as Aladar into a fairytale from another era. The Cinderella story is immediately associated with learning disability in my mind. The narrative tells of a family member who is kept at home and excluded from special events and personal relationships. However, Jack's retelling introduces a threatening tone, one of a fear of incarceration at the hands of a step-mother, which represents a likely transferential reference to the therapist and to the therapy environment, as described earlier, that is located in a hard to reach and abandoned area of the school – an interesting allegorical reference to the contrasting environments of the *Cinderella* story.

The narrative also possesses transitional references. Cinderella is prevented from experiencing a rite of passage into adulthood by the ugly sisters. It is only through the magical intervention of the fairy-godmother that she experiences transformation, yet this is temporary and comes to an end at midnight. It is as if Cinderella enters a state of liminality after her time at the ball where she does not belong as her old oppressed scullery-self or as the partner of Prince Charming. The appearance of the male (Aladar and Prince Charming) in both narratives is important as this figure appears to hold the key to true transition through an Oedipal journey.

Negotiations with the school took place at the beginning of the autumn term to move from 'pilot' status to ongoing provision – not unlike Cinderella's transition. Funding was shared between heatlh and education and work began again. Observations had been made by Jack's class teacher and step-father, noting a shift in his arousal state and behaviour towards others since beginning art therapy, and there was a recommendation that Jack be offered the opportunity to work without the limitation of time constraint.

Figure 8.1 Aladar the dinosaur.

The continuation of therapy

Therapist. Shortly after I resumed art therapy with Jack, Jack's step-father went away for a week. His mother reported that Jack had become even more controlling and demanding at home. Jack's older brother was entering adolescence and Jack was no longer able to 'get his own way', which led to competition and rivalry between the two. Their conflicting needs had been causing some serious clashes at home. Jack's behaviour at school had become rigid and uncompromising again. His teacher expressed her concerns about his verbal attacks and obvious anger and pain being acted out at school.

In the following session, Jack retold the story of *Matilda* (Dahl 1988) in which a little girl's father dies when she is 5 (around the age Jack was when his natural father left). Jack replaced the names with those of his own family members and drew a picture of his step-father with scratches on his face and arm. He told me that a robot, 'Colossus', had come from the underground and killed him, illustrating his story as he spoke. I was made to feel his rage as he sneezed in my face and attempted to put his finger up my nose. He went on to say that it was his mother's fault, using her given name as a way of depersonalising these strong, destructive thoughts and fantasies.

Jack then took on the role of doctor and assigned me the role of nurse, taking 'Simon' (his step-father) to the hospital in an ambulance. When asked if he thought he'd be able to save him, Jack replied in a deep, dramatically sincere voice, 'I hope so'. Matilda, in the Dahl narrative, develops magical control over loss. Jack appeared to be exploring both his ambivalent feelings towards his step-father and his capacity to repair the consequences of his projections.

Supervisor. This period of the therapy is extremely interesting. The absence of Jack's step-father appears to stimulate a powerful Oedipal desire. Bollas (1993) provides a useful insight into the Oedipal struggle. He proposes that all children are aware, at an essential level, that father preceded them in the relationship with mother. This knowledge of mother's pre-existing desire for the father introduces a dilemma for the child, the resolution of which enables the birth of a new self. Bollas sees that this development creates for the child an experience of interaction between two states, that of the initial infant and the new child who experiences mother as an erotic object. The questions about gender differences that emerge at this time give foresight to the path of identification for the child. Therefore, the Oedipal stage, as described by Bollas, dispenses with the frightening castrating paternal object of classical psychoanalytic theory.

This expansion of the triangular space forces the child to be both partici-pant and observer in relation to mother and father. It seems that Jack strug-gles with this, perhaps because of the disappearance of his biological father, and seeks to maintain his infantile relationship to the maternal object. His

Plate 1 'I made this!'

Plate 2 Monkey family.

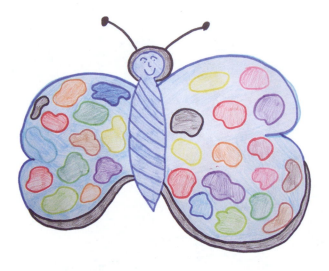

Plate 3 Butterfly.

Plate 4 The Persistence of Memory.

Plate 5 A list of facts.

Plate 6 Bye Zara.

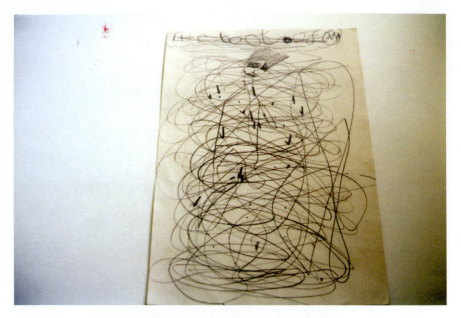

Plate 7 The book of Action Man.

Plate 8 The dress.

Plate 9 Confusion of wishes.

Plate 10 Body.

Plate 11 Birthday.

Plate 12 Growth.

Plate 13 Self – child or adult?

Plate 14 Sleeping fox.

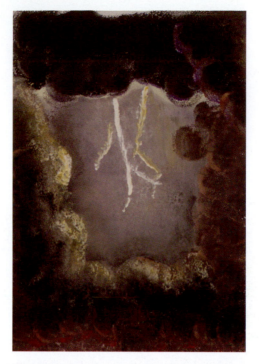

Plate 15 Storm.

Plate 16 Evening scene of moonlight and sea.

powerful and frightening impulses are perhaps linked to his denial of father's/
step-father's pre-eminence in his mother's life and this is perhaps played out
earlier in his wish to rename and restructure the family. These feelings appear
to threaten to overwhelm him and he projects this onto and into the art
therapist's body.

We shared these thoughts in supervision, particularly in the light of the
break and Dot's re-entry into his life. There appeared to be an associated
complication and intensification of his feelings that brought about, on the
one hand, a desire for control, and on the other a reaction to the loss of the
therapist, this latter issue being a conflict innate to term-time school work.

Therapist. Jack had returned, following the summer break, to a new teacher
and shortly after recommencing our work together, I heard from his class
teacher that Jack's mother had been diagnosed with breast cancer.

Although Jack had not been told about his mother's condition, there was a
sense that he did know something as there was lots of talk of 'killer animals',
conveying a sense of danger and being dangerous himself. In the sessions,
he was clearly unsettled and distressed and found it difficult to engage with
the art materials. He lashed out physically and shouted demands at me, but
also sought physical closeness and hugs. One moment that demonstrated
his internal conflict was when Jack took my finger and gently held the tip
between his teeth, pressing slightly. It felt quite primitive and animal-like and,
although the threat was present, there was tenderness and I felt sure that he
would not 'bite the hand that feeds him'.

Supervisor. The feeling in the room was sombre at the news that Jack's mother
had cancer. Jack's lack of conscious knowledge regarding the situation was
rather typical for people with learning disabilities who are 'protected' from the
truth even though the denial would eventually break down as events unfolded.
There is also an assumption that knowing will result in uncontrollable distress.
This is intriguing as it appears that the potential 'innocent' outpouring of raw
emotion represents a threat to the collective non-disabled ego; withholding
the knowledge therefore has a possible defensive function.

Therapist. During the post-diagnosis period, Jack produced several images
of spiders and spiders' webs. At a time when his mother was absent and in
hospital, and we were preparing for a short break due to training commitments, we worked together to reproduce a drawing of a spider's web in string.
We attached string to the table legs, creating the main strands of the web,
weaving and knotting lengths of string between them.

As he was drawing, there was a strong emphasis on the points where each
strand connected, marking it with a *dot* (my name). There was no spider,
perhaps representing the absent mother/my absence. Jack then experimented
with the string to tie me up, and untie me. Although he was able to draw the

design he wanted to create in string, he lacked the confidence to construct it himself. Demanding that I follow his orders, he became the impatient director. He shouted at me for 'not doing it right' with exaggerated sounds of boredom and frustration. This seemed to represent concrete expressions of the sorts of feelings he may have had inside.

Working together we completed the string web and transferred it to the wall. Jack pretended to get stuck on the web and then physically pushed me against it, leaving me 'stuck' there as he went back to class. It felt important to remain 'stuck' to the web and within the art room, as if I/mother might be held there in Jack's mind during the break in therapy.

Three weeks later, following my planned absence the week before, and his class teacher's absence due to illness that week, Jack brought a flashlight with him. We stood inside a walk-in cupboard together, with the flashlight on, pretending we were in a tent. He spoke of ghosts, being scared in the dark and 'nightmare dreams'. It felt womb-like, pressed together in this small dark space, but any attempts to interpret were met by silence. It seemed important to help Jack make connections between his stories and real events, and survive his attacks.

Jack then began drawing, but was frustrated when things 'went wrong', so scribbled over images and turned the paper over. It seemed really important to get things accurate and 'right'. After several attempts, he managed to create a detailed drawing of Buzz Lightyear's nemesis, Zerg, with a close-up of Zerg's teeth (Figure 8.2). The teeth, when separated from the body in this way, resemble mountains or breasts, yet within the body of Zerg they look ferocious and attacking. This perhaps says something about Jack's wish to separate himself, and his mother, from the cancerous breast and the rage he was feeling inside, although I did not know what his conscious understanding of his mother's condition was.

With my gentle interpretation, Jack was able to acknowledge this rage. I spoke with him about finding a way to put the horrible feelings into a picture, so that he could leave them with me in the art room. He seemed uncomfortable as I spoke, changing the subject and telling me to 'shut up', but he did go on to create a picture with a flashlight above a doorway and other shapes which he carefully cut out with scissors. He left the cut-out shapes and took the picture with him. I understood this as further acknowledgement of good and bad parts of himself/the therapist/his mother, and the art-making process enabled him to give some concrete shape to those aspects he wanted and could hold onto.

Supervisor. Jack's adoption of the spider's web motif had a fascinating synchronicity for me as I had recently visited the Tate Modern and had viewed Louise Bourgeois' spider sculpture. Bal (2001) speculates on Bourgeois' references associating the spider with her mother as '. . . comforting, diligent, repairing' (pp. 72–3). Later he contemplates the spider as simultaneously '. . .

Figure 8.2 Zerg.

strange, frightening and motherly. For it recalls the home the mother's body once was, when we had no mastery whatsoever' (p. 73).

These words, and the insight they create, resonate with Jack's webs. They imply the existence of the spider/mother at the same time as describing her absence and act as a means of holding her, and her transferential equivalence, in a sticky membrane. Jack acts this out with the therapist as he casts her into the web.

The reminiscently paranoid/schizoid drama between the 'good' Buzz Lightyear and the 'bad' Zerg indicates a distance from the depressive position within which the observer/participant Oedipal configuration can be experienced. Similar material can also be seen in Jack's apparent desire for the womb, illustrated in his use of the cupboard. It seems that at these times Jack has to evacuate his anxiety in a very concrete act of projective identification, as can be seen in his ambivalent and often physical interaction with the therapist.

Therapist. After the Christmas break a new phase opened where Jack resisted the notion of growing up and decided he wanted to be 8 years old again. He said it was too late for kids to be adults and drew a picture of a 'cuckoo clock' with numbers only going up to eight. Over the coming months, Jack presented material that communicated a strong identification with his mother and the process of her illness. He would arrive with his hood up, hiding his shaven head. This coincided with his mother losing her hair during her treatment. He spoke a lot about death: the death of 'a boy', pretending to die himself and bringing objects such as witches, skeletons and ghosts into his imagery.

As the sophistication of his ideas developed, Jack became less confident in his ability to draw. He also became rejecting and dismissive of earlier images he had made, and adopted an approach whereby we held the pencil together to draw his complex ideas. He would shout at me to move the pencil and was attacking of any praise or encouragement, as he ordered me to draw things for him, under his strict and critical direction.

A good example of this phase can be seen in the following description of the session before the summer break in which Jack made his last image.

Jack wanted me to assist him in drawing his picture which was made with us both holding the pencil, but with Jack in control, guiding it. He seemed to be controlling the therapist/maternal object as if trying to recreate the mother he remembered.

Together, under Jack's direction, we drew a scene with a snow-capped mountain and the thin ledge of a cliff, joined with a rope bridge and alligator-infested water below. There was a cave with a giant spider, things falling from the bridge into the open mouth of an alligator and a crack in the ledge and signs of an impending avalanche. I reflected on how this was clearly a dangerous place to be and was aware of anxieties in the room as we prepared for the long summer break – would he/I/his mother survive?

When I mentioned his mother and the concerns that were around for him,

Jack said, 'She's stupid', and went on to tell stories of skeletons, ghosts and a phantom virus. His image and the stories made me think of the good and cancerous object or breast, and the threat of death.

Jack was very clingy, wanting to be close and connected. He had asked me to draw him on the bridge but then found a safe place, in the cave of the whole and upright mountain. He acted out parts of his story, jumping into my lap and putting my arms around him, saying he was scared.

The ending

When I went to collect Jack for our first session of the new autumn term, he was busy cooking with a teaching assistant. He reluctantly joined me, but 'ordered' me not to laugh or smile. Jack left the session after five minutes and stormed back to class. Apparently he had stopped drawing altogether in class and, for this reason, he told his teacher that he did not wish to return to art therapy. When I tried to discuss this with him, I took a card decorated with a photograph of one of his early 'Aladar' pictures, simply acknowledging our work together. Jack pushed me away and was unable to hear my words. The abrupt nature of the ending left me feeling bewildered and hurt. Jack's apparent taking of control correspondingly left me with feelings of loss and rejection that had often been his experience. Not continuing his sessions served to leave those feelings with me. I hoped the card would act as a non-verbal mark of the end that he could reflect on later.

Supervisor. Interestingly, Jack seems to be experiencing the dilemma described by Bollas (1993) where the child oscillates between being wholly a participant in his relationships and a combination of participant and observer that promotes psychological development. I suggest Jack's solution is sought in the former position. The notion of the cuckoo-clock provokes thoughts about the difference often felt by learning disabled people, particularly if their siblings do not have disabilities, as is the case with Jack. This awareness of difference can also be detected in Cinderella's antithetical qualities to her environmental context.

The last image that heralds the end of therapy and the taking of control by Jack seems to illustrate the anxiety and dangers innate in transition and change. He is both precipitating the ending of his attachment with the therapist, and allegorically his mother, as well as seeking to maintain aspects of connection in the form of his bridge. This act of separation had become inevitable not least because of Jack's realisation that his mother was beyond his control. This is an interestingly common denial innate in the lives of people with learning disabilities. Not being enabled to grow up results in an eternal childlike state where attachments are maintained at a primary level. This sometimes results in the catastrophic severing of attachment at the death of the parental figures.

Another factor for Jack is his awareness of his maturing body and that of his brother before him. His conscious physicality demands change in his infantile wishes for sole relationship with his mother. Although complicated by his identification with the visually ill maternal object, his body connects him to the maleness he and his father/step-father share and points to future transition.

The abrupt ending to the therapy left both therapist and supervisor with powerful feelings of rejection that we could do no more with than bear.

Although Jack's actions enabled him to take control of an area of his life and make a transition from the liminality of the therapy into the new school year, there was also a feeling that we had failed sufficiently to protect the therapeutic relationship through the various breaks that inevitably have an impact on school-orientated art therapy practice.

Conclusions

This chapter has described the sometimes monumental task of growing up as a learning disabled child, where innate difficulties in learning are coupled with powerful social constructs that shape the maturational journey and constrain individualisation.

In addition, Jack's life had been punctuated by interrupted relationships: that with his biological father; the exchange of domestic roles between his mother and his step-father; and his mother's serious illness. This dynamic of loss was played out in the therapeutic relationship. Notably, breaks in the therapy brought about an intensification of this material that ultimately brought the therapeutic relationship to an end. Case (2000b) explores the influence of breaks in therapy and notes that clients sometimes do not return to therapy after an interruption and how the break might be experienced concretely by the child as a catastrophic severing of the relationship in the absence of an internalised representation of the therapist and the therapy.

In this respect, it is difficult to know to what degree Jack's autism, rather than his learning disabilities, influenced his concrete relating. His level of anxiety was certainly related to his concreteness. It would seem that Jack's regression to a paranoid-schizoid state, with its inherent concreteness, was made 'easier' by his autism, though it is important to acknowledge that learning disability is often accompanied by immature ego-structure and the related use of primitive defence mechanisms. There were clearly times where he was able to symbolically express his conflicts within the safety and creativity of the therapeutic relationship. However, breaks were seen, and anticipated, as dangerous, and there is an indication of difficulty in internalising and relating to the therapeutic object in his use of the spider's web, in which the therapist is externally secured and presumably recoverable in the concrete world.

Jack's mother's illness brought similar dilemmas into his home life and it is no coincidence that re-engaging after breaks became more fraught during this period. In a related way, an improvement in Jack's mother's health, and one imagines greater stability in the maternal relationship and home life generally, coincided with a weakening and eventual severing of the therapeutic relationship. Jack's apparent inability to simultaneously bear the idea of two maternal objects is seemingly resolved by the splitting-off and projection of the therapist-mother as the bad object.

For Jack, as for many children and adults with learning disabilities, not having background information about significant life events, such as illness, can hinder the acquisition of life knowledge that subsequently fosters maturity and gives confidence in transition. A vacuum in knowledge can also act as a catalyst for compensatory phantasies that seek to quell the anxiety of not knowing. These phantasies can sometimes be more terrifying than the reality that it has been felt important to conceal from the learning disabled person.

In her introduction to her article on breaks in therapy, Case (2000b) considers the phenomenon where the client, after a break, may appear to have grown in maturity. She notes, however, that this can also be an example of a 'false-maturity' (p. 11) that defends against the experience of loss. In this regard, Jack's change at the beginning of the autumn term and his rejection of art therapy is interesting. There was certainly a feeling of defence, as referred to earlier, yet, at the same time there is balance through an emerging maturity in his associations with his peers and his calmer conduct in class.

As much as 'childhood' is a relatively new concept, so must 'adulthood' become for people with learning disabilities. In this respect, art therapy, as we hope we have shown, has a vital role to play.

References

Bal, M. (2001) *Louise Bourgeois' Spider: The Architecture of Art-Writing*. Chicago: University of Chicago Press.

Bollas, C. (1993) *Being a Character : Psychoanalysis and Self Experience*. London: Routledge.

Carter, E.A. and McGoldrick, M. (1980) *The Family Life Cycle: A Framework for Family Therapy*. New York: Gardner.

Carter, E.A. and McGoldrick, M. (1989) *The Changing Family Life Cycle: A Framework for Family Therapy*. Boston, MA: Allyn & Bacon.

Carter Park, D. and Radford, J. (1999) Rhetoric and place, in the 'mental deficiency' asylum, in R. Butler and P. Hester (eds) *Mind and Body Spaces: Geographies of Illness, Impairment and Disability*. London: Routledge.

Case, C. (1984) 'P' – A case study of art therapy with a child ascertained ESN at a normal primary school: art therapy as psychotherapy in relation to the mentally handicapped. Paper presented at the 'Second Conference on Art Therapy and the Mentally Handicapped', St Albans College of Art and Design, 29–30 November 1984.

Case, C. (1996) On the aesthetic moment in the transference. *Journal of the British Association of Art Therapists, Inscape*, 1(2): 39–45.

Case, C. (1998) Brief encounters: thinking about images in assessment, *Journal of the British Association of Art Therapists, Inscape*, 3(1): 26–33.

Case, C. (2000a) 'Our Lady of the Queen': journeys around the maternal object, in A. Gilroy and G. McNeilly (eds) *The Changing Shape of Art Therapy: New Developments in Theory and Practice*. London: Jessica Kingsley.

Case, C. (2000b) Santa's grotto – an exploration of the Christmas break in therapy. *Journal of the British Association of Art Therapists, Inscape*, 5(1): 11–18.

Case, C. (2003) Authenticity and survival: working with children in chaos, *Journal of the British Association of Art Therapists, Inscape*, 8(1): 17–28.

Case, C. and T. Dalley (1990) *Working with Children in Art Therapy*. London: Routledge.

Dallos, R. and Vetere, A. (2003) *Working Systemically with Families : Formulation, Intervention and Evaluation*. London: Karnac.

Dhal, R. (1988). *Matilda*. New York and London, Penguin Books.

Dubowski, J.K. and James, J. (1998) Arts therapies with children with learning disabilities, in D. Sandle (ed.) *Development and Diversity: New Applications in Art Therapy*. London: Free Association Books.

Evans, K. (1998) Sharing experience and sharing meaning: art therapy for children with autism. *Journal of the British Association of Art Therapists, Inscape*, 3(1): 17–25.

Evans, K. and Dubowski, J.K. (2001) *Art Therapy with Children on the Autistic Spectrum: Beyond Words*. London: Jessica Kingsley.

Evans, K. and Rutten-Saris, M. (1998) Shaping vital affects, enriching communication: art therapy for children with autism, in D. Sandle (ed.) *Development and Diversity: New Applications in Art Therapy*. London: Free Association Books.

Hiller, M. (1984) Art Therapy as a Bridge Between the Handicapped Child and the Learning Situation. Art Therapy as Psychotherapy with the Learning Disabled. St Albans College of Art and Design.

Kellogg, R. (1970) *Analyzing Children's Art*. Palo Alto, CA: Natinal Press Books.

Lindsay, M. (1984) The Role of Transference in Art Therapy with a Severely Mentally handicapped Child. Art Therapy as Psychotherapy in Relation to the Mentally handicapped. St Albans College of Art and Design.

Ofsted (Office for Standards in Education) (2004) *Special Educational Needs and Disability : Towards Inclusive Schools*. London, Ofsted.

Rabiger, S. (1984) Some Experiences of Art Therapy in a Special School. Art Therapy as Psychotherapy in Relation to the Mentally Handicapped. St Albans College of Art and Design.

Rabiger, S. (1998) Is art therapy? Some issues arising in working with children with severe learning difficulties, in M. Rees (ed.) *Drawing on Difference: Art therapy with People who have Learning Difficulties*. London: Routledge.

Rees, M. (1998) *Drawing on Difference: Art therapy with People who have Learning Difficulties*. London: Routledge.

Sinason, V. (1992) *Mental Handicap and the Human Condition : New Approaches from the Tavistock*. London: Free Association Books.

Stott, J. and. Mayles, B. (1984). Art therapy for people who are mentally handicapped, in T. Dalley (ed.) *Art as Therapy: An Introduction to the use of Art as a Therapeutic Technique*. London: Tavistock.

Swain, J., French, S. and Cameron, C. (2003) *Controversial Issues in a Disabling Society*. Buckingham: Open University Press.

Tipple, R. (2003) The interpretation of children's artwork in a paediatric disability setting, *Journal of the British Association of Art Therapists, Inscape*, 18(2): 48–59.

Van Gennep, A. (1977) *Rites of Passage*. London: Routledge.

Warnock, M. (1978) *Meeting Special Educational Needs: A Brief Guide by Mrs Mary Warnock to the report of the Committee of Enquiry into Education of Handicapped Children and Young People*. London: HMSO.

Worden, M. (1999) *Family Therapy Basics*. Pacific Grove, CA: Brooks/Cole.

Chapter 9

Gender disorder in the treatment of a young person in care

Sue Retford-Muir

Introduction

Forty-nine per cent of boys and 39 per cent of girls who are looked after have identified mental health problems. Much of the gender discrepancy relates to younger boys being diagnosed with conduct disorders (Meltzer *et al.* 2003). 'Such factors raise questions about the "gender linked" needs of looked-after children, in particular whether boys are at greater risk. The low presence of men in the care system means that practice can easily become weighted towards the experiences of women and girls' (Wrighton 2006: 3).

This chapter describes how Peter, a young man who was looked after from an infant, explored his gender confusion within twice-weekly, art psycho-therapy sessions over a period of six years. Peter's early relationships and the changing representations of his attachments profoundly affected his sexual development. He had internalised little of a containing mother figure and had a poor sense of self. The attachment to the therapist within the thera-peutic process took a number of years to develop. This formed an essential basis from which Peter felt able to explore and reveal his sexual orientation as he fully entered adolescence. At the age of 13 Peter began cross-dressing and wishing to be and presenting himself as a woman; mainly within the privacy of his art psychotherapy sessions. At 15 Peter went on to abuse another boy which happened in the context of a great upheaval in the structures around him. These external structures had become his container in the absence of internalised resources.

Peter presented his predicament in a sexually explicit way. Some of these instances will be referred to in order to highlight the emotional intensity I was working with as a female therapist. Although art psychotherapists have written widely about sexual abuse (Sagar 1990; Aldridge 1998; Murphy 1998), and also about work with children in the care system (Aldridge 1998; Case 2005), there is little within art psychotherapy literature on gender disorder. I have therefore turned to the specialist literature and analytic theory on the development of sexuality to inform my experiences with Peter (Woods 2003).

The setting

Peter was a looked after child placed in residential care. The therapeutic community where Peter lived provided a 24-hour home and a school for 14 children ranging in age between 10 and 18. All of the children who arrived at the community were usually on full care orders, some with limited supervised contact with parents and usually after successive previous failures in foster placements. There was a high ratio of staff to children (one adult to two children) and each child had two allocated workers. All the care staff attended a sensitivity meeting where they discussed their feelings in relation to the work. Sexual abuse was a common past experience for the children and sexualised acting out, crude language and accusations were common in the children's daily lives and within the therapeutic work.

I worked with Peter for nearly six years. For the last seven months the work moved to a secure unit where a plan was formed to move him to a more permanent home. Throughout, I attended weekly supervision to discuss this work which held and contained my thinking through the difficult times (Dalley 2007). Due to the highly charged atmosphere, the community was prone to falling into chaos. I was glad particularly at such times to have private and separate clinical supervision, which enabled in-depth work to survive within this volatile atmosphere.

Peter

Peter arrived at the community when he was 10. He was a round, soft lad, quite tall, blond, and overweight by a couple of stone, giving him the overall appearance of a large podgy toddler. His coordination was also reminiscent of a toddler, racing unchecked from one thing to another in his own world driven by his impulses.

Peter suffered severe emotional deprivation as a young infant. At birth he had no father and his mother had learning difficulties and was unable to care for him. At home, he was frequently neglected by his mother. Peter was possibly sexually abused by his mother and her partner(s). She herself had been abused from birth to 18 so her handling of Peter inevitably would have been affected by her own sexual and attachment experiences. Peter was accommodated at 2 months old and remained in and out of care, until approximately age 6, when he permanently went into foster care. During this time, Peter was sexually abused by an older foster child.

Peter's mother rejected him when she became pregnant by another man. Peter's step-sister was born when he was 5. His mother later re-established contact with Peter but remained inconsistent and in Peter's mind idealised and unobtainable. This seemed to compound Peter's difficulty with coming to terms with reality.

Before he came to the community, Peter's placements had failed him as they seemed unable to withstand the rigor of his attacks and provide him with containment. His final foster placement had replicated the abuse of his earlier years. Peter had no experience of being contained or loved for being him.

Gender formation and disorder

Freud's theories place the development of masculinity and femininity at the point where the child recognises difference. The boy realises that his penis could be absent and therefore that it can be lost and the girl realises that she has something missing. Breen, summarising Freud, states that the girl and boy develop differently: 'The castration complex (for the boy and penis envy for the girl) refers to the whole constellation of mental processes surrounding this recognition which initiates distinction between the sexes' (Breen and Bott Spillius 1993: 3). She emphasises Freud's view that it is not then a simple question of recognition but how the individual deals with this recognition of difference (Freud 1925). Freud believed that a 'boy's development would be feminine if his fear of castration is so great that he renounces his penis in phantasy' (Breen and Bott Spillius 1993: 3).

Stoller (1968), who coined the phrase 'core gender identity', felt gender identity was formed in the first two years of life, as part of the development of the core self through a number of factors. Breen, interpreting Stoller, says it is 'part of narcissism and was made up of biological force, the sex assignment of the parents' attitudes about the infant's sex, early post natal effects caused by habitual patterns of handling the infant, and sensations especially from the genitals' (Breen 1993: 17). He gives weight to the importance of parental attitudes about the infant's sex, especially those of the mother. The infant constructs these perceptions 'via developing capacity to fantasize, into events, into meaningful, motivated experiences' (Breen 1993 :17). One can assume from Freud and Stoller that the physical and psychological treatment of the child are also responsible for forming the development of masculinity and femininity. Formed in the first years of life, the core gender identity is established permanently by the end of adolescence.

In terms of the development of a healthy male self a positive relationship with a father is central to the child's development of gender identity as a man: 'If the boy has a strong belief in the goodness of his male genitals – his father's and his own – he can allow himself to experience his genital desires towards his mother. When his fear of the castrating father is mitigated by trust in a good father, he can face his Oedipus hatred and rivalry' (Klein 1945: 411); Greenson (1968) thought the threat of fusion with the mother or of engulfment was fundamental. Referring to the mother, 'the male child's ability to dis-identify (from the mother) will determine the success or failure of this later identification with father' (Greenson 1968: 370).

If the child's inherent phantasy life and developing gender identity are in the hands of his parents then one must assume that the initial relationship (for argument's sake the conventional family structure of mother, father and child) with the mother is vital. As the child develops and begins to separate, the gender identity of his parents will have a further forming impact on the child's developing gender identity.

Therapeutic work

Peter was very disturbed on arrival. He was practically mute. He expressed himself through gesture behaviour and his bodily functions (incontinent of both urine and faeces). Initially he was placed on 24-hour one-to-one supervision. His behaviour was highly sexualised towards everybody. He attempted intercourse standing behind staff making sexual motions and trying to touch their genitals. He would also expose himself to adults and tried using hugs for sexualised reasons. Peter awoke several times at night with nightmares shouting 'get off'. He wet the bed nightly and soiled frequently. He would also urinate and defecate in inappropriate places. Peter had outbursts of anger and crying. He also overate to the extreme, stuffing food into his mouth without chewing. He sometimes choked to the point of vomiting. He climbed fences, spat and kicked out at adults. He stole and refused to comply with boundaries. Although he was incontinent he used his faeces to express his aggression and smeared it when upset. His language was like baby speech with infantile squeals. Peter also had poor hearing and, although he had grommets inserted in his ears, this may have affected his language development.

A number of months after Peter had established a relationship with his keyworker and the community life as a whole, I offered him an assessment with a view to further understanding his complex difficulties and whether he could engage in therapeutic work.

Transference, mess and perverse structures: the development of the therapeutic alliance

The beginning of Peter's therapy involved a good deal of boundary-testing. He learnt about art psychotherapy through his experience within the room with me. Essential to containing Peter was my reinforcement of the 50-minute boundary (Dalley 2007). This was part of the establishment of therapeutic boundaries with which Peter persistently battled for the first 18 months of our work together.

Initially he would try and get past me and the adult outside, seemingly wanting to get away. Peter employed other tactics when one manoeuvre failed such as battling over the possession of his images which remained in the room. He employed all manner of manoeuvres to get them. This seemed to be the initial way he expressed his aggression, and I felt in these early stages that he was trying to destroy me. I said this to him. I felt he was also trying to keep at bay any feelings of loss. It was as if any limit I set became a target for Peter's need to control. He would even set up unsuspecting staff to try and get them from me. At times I felt I was absorbing negative transference second-hand from the care team.

Within the sessions themselves I was struck by Peter's pervading sense of non-caring for himself or the objects he now began to use. He was brutal in the way he grabbed at the materials, treated himself and his clothes. I felt ignored by him. He made no response to my thoughts or words and seemed to treat everything with contempt. In the second session, referring to his piece of art work, he said, 'I wanted to give it to my mother [who was visiting] but you won't let me.' I reflected that it felt unfair that I was keeping his image and that they would be safe for him here. In the countertransference, I felt like a depriving mother who was forcing him to give up his objects against his will. But I was determined to help Peter begin to keep things within our relationship, which required holding the negative transference for a while. In further processing the session I reflected on feeling rather brutally used, like a toddler rough-handling its mother. I felt this interaction had a cruel edge to it and that Peter hated me.

Ongoing work

Peter's sessions were established on a twice-weekly basis, and by the fourth session his transference to me began to deepen. He was projecting a very early part of his attachment experience into the relationship with me. He drew in pencil a fence enclosing an oval in the middle of the paper. He then coloured the inside in blue pastel. He said it was a house. He then switched tempo and began to scribble in red felt-pen, inside the fence with great pressure and speed, making aggressive noises and facial expressions. He surprised me with his impatient demand to pass him the paints. He then squirted with unceasing pressure the whole range of colours in turn into the middle of the house. The rush of paint quickly consumed the house. Peter then began to mix the colours with the sharp end of some scissors. This resulted in the production of a brown mixture. Peter then cut the remaining white edges of the paper and put them into the middle of the brown liquid, saying they were 'babies inside mummy'; he then used his hands to further mix the paint and squealed. The liquid swallowed the babies. I reflected how the babies were disappearing into the brown liquid. Peter continued to stir and scratch at the surface until I said it was soon time to stop, to which he responded suddenly by slapping his palms down into the brown liquid. It flew around the room onto the walls, onto him and onto me. I reflected on how upset he was about having to leave and he felt cut off by me. He put the scissors into the middle of the brown liquid. Peter continued to smear and make a mess. I had suggested we clear up together but Peter was having none of it. He seemed triumphant in his facial expression as he left the room before the actual end. I said he was showing me how angry he was with me by leaving me all his pooh to clean up.

When Peter had left I was aware of how frightening this dark womb swallowing all the babies must have been. I thought how in the face of this powerful mother Peter felt he would disappear, indicating how he felt he did not exist without her. Peter was also telling me about his repetitive feeling of abandonment, annihilation and his habitual way of retaliating by using his pooh. In showing his aggression, he might identify with shit being expelled from the session (Klein 1945). Peter also showed that he had been buggered and seemed to be expressing himself in a way characteristic of other children who have been sexually abused. Working with art materials, the therapist is required to hold and contain the actual mess which reflects the messy internal world of the abused child (Sagar 1990; Aldridge 1998; Murphy 1998): 'Often the way in which most satisfaction seems to be found in using art materials is by making a messy mixture which is then spread on any surface. A compulsive need to handle and examine the internal good and bad feelings where good and bad are indistinguishable' (Sagar 1990: 90).

I thought about how Peter might see me as part of him and, at a time of separation, feel great rage but also annihilation. Glasser (1988) suggests that perverse structures of development can be attempts by the infant to solve problems of intimacy. The infant may respond to threats to his

> emotional, psychic, and, in some cases, physical survival by mobilising a particular form of sexual aggression that has at its aim, not the removal or the destruction of the threat, but to retain at a safe distance the parental object on whom of course he depends. This covert aggression, originally self preservative, is turned into sado-masochism because of the conflation of love and hate. Sadism expressing the need to control, whilst masochism serves the need to preserve the attachment relationship.
>
> (Woods 2003: 202)

'Thus the pervert is able to enagage the object in sadomasochistic terms . . . [keeping] the object at a safe distance – a distance which precludes trust and intimacy' (Glasser 1988: 126). As the sadistic mother in the transference with Peter, I had power over him, but he had the ability to get his own back. Peter seemed to both repel me and still tell me about his neediness. He clearly felt annihilated when that feeling took him over. It seemed to develop into a monster once unleashed that consumed everything. It was therefore important I wasn't annihilated.

One year on

A year into therapy, some of these extreme anxieties had become contained. The dominant negative transference was tempered with other experiences.

Peter felt more able to think and reflect on his confusion. The development of his perverse structure began to emerge within the sessions. The painful reality of this is expressed in Plate 7 entitled 'The book of Action Man'. Peter drew the standing figure in a considered manner; the figure has no specific gender. It demonstrated a sophisticated drawing style and seemed to portray himself standing in a space alone. Peter's mood changed during the drawing. He became in touch with a different internal feeling/aspect of his experience. When he came to draw his penis/anus, he began to scribble aggressively over the entire page. Simultaneously he squealed and furiously stabbed the image with a pencil. I commented on how Peter now seemed angry with the figure and I said how painful it must be to be repeatedly stabbed like that. Peter's fury was directed towards himself in the image and depicted a sense of being alone and helpless against his own rage and maybe helplessness against his attacker.

When referring to sexually abused children, Hopkins (1999: 43) recounts a particular dynamic: 'When the source of a child's security is also the source of pain, the child is placed in a position of irresolvable and self-perpetuating conflict. The situation is irresolvable because rejection by the established attachment figure activates simultaneous contradictory impulses both to withdraw and to approach'. Relating to this dynamic of 'never having a good enough containing experience' (Winnicott 1971), Peter remained in the cycle of abuse with his mother who remained inconsistent in her visits and promises, but Peter internally relied on her. I wondered whether I was now, in the transference, the source of pleasure and pain; the one who gave him something only to take it away/abuse him.

Development of containment and control: webs and ensnarement

Eighteen months into therapy, Peter's creative language continued to develop. In one session after a break he started to tape the furniture in the room together. By the end of the session the room was like a web. All the objects and surfaces, including my chair, were attached together. He used Sellotape to seal around the door of the room, sticking the latch together and around the frame; I talked about how it would be nice for us to be stuck together. He then tried to put Sellotape over my mouth. I said no to this but reflected how he wanted me to be quiet. I thought about how he did not want me to speak because this made us separate. Instead of taping my mouth he made do by taping me in between the table and the wall either side of my chair. I was in a sort of stall. In her account of art psychotherapy groups with children, Dalley (1993: 153) discusses one session where the children employ 'yards of string and Sellotape stretching from wall to wall. In one group this culminated in tying one of the therapists to a chair as if ensnared in a web'. Connections were made to making it safe, to using the room as a container and finding the limits of the room. The group felt the need to stick to the therapist, which would enable them never to be separate'.

Once Peter had finished he ran out of the room, leaving me 'ensnared'. His key worker encouraged him back and he said to the worker, 'I hate therapy.' I said he hated me at the moment and wanted me to know what it felt like to be left helpless and stuck over the break. Inside again he climbed into the cupboard under the sink by removing the shelf. He then played hide and seek, wondering if I could see him. When I said I couldn't he said he could see me. I reflected how he was in charge being the one who could see. He then climbed out of the cupboard, turned off the lights and said, 'We can be nice and relaxed.' He then came up to me in the dark and kissed me on the cheek. I suggested that he was making things all right between us again after he was so angry with me. I also thought about this in terms of the boundaries and physical contact between us and his attempts in the session to have physical contact with me; to Sellotape my mouth and to kiss me.

Bick (1968) first defined the concept of adhesive identification. She said this occurred due to the absence of an external containing object available for mechanisms of projection and introjection. The child develops a 'second skin, a phantasy of sticking to an object as opposed to projecting into it. A lapse in the development of a sense of internal space leads to a tendency to relate to objects in a two dimensional way, without depth' (p. 228). It was apparent Peter could not symbolically hold me in his mind and that his need to stick us back together after the break was the only way he could internalise me.

Making progress through play

Peter's attachment relationship with his mother had hardly developed at all. He clearly felt his mother was very powerful and had no father to modify this relationship. Three years into therapy and his relationship with me had become trusting and warm. Peter still struggled with reality. As the sessions continued he made progress in all the areas with which he had difficulties. He was beginning to learn and was motivated to achieve academically at school. He became a good organiser of himself and other children, setting boundaries and explaining rules to other young people. His speech was improving, using words rather than actions to communicate. He was becoming more liked in the house among staff and peers. He was making friends with others and his self-esteem improved. It seemed that Peter was at last able to consolidate his learning, rather like a late latency child.

Woods (2003: 213) mentions how abused and abusing boys' healthy personality may be underdeveloped while the traumatised and persecutory side may be overdeveloped: 'Many of these children have never had the experience of their parents as playmates . . . The young person may experience great despair about his capacity to give pleasure in any manner which is not sexual.'

It was positive that Peter developed a capacity to play and began to see himself as something other than a sexual toy. He devised all sorts and types of games for us to play together such as hiding and reappearing from behind the cupboard after a break, being a magician and reappearing behind a curtain and doing magic tricks. Peter seemed to be exploring all manner of games and play that he hadn't had the opportunity to do before. Our relationship became an established bond that Peter began to look forward to.

Sexual development at puberty

Four years into therapy, when Peter was 14, he entered puberty. He grew tall and skinny very quickly. These bodily changes once again threw him into confusion. There had not been much time for a period of consolidation, which was important for his emotional development. He became fully preoccupied with his body. His interactions with me took on a sexual overtone and his earlier toddler-like intentions to woo me in the many games we shared became outright attempts to seduce me. Peter also began exploring his desire to be female. This behaviour became more overt in the community and in relationship with peers who regarded him with suspicion and sometimes disgust. He was made fun of in the community and bullied; if he had any friendships it was with girls. Some of Peter's behaviours included hanging partly or fully nude from his window, and stealing girls' underwear and girl objects. Peter also began masturbating with his teddy in public. It seemed as if he wanted to disgust or repel people.

In general Peter's previous regressive behaviours had been tolerated from a distance by most of the staff. He was the type of child who stimulated loving and protective feelings in the women and feelings of repugnance in the men. Male workers at the community found it hard to work with Peter. They seemed repelled or unable to make a link with him of any consequence. I wondered if Peter stimulated strong homosexual fears in the men within the community but also that he had nothing in common with them, having himself had no male role-modelling. He had also been sexually used as a woman. Breen talks of how the father's role is fundamental to psychic functioning in that it is the father who introduces reality between the mother and child. Peter had not had this experience. He had never met his father. Another father figure took his mother away and produced a baby sister. His envy went unexpressed as she, like his mother, became idealised. Peter often said 'girls had it good'.

At this time of transition and confusion, Peter embarked on months of using his body as a means to express himself, frequently in an exhibitionistic way. His drive to be female began to feature. He brought sheets from the house and wrapped himself in them like huge dresses. He painted his nails silver and made a pair of shoes out of cardboard. He also made a large paper dress which he decorated with splatters of paint (Plate 8). These two items saw Peter and me through months of role play and exploration of his urge to be female. One day he asked me to bring him some make-up. I wondered about this request, and whether he was wanting me to confirm his feminine identity. If he was a girl would I like him more? He frequently danced and played out his fantasy of being the star performer and winning a prize. I would often be the judge, the onlooker, and he would tell me what to say. I would also reflect to him how he felt he was special, felt loved and wanted to be focused on by me. Peter increasingly became more effeminate and sexually alluring in his manner and actions within the dances and various role plays. Woods (2003: 159) suggests 'that a large part of the damage done to a victim of sexual abuse is the destruction of the boundaries, which help define gender identity, and thus fragmentation might become evident in early adolescence'.

Peter eventually brought his own make-up into the sessions. I explored with him his wish to wear make-up as a young male. He seemed to know he was a young man but was impulsively drawn to wearing make-up. He said women had things better. I thought about Peter's sister who was still at home with his mother. I also thought about him being more identified sexually as a female, having been abused by males and possibly his mother, and in terms of his peer friendships. A further complexity for the boy in terms of his developing gender is specifically in his transition between pre-Oedipal and Oedipal phases: 'Although the boy does not have to change his love object like the girl (from breast to penis) he does have to change the character of his relation to the primary object from an oral receptive sucking to an active aggressive penetrating and discharging relationship' (Payne 1939: 22). He seemed to see me as the penetrating object rather than himself. Peter often became sexually aroused while dancing, and on one occasion he bent over a cushion and offered his bottom to me. He said in a tone with some aggression in it, 'Fuck me up the arse.' I said I wasn't going to do this to him; this wasn't the way we related to one another but I knew that he was aroused and that this had happened to him before. Typical of Peter's defensiveness, he got cross and ashamed and moved onto something else. According to Woods (2003: 182) although 'the development of perverse pathology may be laid down in previous years it does seem clear that the trajectory for perverse behaviour begins in adolescence'. Clearly Peter's early experiences and difficulties were now being recharged by the onset of puberty and his interpretation of his sexuality lay within his past abuse.

Laufer and Laufer (1984: 6, 10) refer to the central masturbation fantasy which:

> contains the various regressive satisfactions and the main sexual identifications . . . With the maturation of the genitals the fantasies take on new meaning and the body becomes an active participant in the gratification of sexual and aggressive fantasies. In pathological sexual development within adolescence, the pre-genital wishes override genitality whereas in

healthy development the adolescent has an 'unconscious awareness' that he/she has a choice to have some control of these wishes.

For Peter I think there was no sense of control. His body drove him like a child behind the wheel of a huge car. Starting his therapy at 10 there was little time for him to consolidate his childhood experiences into latency and build an emotional foundation from which to develop into adolescence.

Transsexual identity

Four and a half years into therapy, Peter brought his central masturbation fantasy which had now evolved into a transsexual identity (Stoller 1985). He came to his session carrying high-heeled shoes in his size, a mini-skirt and a large pink T-shirt, which he claimed he had bought with his key worker. Peter squeezed himself into these clothes as he had put on weight and was tall and round. It not only looked odd from the point of view of the gender difference but also because the skirt was too small. He had to leave the skirt undone. As I had to be clear that this did not mean he could remove his other clothes, he bunched them under the skirt. Dressed in his new clothes, Peter paraded proudly around the room, one hand on his hip and the other raised, his chin lifted. He painted his face and said his name was Charlotte. Charlotte then began to make advances towards me, coming to sit on my lap. I said I did not wish to reject him but I could not allow him to sit on my lap in this way. Maybe we could find other ways for him to tell me how he felt right now and what he wanted. Charlotte leaned back on the table and put his/her hand behind his/her head to look alluring. I commented on how he/she was feeling sexy and wanted me to find him/her sexually attractive. Peter said nothing but continued to blow me kisses. I repeated how he/she was being sexy and trying to get me to respond to him. I wondered who I was. I certainly felt very uncomfortable. Glasser (1964: 290–1) states, when referring to the sadistic pleasure of the pervert, that a vital component of this is:

> the implication that the object is experiencing what the individual wants her to experience. This is reassuring in a number of ways. It removes the sense of uncertainty as to what the object may be experiencing: this uncertainty is a significant element in the relationship with the mother . . . a further significant interplay with the object is that of revenge on the mother.

Glasser states that sexualisation can protect the individual's 'core complex' from such overwhelming threats as fears of annihilation, abandonment and loss.

Chasseguet-Smirgel (1974) suggests that the sexual deviant minimises the role of the father while creating the illusion that he himself is the main object of the mother's sexual interest. I felt that Peter was recreating a sexualised variation on the theme of him being preoccupied with his mother and his mother being preoccupied with him. It felt like a homosexual seduction, but from previous sessions he seemed to see me as the one who would penetrate him. I felt robbed of my own sexuality. Woods (2003: 167), in his moving case study of Sam who had a gender disturbance, talks about how Sam 'implicitly invit[ed] me to have sex with him, as though he was female. I experienced this as an intrusion into my being, an attempt to get into my heterosexuality'. Woods goes on to talk about his then wish to 'get rid of him' (p. 167) and how on further reflection he saw Sam as 'the embodiment of a particularly primal scene and mother as all-destroyer'. Woods concludes that the emotional connection for Sam with the 'idea of becoming a woman could be seen as an attempt to get the love he wants whilst avoiding the castration power of the woman' (p. 169).

Interspersed with this long period of role play, Peter put his wishes to be penetrated into drawing form (Plate 9). The fantasy represented his wish for a young person in the community to penetrate him and 'suck his dick'. This particular lad, although also sexually abused, had made the difficult journey to 16 and found his masculine sexuality (he had also attended art psychotherapy). He was tall, handsome, had girlfriends, played rugby and carried himself in a very masculine way.

I think that Peter was using his sessions to explore what could now be called a perversion, although Glasser might suggest that with the looked-after child they might not have the 'cohesion and integration of the pervert's make-up and in the impermanence of their form of sexual deviance, which now takes this form and then that' (1964: 294). Whether permanent or not, Peter's perversion seemed to fit Stoller's definition which implies 'unconscious conflict; inability to indulge a forbidden, pregenital sexual activity is resolved by using a perversion as the conscious manifestation of compromise' (Stoller 1979: 109–10). Cross-dressing was one such example. Stoller further defines perversion:

> in order for the individual to resolve the ever present unconscious conflict and to permit potency and the capacity for sexual gratification to persist, one's unconsciously desired objects must be changed, intrapsychically reinvented . . . this involves splitting, fetishization and dehumanization . . . one must restore one's sexual pleasure, triumph over the original object.
>
> (p. 110)

This seemed to explain Peter's present behaviour but also explain past behaviours of repetitively needing to triumph over me in games, competitions and puzzles. I wonder if Peter was now triumphing over his abuser, constantly trying to seduce me (certainly making me feel uncomfortable), dehumanizing us both and cross-dressing as a means to dealing with his desire to be penetrated:

> Disturbances in an individual's ability to function healthily in sexual relationships are commonly related to sexual abuse. Some children experience profound effects on their sexual identity . . . During a normal socialization a boy accepts authority as part of normal life and hopes one day to develop into an adequate male . . . he must first have enough confidence in the fact that he is not going to be destroyed by those over him and secondly, a capacity to accept the loss of his first object of desire, represented as the oedipal mother. In an abusive environment the young boy will find it impossible to negotiate these stages of development.
> (Woods 2003 :159)

Peter persistently defended against reality in the sessions. He did not wish to think. He wanted to maintain a bubble around the two of us, recreating the original early maternal relationship. If I spoke or tried to think about it Peter would tell me it wasn't real. Due to his deprivation it was hard for Peter to symbolise and think. His age now made this even more difficult. Stoller (1985) writes about the relationship of the transsexual boy and his mother, suggesting that their gender identity may come about through mothers who treated their sons as 'extensions of themselves', hence the boy's underdeveloped sense of masculinity. Greenson (1968: 372) states that:

> the oedipal situation in primary male transsexualism is different from that of other boys, for there is no oedipal conflict. In order for oedipal conflict to occur in a boy, he must desire to possess his mother and have that desire thwarted by his father, with the result that a conflict between the desire and the danger is established. But the transsexual boy does not want to possess his mother; instead he would be like her. There is no erotic component to the relationship.

Stoller (1985) describes the environment within which a boy may develop into a transsexual. The birth of a baby boy to the transsexual's mother would be an event that makes her feel life is worth living. She has in her possession in her son 'the perfect phallus'. She needs her son as an extension of her own body, always under her control. By never separating enough to disturb her, both parties therefore avoid any conflict. Stoller (1985: 26), referring to Freud, stresses the importance of conflict in the development of the child's sexuality:

> if the blissful conditions of intrauterine life and the early symbiotic fusion were not invaded, maturing ego functions would not emerge. These functions need, in addition to a biologic epigenesist, the goad of

dissatisfaction – trauma, frustration and other pain. The oedipal conflicts exemplify how painful reality forces the psychic apparatus (that is,
the child) to modify itself in opposition to its own self-centred, pleasure
driven, pain-avoiding bent to float dreamily in the tensionless maternal
soup. Humans, prodded by biology and reality, are doomed/privileged to
invent themselves out of the struggle between the opposing demands of
bliss – that is stasis – and growth.

I felt this was a difficulty in the therapy where Peter would not think with
me about what was happening but rather continue enacting; he would cut off,
the subject would be closed and the connection lost. At such times I felt a
physical sensation of being wrapped up or lulled to sleep.

Transsexuals present a rigid defence and avoid thinking about meaning:
'childhood experiences, the unavailability of symbolisation, are all features
of the transsexual who believes that if only he/she were given the body of
the other sex then the true self will be realised' (Woods 2003: 162). A male
infant's feminisation would have been bestowed upon him in the first two
years of life. Coates and Moore (1997) describe how in psychotherapy with
traumatised children, they frequently came across the transsexual fantasy
as embodying reparative wishes; a good object had been split off from any
destructive feelings and constructed as an all-gratifying maternal figure.
Woods (2003: 163) describes this in another way as in the case of the abused/
abuser: 'the boy's own body may have been the source of pain, except in so far
as it is felt as if it were a sexualised part of the mother. Thus the boy attempts
to deal with his fear of abandonment though mourning is impossible.' The
transsexual boy is stuck with the fantasy that he is both male and female.
Forgoing this fantasy that one is more than one sex is part of the maturational process towards a singular sexuality: 'This then is the therapeutic
task, to facilitate the process of mourning, for the sex which the adolescent
cannot be, and for the maternal love he never had' (Woods 2003: 163).

I thought about why Peter would put up such resistance. Establishing
gender identity could be seen as being based on a 'capacity for grief at the
unfulfilled aspect of the self, and hence finding the capacity to seek it in the
other' (Woods 2003: 161). A young person like Peter with a gender disorder
and with little capacity for mourning would find differences between the sexes
as 'reminders of deprivation instead of possibilities of pleasure, envy rather
than desire, rage not love' (Woods 2003: 161).

Crisis in the community

A crisis occurred in the community when a new director arrived who
reassessed many of the children. He had expressed concern about Peter, felt
his behaviour was bizarre and wondered if he should continue to be at the
placement. Peter also faced the dilemma of separation and leaving the home

and his therapy as he was approaching 16. Many meetings at various levels had occurred within the community to discuss the next placement for Peter as it was acknowledged that he would need a supported living arrangement. I also spent numerous sessions in supervision thinking through how Peter might negotiate this impending task of transition and separation and move into independence and adulthood (Dalley 2007). We speculated that Peter might do something dramatic as very few children left the community in a managed way without getting 'chucked out'.

With all the changes, Peter began to feel unsafe. I was away on leave and his key worker was absent. In particular he felt uncontained by the arrival of the newcomer, the new father figure, who questioned his place in the community which had become his home, the closest he had experienced to a family. It was during this time that Peter sexually assaulted another boy, a younger, smaller child with a history of sexual abuse. Peter ran to the safety of penetration to try and scramble back inside somewhere safe. He was seen as the perpetrator and, as he was still under 16, immediately sent to a secure unit.

Woods, referring to the effect that sexual abuse has on the male infant at the time his core gender identity is establishing itself, suggests how this is a particularly fragile area for the boy because of the threat penetration may have to his male sexuality; it 'may contribute to the underlying psychopathology that might perpetuate their abusive behaviour. It is as though they need to attack another in order to preserve a fragile sense of identity' (2003: 154).

In Peter's new placement, I negotiated to continue his therapy weekly for the next seven months. It was important to work towards an ending with Peter, who had been so abruptly removed from the community that had become his home for so many years. He had resolved his separation dilemmas by finding a more secure place to live where there were people to look after him, literally to lock him in. Ongoing child protection proceedings and the impending court case prevented me from exploring the detail of recent events. The unpredictable and long drawn-out court proceedings finally decided his sentence with recommendations for his next placement. This work brought some understanding and enabled Peter to link up with good parts of himself that had evolved while he had been in the community rather than bury it all in the severed ending, having shame and fear of the events and the aspects of himself which had committed the offence.

In this ending phase Peter reminisced about the community and expressed some hatred and anger for the place and people. The experience seemed to make him grow up very quickly while the security of his new setting offered him more physical containment. He seemed better able to talk, think and reflect. He developed more external signs of adolescence and a more masculine appearance. He was now well over six foot, wore a baseball cap and was concerned about designer labels. It was however still hard for him to control his childlike impulses and I wondered how consolidated was this tentative masculine identity. Peter's final images were like maps or intestines and seemed to be about me finding him again and about his own internal journey. Plate 10, made in the last few sessions, represents the degree of confusion Peter had about his own body. He was neither male nor female. Alone, a sort of all-encompassing sexual being, asexual and self-sufficient. We looked through his art work as planned and Peter took the clay models he had made when he was 11 but wanted me to have the rest. We were able to say goodbye. Our ending occurred in a thoughtful and secure way. Peter was in a place where he could acknowledge this and was able to move on.

Conclusion

I was left wondering how Peter would manage his gender disorder as a young adult. His final image (Plate 10) so graphically conveyed his predicament. He felt both male and female, neither one nor the other. This made me think about how Peter, who never knew his father, became part of a care system where the male role became marginalised. It is a common problem for boys in care that there is a lack of strong male role models. They become 'father hungry', often 'hidden behind a façade of anger or apathy, [with] either scapegoating or idealisation of the absent father leading to negative identifications' (Wrighton 2006: 2). Talking of the 'gender-linked needs' of boys in care, Wrighton describes how boys 'need to legitimately express their tendency towards physicality, which among other things can facilitate the acquisition of skills' (p. 3). However, 'Male foster carers and adoptive parents often say agencies focus on the negative "risk-led" aspect of their involvement . . . the parenting task, be it foster or adoptive parenting, is still seen as the woman's role (p. 1). The problem for Peter was that the male staff caring for him during his adolescence found it hard to understand him and tolerate their own fears and the challenges that Peter presented them with. Having left a community that was predominantly female, in his new placement Peter was secure but immersed in a male environment where his peers were boys and his carers male. Paradoxically this may have placed Peter at greater risk of abuse, or of becoming the perpetrator of abuse.

By abusing others, Peter could avoid feeling powerless. In his situation of feeling potentially so rejected he could also demonstrate to parental figures the extent of the abuse perpetrated on him. Peter's offence made his problems more conscious and allowed him access to greater safety in the near future and probably for his adult life.

References

Aldridge, F. (1998) Chocolate and shit: aesthetics and cultural poverty in art therapy with children, *The Journal of the British Association of Art Therapists, Inscape*, 3(1): 2–9.

Bick, E. (1968) The experience of the skin in early object relations, *International Journal of Psychoanalysis*, 49: 484–6.

Breen, D. and Bott Spillius, E. (eds) (1993) *The Gender Conundrum: Contemporary Psychoanalytic Perspectives on Femininity and Masculinity*. London: Routledge.

Case, C. (2005) *Imagining Animals: Art, Psychotherapy and Primitive States of Mind*. London: Routledge.

Chasseguet-Smirgel, J. (1974) Perversion, idealization and sublimation, *International Journal of Psychoanalysis*, 55: 349–57.

Coates, S. and Moore, M.S. (1997) The complexity of early trauma, representation and transformation, *Psychoanalytic Enquiry*, 17(3): 286–311.

Dalley, T. (1993) Art psychotherapy groups with adolescents, in K.N. Dwivedi (ed.) *Group Work with Children and Adolescents*. London: Jessica Kingsley.

Dalley, T. (2007) Piecing together the jigsaw puzzle: thinking about the clinical supervision of art psychotherapists working with children and young people, in J. Schaverien and C. Case (eds) *Supervision of Art Psycotherapy: A Theoretical and Practical Handbook*. London: Routledge.

Freud, S. (1925) Some psychical consequences of the anatomical distinction between the sexes, *Standard Edition of the Complete Psychological Works of Sigmund Freud*, vol. 19. London: Hogarth Press.

Glasser, M. (1964) Aggression and sadism in the perversions, in I. Rosen (ed.) *Sexual Deviation*. Oxford: Oxford University Press.

Glasser, M. (1988) Psychodynamic aspects of paedophilia, *Psychoanalytic Psychotherapy*, 3(2): 121–35.

Greenson, R.R (1968) Dis-identifying from mother: its special importance to the boy, *International Journal of Psycho-Analysis*, 49: 370–4.

Hopkins, J. (1999) Some contributions on attachment theory, in M. Lanyado and A. Horne (eds) *Child and Adolescent Psychotherapy*. London: Routledge.

Klein, M. (1945) The Oedipus complex in the light of early anxieties. in *Love, Guilt and Reparation*, London: Hogarth Press (reprinted 1975).

Laufer, E. and Laufer, M.E. (1984) *Adolescence and Developmental Breakdown*. New Haven, CT: Yale University Press.

Meltzer H. (2003) *The Mental Health of Young People Looked After by Local Authorities in England*. London: Office for National Statistics.

Murphy, J. (1998) Art therapy with sexually abused children and young people, *The Journal of the British Association of Art Therapists, Inscape*, 3(1): 10–16.

Payne, S.M. (1939) Some observations on the ego development of the fetishist, *International Journal of Psychoanalysis*, 20: 161–70.

Sagar, C. (1990) Working with cases of child sexual abuse, in C. Case and T. Dalley (eds) *Working with Children in Art Therapy*. London: Routledge.

Stoller, R.J. (1968) *Sex and Gender*, Vol. 1 New York: Science House.

Stoller, R.J. (1979) Gender disorders, in I. Rosen (ed,) *Sexual Deviation*, 2nd edn. Oxford: Oxford University Press.

Stoller, R.J. (1985) *Presentations of Gender*. New Haven, CT: Yale University Press.

Winnicott, D. (1971) *Playing and Reality*. London: Routledge.

Woods, J. (2003) *Boys Who Have Abused*. London: Jessica Kingsley.

Wrighton, P. (2006) The role of male carers in adoption and fostering, *BAAF Adoption and Fostering*, 49: 1–8.

Chapter 10

Paranoia and paracosms: brief art therapy with a youngster with Asperger's syndrome

Robin Tipple

Introduction

The work in this chapter was undertaken in a paediatric disability service. This is a specialist multi-disciplinary service which provides comprehensive assessments and diagnoses for children and families, and advice to other services and professionals in relation to therapeutic intervention and management, for a range of neurological difficulties, but focusing in the main on autistic spectrum disorders. Occasionally the service offers brief interventions where there is a deficit in local services and where it is thought that a brief period of therapy or behavioural work with the family might be helpful.

Through the presentation of a case study, a short-term art therapy intervention lasting for 12 weeks with a young man diagnosed as having Asperger's syndrome, I will show how I have developed this model of working with youngsters who have such a diagnosis. I hope to show that brief art therapy *can* be useful, while recognising that all cases are individual, in terms of the approach to the work, as well as in terms of the outcome and value.

Autism and Asperger's syndrome

Kanner (1943) first identified autism when he described a group of children who demonstrated a lack of 'affective contact' to people, were extremely withdrawn socially, actively avoided social contact, did not use language to communicate, appeared intent on maintaining sameness and were resistant to change. Wing and Gould (1979) argued that autism should be regarded as a continuum of impairments, in social understanding and interaction, in communication and in the use of imagination. In autism the presence of these social impairments is accompanied by rigid and repetitive patterns of behaviour.

At the same time as Kanner's work in America, Hans Asperger was reporting on another group of children in Vienna whom he subsumed under the term, 'autistic psychopathy' (Asperger 1944). His group of children were socially isolated and like Kanner's group they had problems in using language and had a dislike of change. However, Asperger's children differed in that all his children had developed speech before school age, and usually had large vocabularies. Their social isolation was not as extreme as the children described by Kanner but their approaches to others tended to be regarded as inappropriate. Asperger also reported that his group of children had originality of thought. Wing (1991) argued for the inclusion of Asperger's syndrome into the autistic continuum. Asperger's findings have now been incorporated into the diagnostic manuals under his name.

Theory and technique

Although working within the predominant medical, neurological and cognitive discourses that relate to autism when assessing children (Tipple 2003), to help maintain a more psychodynamic approach when undertaking brief interventions, I have made use of the insights of child psychotherapists and other psychoanalytical writers (Klein 1930; Meltzer 1975; Lacan 1977, 1998; Alvarez 1992; Tustin 1992; Hobson 1993; Evans 1996; Alvarez and Reid 1999). The literature demonstrates how the absence of clear expressions of feeling on the part of the autistic client can make the transference and countertransference difficult to explore. The need for close observation and attentiveness to small changes is emphasised as is a need to be active on occasions, to show interest, to end repetitive activities, 'to mobilize the suspended attention of the child in its autistic state, in order to bring it back into transference contact' (Meltzer 1975: 15). I would also like to add that activity is sometimes needed to mobilise the suspended attention of the therapist, who has to endure repetitive behaviours that generate hypnotic somnambulant states. All this is about being 'live company' (Alvarez 1992). Alvarez argues that psychotherapeutic technique should be developmentally informed: 'Interventions must reach the child in a "language" or form that is appropriate to the (possibly very early) developmental level at which he is functioning' (Alvarez 1999:60). Art therapists, Evans (1998) and Evans and Rutten Saris (1998), also call for activity or intervention on the part of the therapist to promote development and change from repetitive activities, and to encourage interrelatedness.

Brief art therapy

Assessment is brief work of a kind. In her account of assessment, Case (1998) emphasises how a 'brief encounter' with an understanding adult can be helpful for children and adolescents. She presents such brief encounters as 'unconsummated affair[s] of great intensity', the transference presenting itself through the images produced. These images refer to 'pictures' that are constructed from conversations with the child's parents, images that arise from the countertransference, as well as images that are produced through the use of art materials. Case's assessments generally last for three sessions, although she argues that six weeks is often more helpful to some adolescents. She reserves the word 'exploration' for this work and recognises the difference between this assessment and brief work – the kind of brief work that constitutes a treatment.

Mostly the art therapy literature about children or youngsters who have an autistic spectrum disorder describes work which lasts for considerably longer than 12 weeks. Henley (2001) argues for long-term treatment in order to work through the threat of annihilation. Case (1998) describes working with an autistic child for a year before she could 'even have a stab at writing an assessment'. And indeed there are significant contraindications for brief art therapy in relation to our client group, because individuals with autism and Asperger's syndrome have difficulty with play. Often their play is regarded as repetitive and lacking in symbolic and interpersonal content (Wulff 1985; Libby *et al.* 1998). They have difficulties in generating ideas (Turner 1999) and when creating imaginary situations they may rely heavily on previous models, being interested in amassing information, as opposed to constructing novel narratives or exploring character and motive. Such difficulties can create problems for any form of art therapy.

Important to my thinking and approach to brief art therapy has been the idea of 'the dynamic focus' (Schact *et al.* 1996). This is a method of 'gathering and organising information and systematically incorporating' the same into the therapy (p. 171). The focus should be identified by the therapist and client together. It may be seen by the therapist as representing a symptom, or an intrapsychic conflict, a developmental impasse, an interpersonal dilemma or a maladaptive activity. There does not appear to be any agreed method or strict protocol for establishing a focus but two principles remain important to Schact *et al.* Firstly, the 'arena for construing life experience' is regarded as 'interpersonal' and involves transactions with significant others. Secondly, the mode in which the focus is expressed is narrative, presented through a sequentially organised account of experiences and actions. Stories are interpreted as versions which are not necessarily true but which help to make sense of experiences. There may be a failure on the part of the therapeutic dyad to develop a focus in brief psychotherapy, but such failure can lead to further questions which may be helpful in framing problems and suggesting solutions. This is of course a way of remaining optimistic.

Establishing a focus when using art materials suggests the need for interpretation, or the translation of visual imagery into verbal form. Some misunderstanding is almost always present when translations are attempted and, if not used circumspectly and with care, translations in art therapy, and in psychotherapy, can feel like 'a form of control, if not outright bullying' (Phillips 2000). Phillips goes on to say that the 'only good translation is the one that invites retranslation' (p. 146) and in this sense it is important to give the patient 'something that can be used'. In brief art therapy, interpretation translates as giving the client some comment on the work that can be responded to, which can lead to further associative material. As Case (1998: 32) argues in relation to assessment, 'if it is possible to understand something of what the client experiences, and feed it back, then some forward movement can take place'.

Finally I would want to agree with Mann (1996) that it is important to be aware of time in its existential import when considering brief work. Existential time should be regarded as different to categorical time, the time measured by clocks and the calendar. Intensity of experience is capable of stretching time into an apparent infinity, and at such moments death ceases to threaten life. Mann suggests that in adolescence a conflict emerges between this belief in limitless time, often experienced in childhood, and the realisation that time is limited, that there is a limited time for making decisions.

Case material

Jimmy was referred to Chestnut House by a local paediatrician, who had provisionally diagnosed Asperger's syndrome and was looking to our specialist service for confirmation. Jimmy's parents had long felt that Jimmy had social difficulties of an unusual kind. After an initial appointment where an early history was constructed with Jimmy's parents, the diagnosis was confirmed. The diagnosis came more as relief than a shock for the parents.

As the service wanted to understand Jimmy better, he was asked to return for further assessment. This included meeting with the art therapist in order to assess whether he might be able to use art therapy to enable him to express anxieties and explore difficulties.

Jimmy lived at home with his mother, his father and his younger brother, aged 13. He had two sisters in their 20s who were not living at home. Jimmy's oldest sister did have some dyslexic problems and social difficulties as a child but there were no other reported difficulties within the family. Jimmy was 16 when he undertook his art therapy assessment. He had been described as 'quirky and a loner' – a fairly typical description for youngsters with Asperger's syndrome. At the time of his referral he was thought to be suffering from depression. Jimmy had difficulties with his peers from the beginning of school life. For example, he liked to recite the lines of comedy programmes and wanted other children to join in, and if they got the lines wrong he became angry. He experienced bullying and his parents withdrew him from school in Year 9 as they were unable to get the help for him that they felt he needed. Apart from playing computer games with a neighbouring child aged 8, whom he had known for a long time, Jimmy remained isolated at home and would not go out into the village where he lived, because the village children teased him. His parents reported that he had become 'Mr Fixit for the family PC', but his topics of conversation were limited to Warhammer, computers and Python.

Assessment session

I met Jimmy briefly in the family room before the start of his art therapy assessment. A tall slim boy with dark hair, well dressed and handsome, he did not appear odd and it was hard to imagine him as the victim of village ridicule. As soon as we had been introduced he began confidently, and without reserve, to show me his Warhammer figures which he had brought along for this purpose. These small figures were very carefully and meticulously made.

Once in the art room I gave him an opportunity to initiate activities and soon he was focused, in a very self-absorbed way, on a drawing of 'Marshal Vortigen', ignoring me as he concentrated on shading gently with his pencil. He explained that he wanted to use pencil as he felt that he was good at shading and later told me that he was having difficulty with the three-dimensional aspect of the helmet. In particular he was not sure how to draw the long cubical tube that ran along the bottom of the helmet. However, after asking for a white crayon and accepting Tippex as a substitute when the crayon failed to cover the pencil, he reached a satisfying end with his drawing. Jimmy asked if he could take the drawing home with him and we agreed to photocopy it at the end of the assessment. After giving the picture a title and adding his name, he indicated that 'Marshal Vortigen' was the identity he assumed when he played the Warhammer game. Jimmy pointed out the scar or dent on the helmet, showing where it was punctured in battle, and the 'special gothic writing' on the other side which detailed the wearer's exploits.

Looking at the helmet (Figure 10.1) we can see that it is held in place, or held together, with large screws and rivets. It gives the impression of fitting the contours of the face closely. For instance, there are indentations under the eyes or eye holes, shown by darker shading, that appear to follow the eye socket of a face. A black cross on the forehead and on a chain hanging from the bottom of the helmet advertises an identity or allegiance of some sort. Cubical tubes run along the jaw line. One eye hole is large and round and surrounded by some sort of mechanical apparatus; perhaps there is an ocular instrument of some kind fastened onto the helmet, perhaps it gives the wearer of the helmet special vision. The other eye hole is more sinister looking, a narrowing of the eye as in aggression and evil intent.

Jimmy wrote novels about the Warhammer world and I have included the following extract from one of these which he shared with me, which gives the Marshal Vortigen helmet context:

> The space marines of the imperium are not normal humans, they are super-human capable of great strength and quick reflexes. And every single space marine wears power armour, this great shell of ceramite and adamatium shields the space marines from a blast that could kill a normal man in less than a second. With the best skill, weapons, armour and

arshall Vortigen.

Figure 10.1 Marshal Vortigen.

experience the imperium has to offer, the space marines are the last hope
for survival in a hostile universe.

As can be seen in the assessment, Jimmy presented himself in two forms,
firstly as an able individual, good at drawing and shading, but being willing
to recognise difficulties, seeking and accepting help when drawing problems arose. Secondly, imaginatively, he presented himself as an aggressive
helmeted warrior, one who had fought many battles, one who was well
armoured and protected against 'a hostile universe'. The immediate question
that arose here was whether Jimmy would be able to relate to the symbolic
element in his imaginative constructions; would he be able to relate his
alter-ego identification to his experiences?

After this assessment an arrangement was made between his mother, the
multi-disciplinary team, myself and Jimmy, that he should attend fortnightly
for 12 sessions.

First session

As might be expected, Jimmy began his first session by talking about
Warhammer. He started with an account of the 'inquisitors' who were a
secret organisation responsible for ensuring that good prevailed in the universe. Jimmy told me that he had started on his next novel which was centred
on the inquisitors and the attempt by Marshal Vortigen to join their special
guard. He also told me that he had placed his Marshal Vortigen picture
produced during the assessment on the wall in his room.

Being afraid that the 'conversation' about Warhammer could grow and fill
the space to no purpose I reminded him of our task and asked how he had
been since we last met. Things hadn't been too bad but he said that he very
much wanted to tell me about his feelings towards his mother. His first
complaint was that his mother badgered him. She asked him what was wrong
when he was looking sad but basically feeling all right, 'not necessarily happy
but OK'. He said that she insisted on knowing what was wrong, 'it happened
just now in the waiting room'. This made Jimmy feel angry because she would
not believe him when he said he was feeling OK. Then Jimmy said that
because his mother insisted that he tell her if he felt sad, when he did want
to tell her she grew angry and complained. Jimmy said she spoke in the
following terms: 'Why do you have to be depressed, you've no reason to be
depressed.' His second complaint was that his mother favoured his younger
brother, Peter, over him. Next he reported a row involving his sister's boyfriend and his mother who expressed her disapproval that Jimmy had made
contact with them.

Things had been bad for some time and he said he hated his mother. Jimmy
said that if his mother was here in the room and heard the things he said she
would 'blow her top'. He could talk to his father but he did not think that his

father could do anything about his mother: 'There's nothing I can do', he said.

I commented that the situation of being at home all day with his mother was bound to create difficulties and Jimmy then said that he couldn't go outside because he would be attacked. Everybody in the village hated him.

Jimmy next went on to complain about Peter, his younger brother. He could not understand how he could hold the views that he did. He was shocked when Peter cheered in the film *Saving Private Ryan* when the Germans who surrendered were shot. Jimmy felt that in disputes with Peter he was not treated fairly.

I fetched some paper over to the table in the hope that Jimmy might become engaged with the art materials, but he kept talking and we went five minutes over time.

As can be seen from the above material a dynamic focus, stories that were constructed from his experiences of interpersonal exchanges with significant others, had been presented. Jimmy had described himself as trapped in a double bind in relation to his mother. She wanted him to tell her when he felt sad, but she got angry if he did but also if he didn't. However, his mother was placed in a bind by Jimmy. For instance, he wanted her to approve of him contacting his sister, but if she did approve he would feel she was being insincere. We might ask what Jimmy wanted from his mother. And what did he think his mother wanted from him? Jimmy's father was represented as ineffective and his brother as an enemy. I wondered how this related to the emerging transference and the Warhammer world, where the bad was exposed by the inquisitors, so that the good could prevail.

Second, third and fourth sessions

The pattern of long monologues, established in the first session, remained a feature of Jimmy's therapy. He was reluctant to use the art materials, chiefly it seems because he had insufficient time to achieve the results he might have desired, but also because describing space marines and other creatures, listing their attributes and rehearsing his knowledge of the Warhammer world, was captivating and led to reverie. He also, I think, took pleasure from complaining about the shortcomings of his family, listing his grievances relentlessly.

In the second session Jimmy explained how the space marines were created. They were genetically engineered creatures but the 'Lords of Chaos' had interfered with their growth and sown discord in some way.

In the third session Jimmy talked about the different kinds of space marine. The space marines were expected to swear an oath of allegiance to the Emperor, however loyalty was not always guaranteed as, through the interference of the Lords of Chaos, betrayals took place. The universe of Warhammer was forever at war, the forces of darkness and evil fighting with the forces of the Emperor.

In this third session Jimmy began another drawing of Marshal Vortigen, this time a full-sized figure (Figure 10.2). He looked at a Warhammer magazine he brought with him for some help, but his figure was not an exact copy. This drawing was taken home, with my support, to be completed.

Jimmy showed me his completed drawing in the fourth session. He pointed out that he had managed to get the figure on the paper without adding an extra sheet. He was pleased with the figure who is portrayed in violent action with a machine-gun.

Fifth session

The characters Jimmy wanted to tell me about in this session were the 'Eldars' and the 'Tyranids'. The Eldars had developed a big empire and had gained technological powers which enabled them to create life on dead planets, but they also possessed 'psychic' powers. The Tyranids were locust-like creatures which stripped planets of their atmosphere; 'nobody knows how they do this', Jimmy said. He showed me images of the Tyranids in his magazine, creatures with very large jaws filled with rows of shark-like teeth; they also had claws.

There was an urgency in his talk about Warhammer in this session and I felt that this signified some anxiety and decided to introduce the symbolic through some interpretative comment, some translation. I said that I thought he was wondering about me, whether I was an Eldar with psychic powers, or an inquisitor – how far was I to be trusted? Was I on the side of the Emperor or the Lords of Chaos? I pointed out that the Warhammer world was full of betrayal, He couldn't trust anybody any more he said, especially not boys of his own age. I then commented on the Tyranids and said how they seemed to represent, for him, a kind of mindless destruction. Acting without thinking, they were very dangerous creatures.

Following a brief period of silence I suggested some painting together to which he agreed. I painted a Tyranid while Jimmy attempted an Eldar (a symbolic change of place perhaps). Jimmy was surprised that my blotchy painting could be made to look like a Tyranid and he compared it to one of the silhouettes in his magazine.

After the painting, Jimmy talked about his family. He felt the family was divided into two: his mother and his brother in one half, himself and his sisters and father in the other half. His mother had turned against his sister's partner and this had caused a division in the family. His father stayed neutral in this dispute.

Sixth session

I was held up in a team meeting and we started ten minutes late. I offered Jimmy the ten minutes at the end of the session. He had waited patiently – or

Figure 10.2 Marshal Vortigen (full-size).

at least showed no immediate outward signs of having been put out by waiting.

He did not talk about Warhammer today, but instead told me how he had spent some time over the holiday at his grandmother's, on his own, where he had been playing war games on the computer with others over the net. Jimmy said that he liked interactions via the net because 'you didn't have to face people and you know exactly what the rules are'. Jimmy provided more detail about the game through drawing. He then talked about reaction times and the 'delay' that occurred when the computer processed an action. I reminded him of the delay today, which I stressed was really the result of my breaking of the rules. Jimmy said that he had no particular difficulty with this. Then he spoke about his father having nerve trouble in the side of his face, but he was going to work. The chief difficulty was with his mother, he reported, who told him that she wanted to live in Italy. Jimmy said he was not keen on this but was more concerned that his mother should forgive his sister's boyfriend. He also related a story about a neighbour who lit a fire and whose smoke entered the house of an old lady and suffocated her. His mother remonstrated with this neighbour who then became violent towards her.

We discussed his mother's likely feelings but I felt that it was Jimmy's disavowed violent feelings about the therapist who is late which were seeking articulate form in some way. I had not been very helpful. My lateness was an attempt to avoid the anticipated monologue and the struggle to stay awake. I think that it was the feared Tyranids, something unforgiving in Jimmy's unconscious oral aggression, that aroused anxiety in me, a representation of Jimmy's anxiety that lay just below the surface. In retrospect I can now compare my countertransference to the old lady who is suffocating.

Seventh session

This session was entirely given over to Warhammer. Jimmy wanted to show me the 'Tau' who were survivors from a destroyed planet. The Tau did not have psychic powers and they were vulnerable in battle, especially when fighting took place at close quarters. Although not strong physically they were very good at shooting from a distance. He next described a savage race called the 'Kroot'. The Kroot were something between the Tyranids and the Tau.

During the talking he drew weapons, concentrating on a very large gun whose barrel was mounted on a vehicle called the 'Pthrassquirillel' – this was spelt out. As well as the gun he focused on the Tau's helmets which he felt he could not get right.

Again I struggled to stay awake during the monologue but in order to clarify the structure of the Warhammer world and to keep my thinking alive, I presented him with an account of the order of beings that he had given to me. From the top downwards we have the Emperor, the Eldar (the Eldar apparently were responsible for the existence of the Lords of Chaos), next followed the inquisitors (detectives Jimmy pointed out), then space marines, then the Tau, followed by the Kroot and finally the Tyranids. The Tyranids, he told me, had no intelligence and nobody quite understood how they managed to organise themselves as well as they did. The Eldar, the inquisitors and space marines had psychic powers, they could read other minds – this was through luck – through having gained something from the gene pool, Jimmy indicated.

I explored with Jimmy at this point his own powers of understanding, or not understanding, others. He felt that the difference between himself and others was not that he had something others did not have, but that he had something missing – that was what made it difficult. This seemed to be an important insight and Jimmy did, at this moment, seem to be attempting to place himself in the world, to understand exactly what order of being, or kind of person, he could claim to be.

Eighth and ninth sessions

In the eighth session Jimmy began by showing me pictures, from his Warhammer magazine, of the weapons and helmet that he had been trying to produce in the previous session. He then discussed his mother's wish to go to Italy which he did not approve of.

Being aware that this was session number eight I began to experience some anxiety and urgency which led me to suggest to Jimmy that maybe at the end of the therapy we could have a meeting with the psychiatrist in the assessment team and his mother and, in this meeting, he could discuss his future and raise issues with his mother. This idea was met with silence from Jimmy.

In the ninth Session Jimmy talked about his mother again. He said that he would be going with his mother and Peter to Italy over Christmas but he was not looking forward to it. He complained again that his mother was a 'hypo-crite'. She got angry when he corrected her and she asked to see his cartoons but had never made time for them and was not really interested.

I reminded Jimmy of my suggestion of a meeting with the psychiatrist and his mother. I said that I thought that this suggestion was not very welcome. Jimmy said that if he spoke of his feelings to his mother she would get very angry and ostracise him, in the way that she had his sister.

He suggested his mother was in 'denial' and explained this word by refer-ring to a boy he knew who was gay and whose mother refused to accept this. Jimmy gave this as an example, he is not gay, but his mother does not accept him. Jimmy was not able to say what his mother would have to do to show 'proof' (Jimmy's word) of her love.

Tenth session

The Warhammer magazines were used by Jimmy again, this time to show me a type of space marine which was 'more human' than usual. These space marines were excellent fighters because they had spent their lives on hostile planets. These humans had to learn trust in order to survive a hostile environment, for instance they had to allow a fellow marine to 'cut leaches from their bare throats with a swift movement of a knife'.

After we had looked at the pictures together he described a dream. He had dreamt that he was in a tunnel the walls of which were made of skin or flesh. There were boils on this skin, some of which had burst. It was very dark in the tunnel and there seemed to be no way out. After the description Jimmy appeared sad and he said that others did not know 'what it was like'; what it was like to be bullied for example. I said that I thought that the dream did seem to express feelings about his isolation, his being alone, and that he also appeared to be in a very hostile world, like the 'more human' space marines. I reminded him of how the space marines needed to trust each other and I suggested that perhaps trusting me was an issue – could he trust me to help when I couldn't share this experience, when I didn't know what it was like in the tunnel? Jimmy then talked about Peter. He was pleased that his mother had got angry with Peter when on the plane going to Italy.

Perhaps being in the tunnel represented the experience of adolescence. It certainly did seem to express something of his depression and lack of hope. In the Warhammer world the space marines were able to survive a hostile world through their fighting capacities and camaraderie – in this sense the Warhammer world might represent wishful thinking that had replaced hope.

Eleventh session

Jimmy used this session to give me further reports about his mother which took the form of a catalogue or list of shortcomings, but this time there was some interjection of positive comments, and this seemed different. He also allowed me to structure his thinking by identifying questions or items we might address in a family meeting.

He felt that there was difficulty in understanding Asperger's syndrome. His mother made him feel like a child when she commented on Asperger's. He thought that she did not give him credit, but (and this felt like a shift in his thinking) he did recognise that she was trying to help.

Jimmy said that his mother had sold the house. He thought that he might live with his aunt. Although he liked this idea he felt that this would mean he would never be able to speak to his mother again. He also spoke about his anxiety in relation to a family meeting. He thought his mother would go mad if he said the things he wanted to say.

Twelfth session

I wanted to look through the art work that had been produced but Jimmy was not interested in this idea. Instead he chose this last session to discuss his relationship to his peers and to think about the future. His peers were full of evil intent and things had been very bad for him since the age of 11. They were getting worse not better.

I asked about his thoughts in relation to the therapy. He said that he thought it was good to come and talk, to have somewhere where he could talk about things. He thought that he could get on with adults in the workplace but he didn't see how he could get on with his peers, with other youngsters.

I spoke to Jimmy's mother briefly at the end of the therapy and she commented, in Jimmy's presence, that she was having more problems with Peter at the moment.

Discussion

There are perhaps three kinds of image that interest us when undertaking this kind of work. Graphic images, that is, pictures and designs, and sculptural products; verbal images, that is, metaphors and descriptions; and mental images – dreams, memories, ideas and phantasms (Mitchell 1986). Graphic images appeared in the magazines that Jimmy introduced, and in his pencil drawings, and there was considerable verbal imagery which appeared in conversational exchanges and in his reported dream. However, when thinking about my countertransference response to his imagery and interactions, I was struck by the numbing effect of Jimmy's monologues. His lists seemed to be directed towards overloading the mind of his listener, leading to the cessation of thought. In order to stay 'active' and 'alive' while Jimmy spoke about his Warhammer world, it was necessary to be firm and persistent and break into the monologue, hopefully in a productive way. The overload of information and rapidity of speech could be regarded as a symptom of anxieties that could not be thought, just as the imagery could be regarded as his impulses and phantasies in a disguised form. However, it was difficult to offer him a translation of his images that he could respond to.

Ricoeur (1991) argues that when 'imagination' is at work through thought, this 'produces itself as a world'. The Warhammer world is not the product of Jimmy's working imagination but a ready-made world. However, as his novel and his invention of Marshal Vortigen shows, Jimmy's thought was nevertheless at work in this world. Such worlds, 'paracosms' as they can be called (Cohen and MacKeith 1991), have been invented and enjoyed by children and adults for a long time. The Warhammer world, like other paracosms, is a systemised world. This might account for its appeal to youngsters with Asperger's syndrome, as there is information that can be listed, remembered and retold.

But what is striking is also the paranoid/schizoid structure. In this world, good is perpetually at war with evil. Henley (2001), in his account of work with children who have Asperger's syndrome, draws attention to annihilation anxiety expressed through art production, for example, through 'mechanical components' which 'assumed anthropomorphic form' (p. 115). In the War-hammer world the space marines are part-human, part-machine, with hard outer exteriors, like crustaceans. But the Warhammer creatures are varied. There is an order or ranking within the paracosm. Tyranids seemed to give shape to some fundamental aggressive oral sadism, whereas the Tau exercised phallic power through the use of a very large gun. In the dream we have some symbolic expression of anxiety, of being in a dangerous place, from which it is impossible to escape. This may be an expression of Jimmy's fear of his own aggressive drives and destructive wishes. Feeling trapped was also another significant aspect of the countertransference feeling in relation to the monotony of Jimmy's monologues.

Blackshaw *et al.* (2001) argue that paranoia in Asperger's syndrome arises from confusion, from 'not understanding the subtleties of social interaction'. They suggest that it represents a perplexity rather than psychotic and per-secutory delusion. In part we gain an impression of this kind when we con-sider the other world that emerged in the sessions, the 'real' world of Jimmy's family relations which was presented through verbal imagery. In this world, Jimmy portrayed himself as a misunderstood victim. It appeared impossible for him to communicate his feelings to his mother, who was in any case 'hypocritical' and placed him in impossible binds. His ineffective father could not help and his brother was evil – as were all his peers. All good resided in his sister who had been ostracised by his mother. In his account, Jimmy's family appeared mechanical. This portrayal reflected his difficulty with the ambigu-ities of social exchanges, a lack of awareness of emotional expression in communications, rather than being a true account of a system that was rigid and unforgiving. For instance, the tendency to treat people as either for or against him was present in his accounts of his experiences in the workplace. Towards the end of the intervention, there were some shifts in this imagery. The space marines had become more human and they had learned trust; difficulties were not faced alone.

Outcome

To evaluate this work, outcome measures were introduced. Jimmy com-pleted the CORE (Clinical Outcome Routine Evaluation) self-report ques-tionnaires at the beginning and at the end of the therapy. Although Jimmy reported a significant increase in problems, and a deterioration in his feeling of well-being, this marked a shift in understanding his emotional world and in his ability to express this. The risk element in the CORE decreased and his scores moved from the clinical population towards the non-clinical, remaining just on the borderline. The risk of self-destructive action had decreased.

The family meeting that I hoped for never materialised. Jimmy moved to Italy with his mother, brother and father. I wrote to him and his mother a

Figure 10.3 New character.

year later. Jimmy sent me some drawings back. His mother wrote that he was enjoying Italy and had made a friend in an internet café. The drawings were of a new character, a magus or magician of some sort, not armoured but still reliant on mechanical and electrical devices (Figure 10.3). Although the aesthetic reminds me of Maclagan's account of the work of an anorexic client (as does Figure 10.2), with the emphasis on control (Maclagan 1998), this figure has more organic content than the Marshal Vortigen figures.

References

Alavarez, A. (1992) *Live Company: Psychoanalytic Psychotherapy with Autistic, Borderline, Deprived and Abused Children*. London: Routledge.

Alvarez, A. (1999) Addressing the deficit: developmentally informed psychotherapy with passive, 'undrawn' children, in A. Alvarez and S. Reid (eds) *Autism and Personality: Findings from the Tavistock Autism Workshop*. London: Routledge.

Alvarez, A. and Reid, S. (eds) (1999) *Autism and Personality: Findings from the Tavistock Autism Workshop*. London: Routledge.

Asperger, H. (1944) Autistic psychopathy in childhood, trans by U. Frith, in U. Frith (ed.) *Autism and Asperger Syndrome*. Cambridge: Cambridge University Press, 1991.

Blackshaw, A.J., Kinderman, P., Hare, D.J. and Hatton, C. (2001) Theory of mind, causal attribution and paranoia in Asperger syndrome, *Autism*, 5(2): 147–63.

Case, C. (1998) Brief encounters: thinking about images in assessment, *Inscape*, 3(1): 26–32.

Cohen, D. and MacKeith, S.A. (1991) *The Development of Imagination – The Private Worlds of Childhood*. London: Routledge.

Evans, D. (1996) *An Introductory Dictionary of Lacanian Psychoanalysis*. London: Routledge.

Evans, K. (1998) Shaping experience and sharing meaning – art therapy for children with autism, *Inscape*, 3(1): 17–25.

Evans, K. and Rutten Saris, M. (1998) Shaping vitality affects, enriching communication: art therapy for children with autism, in D. Sandle (ed.) *Development and Diversity: New Applications in Art Therapy*. London: Free Association Books.

Henley, D. (2001) Annihilation anxiety and fantasy in the art of children with Asperger's syndrome and others on the autistic spectrum, *American Journal of Art Therapy*, 39 (May).

Hobson, R.P. (1993) *Autism and the Development of Mind*. Hove: Laurence Erlbaum.

Kanner, L. (1943) Autistic disturbances of affective contact, *Nervous Child*, 2: 217–50.

Klein, M. (1930) The importance of symbol-formation in the development of the ego, in *Love, Guilt and Reparation and other Works 1921–1945*. London: Virago, 1988.

Lacan, J. (1977) *Ecrits – A Selection*, trans A. Sheridan. London: Routledge.

Lacan, J. (1998) Of the gaze as *objet petit a*, in A. Sheridan (trans) *The Four Fundamental Concepts of Psycho-analysis*. London: Vintage.

Libby, S., Powell, S., Messer, D. and Jordan, R. (1998) Spontaneous play in children with autism: a reappraisal, *Journal of Autism and Developmental Disorders*, 28(6): 487–97.

Maclagan, D. (1998) Anorexia: the struggle with incarnation and the negative sublime, in D. Sandle (ed.) *Development and Diversity: New Applications in Art Therapy*. London: Free Association Books.

Mann, J. (1996) Time limited pschotherapy, in J.E. Groves (ed.) *Essential Papers on Short-term Dynamic Therapy*. New York: New York University Press.

Meltzer, D., Brember. J., Haxter, S., Weddell, D. and Wittenberg, I. (1975) The psychology of autistic states and of post autistic mentality, in D. Meltzer *et al., Explorations in Autism: A Psychoanalytical Study*. Oxford: Clunie Press/ Roland Harris Educational Trust.

Mitchell, W.J.T. (1986) *Iconology – Image, Text, Ideology*. Chicago: University of Chicago Press.

Phillips, A. (2000) *Promises Promises – Essays on Literature and Psychoanalysis*. London: Faber & Faber.

Ricoeur, P. (1991) A Ricoeur Reader – Reflection and Imagination, ed. M.J. Valdes. London: Harvester Wheatsheaf.

Schacht, T.E., Binder, J.L. and Strupp, H.H. (1996) The dynamic focus, in J.E. Groves (ed.) *Essential Papers on Short-term Dynamic Therapy*. New York: New York University Press.

Tipple, R.A. (2003) Interpretation of children's artwork in a paediatric disability setting, *Inscape*, 8(2): 48–59.

Turner, M.A. (1999) Generating novel ideas: fluency performance in high functioning and learning disabled individuals with autism, *Journal of Child Psychiatry*, 40(2): 189–201.

Tustin, F. (1992) *Autistic States in Children*, revised edn. London: Tavistock/Routledge.

Wing, L. (1991) Asperger's syndrome and Kanner's autism, in U. Frith (ed.) *Autism and Asperger Syndrome*. Cambridge: Cambridge University Press.

Wing, L. and Gould, J. (1979) Severe impairments of social interaction and associated abnormalities in children: epidemiology and classification, *Journal of Autism and Childhood Schizophrenia*, 9: 11–29.

Wulff, S.B. (1985) The symbolic and object play of children with autism: a review, *Journal of Autism and Developmental Disorders*, 15(2).

Chapter 11

Seen and unseen: art therapy in a girls' comprehensive school

Carole Welsby

In the early 1990s art therapy made a quiet entrance into the local girls' comprehensive school. It was a small and tentative beginning. Over the following years, against a background of continual change in education, it has grown and matured; much like the pupils. Art therapy is now seen as a valuable part of the pastoral care system, rooted in the school community. Few mainstream schools employ a professionally qualified therapist; over-worked and under-trained year coordinators usually perform this role. The more needy students are referred to the local child and family services where waiting times are often long. This is a picture repeated throughout the country; provision for the emotional and mental health needs of our most vulnerable young people is inadequate.

The school

Schools, like society, include all their members, but this school includes only the girls. There are very few single-sex schools remaining in the state sector and the demand for places here is high. One of the main reasons given by parents for choosing an all-girl establishment is the enhanced academic achievements of its students; another is the absence of boys.

The school caters for 1130 students between the ages of 11 and 18. It is on two sites, just over a mile apart; one for girls in Years 7 to 9 and the other for those in Years 10 to 13. The school receives students from a large and diverse catchment area and there is a large proportion for whom English is not their first language. About two thirds are classified as white, including many of Greek and Turkish origin, while the remainder come from a range of other ethnic backgrounds, such as the Bangladeshi and Afro-Caribbean girls. This makes for challenging and exciting art therapy work: 'Specific initiatives to support girls need to recognise differences in needs between girls, related for example to ethnicity, sexuality, maturity and out of school responsibilities' (Osler *et al.* 2002: 5).

The students bring with them very different experiences of life and learning; from the newly-arrived asylum-seeker to the profoundly deaf girl; from the student with learning difficulties to the one hoping to read medicine. The majority will manage well in school while a small number will not. Some of these girls will be referred for art therapy.

School-based art therapy

As the art therapist I am part of the school's pastoral team. This is an experienced group of staff, led by a deputy head. Requests for student support are discussed here and referrals made to the most appropriate services; there are always more requests for art therapy than can be met. These requests cover a broad and often complex spectrum of need and there is sometimes a fine line in school between what is perceived as a physical, sensory, learning or emotional and behavioural difficulty.

Once the referral has been accepted the student will be introduced to me by a colleague who knows her well. Prior to this I will have informed the parents or carers about the nature of the work and will have received their permission to start; further meetings will be arranged as necessary. The student and I will work together for four, 50-minute weekly sessions, before deciding whether or not to continue; very few indeed choose not to proceed. Art therapy may then continue for weeks, months or even years and will always be confidential: 'Children who have neither been allowed their feelings nor owned their internal experiences will make dramatic improvements if their unconscious expression is valued' (Sinason 1991: 17).

As a subject art is well taught and highly regarded in the school. Because students are familiar with art materials, those referred are generally at ease with the creative process and do not have the resistance that some adolescent girls might bring. Art therapy sits well in this environment: 'Interventions and support for individuals identified as vulnerable need to be discreet and sensitive as girls and young women are often concerned about peer reactions and reputation' (Osler *et al.* 2002: 5).

There is never an 'ideal' time in the student's day to attend art therapy; it is always a compromise. One can understand the reluctance of teachers to release girls from lessons, but once the purpose of the work is explained cooperation usually follows. This is a sensitive area for those trying to establish school-based art therapy, and negotiating the hurdle of withdrawing from lessons is probably best achieved by the therapist's line manager or a senior member of staff.

An important part of my role is liaising with and supporting those staff who teach the girls referred to me. Teachers become distressed by troubled students and a 'confidential' word of explanation, or a different perspective on a problem, can lead to a better understanding and may bring about a positive shift in the work: 'A teacher affects eternity; he can never tell where his influence stops' (Adams 1907: Ch. 20).

Although my work is school-based, I avoid professional isolation by being in regular contact with the local Child and Adolescent Mental Health Services (CAMHS), and the Educational Psychology Service. Such links and consultations allow me to act as a bridge between the school and outside agencies. This is very much in the spirit of *Every Child Matters* (DfES 2003) and leads to better communication and improved outcomes.

Adolescence

> Advice to society could be: for the sake of adolescents, and of their immaturity, do not allow them to step up and attain a false maturity by handing over to them responsibility that is not yet theirs, even though they may fight for it.
>
> (Winnicott 1971: 146)

The main focus is on the adolescence of girls; it is where my experience and my work lie. I have a room for art therapy on both school sites. At the upper school (14–18 years) it is on the first floor and overlooks an outside area where the girls pass back and forth. From here I quietly observe their adolescent behaviour where it is freed from the restraints of teachers and parents and, perhaps more importantly, freed from the presence of boys. I see girls rushing by in large, noisy and sometimes quite threatening groups; some move more leisurely, in smaller numbers. Best friends pass by arm in arm, deep in private conversation, while a few walk alone, isolated and silent.

It would seem that all female adolescence is represented here, but this is a diverse community and adolescence is an evolving concept which can vary from culture to culture. This important transitional stage is particularly influenced by family and friends, by beliefs and traditions, and may be marked by rites of passage. All the girls, in their individual ways, are growing, changing and moving towards their own sense of identity and vocation, a large part of which is played out in school.

The fifth edition of the *Shorter Oxford Dictionary* defines adolescence as 'the process or condition of growing from childhood to manhood or womanhood; the process of growing up'. Adolescence can be divided into three sections. In school, early adolescence is lived out in Years 7 and 8, the 11- to 13-year-olds, when the transition from primary school and the making and breaking of friendships are of immense importance. Mid-adolescence is the 14-, 15- and 16-year-olds, when independence, group loyalty and sexual exploration, combined with the stress of examinations, make for a challenging mix. Late adolescence usually takes us into calmer waters, where the 17- and 18-year-old sixth formers have surprisingly metamorphosed into engaging young women. They bear little resemblance to the students they once were in Year 7; time alone, it would seem, has worked its magic.

But adolescence is a wide and complex subject, beyond the scope of this chapter. Among the key theoretical frameworks which conceptualise this period are those of Freud and Erikson, Klein, Winnicott and Bowlby. Although formed and informed by the writers' own particular disciplines, they all add to our understanding of this critical phase of life. For example, Anna Freud (1958), exploring her father Sigmund's theories on adolescence, says that it is primarily a time of resurgence and reworking of Oedipal issues.

Blos (1967: 163) suggests that the primary focus is on issues of separation/ individuation and states that, 'What is in infancy a "hatching from the symbiotic membrane to become an individuated toddler" (Mahler), becomes in adolescence the shedding of family dependencies, the loosening of infantile object ties in order to become a member of society at large or simply, of the adult world.'

Writing more recently and taking a broad perspective, Rutter and Rutter (1993: 3) say that:

> ... there can no longer be a single theory which constitutes a final explanation of maturation; most theories pay lip service to the role of genetic factors; biological maturation; and the relevance of brain pathology. Rarely an attempt is made to provide any form of integration ... As a consequence of these neglects there has grown a need to create new concepts and a fresh approach.

Although our understanding of adolescence is being furthered by advancements made in medical technology and research, particularly in the area of neuroscience, nevertheless one of the main tasks of adolescence remains the same: that is the search for, and the formation of, identity.

Erikson said much about this stage of development in his book *Identity: Youth and Crisis* (1968: 165). He writes, 'an optimal sense of identity ... is experienced merely as a sense of psychological well-being. Its most obvious concomitants are a feeling of being at home in one's body, a sense of "knowing where one is going" and an inner assuredness of anticipated recognition from those who count.'

Many of the girls referred to me for art therapy will be unable to identify with Erikson's words. They are ill at ease in their bodies; they do not know where they are going and have no inner assuredness of anticipated recognition from those who count. For them, moving through adolescence is particularly difficult and from experience I know that most will have major problems inside, and frequently outside, the home.

The reasons for fractured families and the effects on their members are many and complex and are the subject of ongoing national debate. Those most frequently met here in school are:

• the mental or physical ill-health needs of a parent, sibling or the student herself;
• the death of a mother or father;

- the break-up of a marriage;
- the introduction of new partners and perhaps the formation of a new family grouping;
- abuse of drugs and alcohol;
- domestic violence, physical/sexual abuse;
- families struggling between cultures;
- poor parenting – too rigid, too lax, too absent.

The girls' attempts to manage painful and confusing situations often lead to damaged emotions, damaged bodies and impaired and challenging behaviours. Unresolved conflicts are acted out daily in the classroom and if not addressed now will be carried forward into later life. Some of the girls in school compel our attention, demand to be seen, by being loud and aggressive; by bitching and bullying; by flouting rules and authority; by stealing, lying and other antisocial behaviour. Others, who equally deserve our attention, but whose pain remains unseen, may slide into depressions or self-harm, become too fat or too thin. They fall behind with school work, withdraw, and seek refuge in absence and school-refusal. Girls who are abused feel anonymous; they feel they cannot be seen or recognised.

From my work with troubled students I know that where school is a secure base, it acts as a protective factor. This good-enough, facilitating environment, to use Winnicott's term, goes some way in compensating for deficiencies in other areas of the girls' lives and art therapy has the privilege of being part of this: 'There are genes which determine patterns and an inherited tendency to grow and to achieve maturity, and yet nothing takes place in emotional growth except in relation to the environmental provision, which must be good enough' (Winnicott 1986: 151).

In the following case studies I look at the journeys made by two students. Ellen's needs were clear from the start; her father was terminally ill. Kate's needs were very unclear. She was an enigma who was slowly and silently dropping out of school.

Ellen

The following was a notice read out at the weekly staff briefing:

> Please be aware that Ellen's father is now extremely ill. His illness has lasted many months and the prognosis is that he will live for only a few more weeks. Ellen has tried hard to maintain her work levels but her mother feels she has done as much as she is able. Ellen is worried that she has not worked hard enough over the summer break. Clearly over the next few months life will be very difficult for her. Please allow her to judge what she can manage.
>
> (Year 10 coordinator)

It was at this point in her father's illness that Ellen was referred for art therapy. It was clear from the notice that she was a conscientious student, and it was known that she had a caring mother. She was part of a loving family; English and middle class. Ellen was 14 years old with an older brother of 16 and a younger one of 10; both her parents were teachers. She had just entered Year 10 and was about to begin her GCSE courses. Ellen's father had a brain tumour and had been ill for over a year. He now had no speech and only a little movement; communication was through sight and touch. Treatment was no longer viable and he was being nursed at home. Although I had considerable experience of bereavement work in school, I had never accompanied a girl towards the death of a parent and then continued on the journey afterwards. This was an unknown experience for both of us.

> In order to arrive there,
> To arrive where you are, to get from where you are not,
> You must go by a way wherein there is no ecstasy,
> In order to arrive at what you do not know
> You must go by a way which is the way of ignorance.
> (Eliot 1963: 201)

I divide Ellen's art therapy work into three parts – before her father's death; the months following and the final school term. I make only brief reference to the large amount of literature available on bereavement, concentrating for the most part on Ellen's journey through a selection of her images.

First session

> A time to tear . . .
> A time to be silent
> (Ecclesiastes 3: v. 7)

Ellen was a polite and pleasant student, tall and fresh-faced. There was nothing modern about her hair, her shoes or the way she wore her school kilt. Ellen looked sensible and reliable, not typical of the students who usually came through my door.

Following a short introduction she said, 'I just want to tear paper' (Figure 11.1).

She worked slowly and deliberately, tearing, twisting and sticking. While doing so Ellen told me a little about herself – she puts a brave face on it; it is painful to look ahead in class; she is taking a day at a time but her imagination gets the better of her and she feels overwhelmed. Her older brother is emotionally restrained, while the younger loses himself in sport. Ellen is aware of the heavy burden her mother carries. Her maternal

Figure 11.1 I just want to tear paper.

grandparents live close by and the family has a circle of supportive friends. Her father is musical and is now just able to control his breath to play his harmonica. Ellen spoke in measured tones; she was somewhat detached and for the rest of the session worked in silence, lost in the process and oblivious of time.

I was careful not to intrude into the private and silent space she had created. In bringing the session to a close I knew I would jolt her back into reality, into the pain of the present. Ellen did not hear the school bell signalling the end of the day and was surprised at my request to bring her work to a close.

'You knew what you wanted to do?' I asked.

'Yes,' replied Ellen, 'tear and tear and tear. I'm probably angry.'

I agreed with her. There was no emotion in her voice and she offered no comment on her work. Her grief was unspoken, but she had communicated her anger and anguish in the twisted, torn papers stuck down in three-dimensional form; an attempt to control, to give substance to her fragmenting world. (I realised the word tear (ta¬r) – ripping and pulling apart is also the word tear (te¬r) – an expression of grief.)

As Ellen was leaving she hesitated at the door, unsure whether to go or not. This was to become a familiar pattern.

Second and third sessions

The day was hot and my offer of a glass of water was readily accepted. This was to become symbolic of the art therapy space which Ellen later called her haven. She said much of the summer break had been unreal; it was spent in hospital-visiting, though she did get away to Guide camp. She loved Guides and felt supported by the group. Ellen chose to paint, and worked in silence. She painted sand and sea with waves which resembled four swans, with heads bent low, silently moving out of the frame; the mother at the front, followed by her three children. The image, tender and desolate, was abruptly cut off in the middle, like her father in his illness.

> The silver swan, who living had no note,
> When death approach'd, unlock'd her silent throat;
> Leaning her breast against the reedy shore,
> Thus sung her first and last, and sung no more.
> (Gibbons [1612] 1975)

Ellen gradually revealed more of the relationship with her father. They had a strong and warm attachment. With the threat of his loss there was a growing idealisation of him and perhaps a resurgence of Oedipal issues. Was there a rivalry between mother and daughter for the love of this man? I learnt he was a design and technology teacher who had made gifts and birthday cards for his children and Ellen asked if she might take some art therapy work home to show to her mother. This was an unusual request from an adolescent, and one that I would normally refuse, but in these circumstances I agreed. I wondered if Ellen felt that a therapeutic relationship with me would be a betrayal of her mother. Perhaps taking some work home lessened that fear by breaking the confidential space.

In the midst of the family's pain her younger brother celebrated his eleventh birthday, complete with party and a West Ham football cake, made by his mother. Ellen used the birthday theme in her next image – pastels on black paper (Plate 11). She placed a party-hooter next to a lighted and a snuffed out birthday candle and, seeing the significance of this in relation to her father, said there were times when his light was still there. Ellen hesitated at the door as if to speak. It was the end of the school day and she walked ahead of me down the corridor, keeping a distance, but turning to say goodbye.

In the next session, Ellen cut and tore brightly coloured tissue-paper, weaving and sticking the delicate strips into a fence-like structure; a barrier. In order to avoid a sticky mess she exercised great control over the materials, just as she did over her emotions. Ellen needed to keep a barrier between us and I needed to respect that. As she left she lingered at the door.

Ellen was absent from school the next week and on the following Tuesday her father died. It was a month before Christmas.

Following her father's death

Ellen, like her brothers, returned to school two weeks later and her mother would return to work after Christmas. I knew that Ellen was a Girl Guide, and Guides were, and perhaps still are, exhorted to 'smile and sing under all difficulties'. From the insight gained from the art therapy, I wondered if this 'Middle England' response would be the family's way of managing their terrible loss and whether Ellen, therefore, would be able to take sufficient time and space in which to mourn.

> A time to weep
> A time to mourn
>   (Ecclesiastes.3: v. 4)

There was little change in Ellen's outward appearance. She described her father's secular funeral which had been full of family, friends and music; a celebration of his life. She had cried.

Ellen was quiet during the next session and worked in clay, producing a small tile with a balanced and intricate design. Although small, it felt grand and monumental; a tribute to her father (she later took it home).

Although Ellen was in school, she did not attend the last session of term. Christmas festivities were in full swing and the holidays about to begin. She was numb, and did not want another ending.

The new year – spring term

The building was warm but Ellen entered wrapped up in scarf, coat and gloves; protecting herself from some invisible cold. She wiggled her colourful gloves at me in a friendly manner – they had been a Christmas gift. The holidays had been OK and old family friends had taken her to the ballet and the theatre. Ellen removed her outdoor-wear, willing to be seen. She cut coloured sugar-paper into long strips and cleverly wove them together into a kipper tie shape (Figure 11.2). She light-heartedly held it to the collar of her school blouse. Here was the male symbol, her father, worn around her neck and woven into her very being. We would keep alive the good object and the good memory.

Ellen continued to weave in the next session and chose black and white paper, weaving the strips together as if integrating life and death.

For the first time a figure appeared in Ellen's work (Figure 11.3). It was the back view of a girl looking out to sea, her hair falling into a tie shape. She said the girl was about her age. She looks out onto a vast and empty ocean, scanning the horizon. She is alone, but the wooden, protective structure at the end of the pier reaches only as far as her shoulders; the barrier is dropping. We verbalised the powerful feelings of emptiness and loss embodied in this image; Ellen's response was palpable and there followed a positive shift in the work: 'It is quite useless for us to speak from our head to the head of a sick person, and expect it to be taken up at any emotional level. Only the image will suffice' (Champernowne 1968).

Summer term

Six months had passed since her father's death and Ellen drew a room, three-dimensionally, as though trying to see things in perspective (Figure 11.4). The doors open wide onto a pathway, stretching into the distance. On the left are famous paintings – Mondrian, Klee, Monet *et al.*, and on the right is Ellen's art therapy work. The room resembles an art gallery and is full of symbolism.

'Will you take the road or remain in the gallery?' I asked.

'I ought to go, but I want to stay,' she replied.

I likened this to her hesitancy when leaving our sessions. Did she want to go, or to stay?

With all the intensity of an adolescent girl she said she wanted to stay forever, but then came this profound statement: 'I had to face the reality outside the room but felt maybe that the reality was inside the room.'

> The pain experienced in the slow process of testing reality in the work of mourning thus seems to be partly due to the necessity, not only to renew the links to the external world and thus continuously to

Figure 11.2 Kipper tie.

Figure 11.3 Girl looking out to sea.

Figure 11.4 Art gallery.

re-experience the loss, but at the same time and by means of this to rebuild with anguish the inner world, which is felt to be in danger of deteriorating and collapsing.

(Klein 1986: 156)

Autumn term: Year 11

Major building work had finally started in the school and, as planned, my work room was demolished. The replacement was a room with a view; high up and looking out over the playing fields of the neighbouring boys' school, where Ellen's older brother was now a sixth-former. Sharing this view together over the following weeks strengthened the therapeutic relationship, and as autumn turned to winter, mirrored the loss of Ellen's father, almost a year ago.

At the beginning of the school year, Ellen, like all Year 11 students, had been on three weeks' work experience – hers was a coveted placement at a West End theatre. This, together with the summer holiday, meant that eight weeks had elapsed since our last session, but the long gap in therapy was not as detrimental as I had feared. Crucial to this was the richness of Ellen's cultural life – foreign travel, the theatre, books, Rangers (older Guides) and friends and family, in sharp contrast to the barren lives of many of the girls who came to art therapy.

It was a bright autumn day and Ellen noticed fewer leaves on the trees. She carefully painted a patchwork of coloured squares, roughly placing black borders along two adjacent sides, giving the image a shadow. Jung emphasised the importance of being aware of shadow material and of incorporating it into conscious awareness. Although Ellen's grieving was mostly unspoken she had always expressed herself in the actual art process, and here the dark shadow of mourning presses down, but does not obliterate life's colours.

I wondered if the shadow might also symbolise her mother, because I was acutely aware of the difficulty of allowing sufficient space for Ellen's pain. There was a barrier, a line I was careful not to cross. Was this an echo in the transference of the relationship between Ellen and her mother? Was her mother unable to give space to her daughter's pain, and was this my problem also?

Autumn advanced. We stood at the open window taking in the view. It was the day before the first anniversary of her father's death.

Ellen layered down tissue-paper, creating new colours when one overlapped the other, building it up like a house, rebuilding, recreating herself. It had a tall green door. Would she be hesitant in opening it?

Mock GCSE examinations were upon us; work for Year 11 students intensified and their school year would end in early May. I wanted sufficient time to think about an ending with Ellen and gently broached the subject. I should not have been surprised that she wanted to end at Christmas, only a few weeks away, for she needed to take control of the ending in order to avoid feelings, to lessen anxiety. In order to create some space I suggested a review after Christmas, but before then a meeting was arranged with her mother.

The meeting

Ellen's mother was late, and while waiting we stood at the open window. We reminisced. Ellen was able to say that she had always found difficulty in putting feelings into words and art therapy had been a haven.

Ellen's mother arrived; she was a tall, confident woman and although we had spoken several times on the phone, this was our first meeting. As happened at the beginning of therapy, Ellen wanted her mother to see her art therapy work, not a usual adolescent response, but one taken by Ellen to avoid a feeling of betrayal towards her mother.

And then it happened; looking at the images holding the pain her mother stated, 'That's not you,' but looking at the defensive, surface paintings said, 'Now that's you.'

The comments confirmed my thinking. Her mother could not pick up on, could not hold, the sensitive pain of her daughter and Ellen had greatly needed the private, expressive space, which art therapy had afforded her. She was right to call it her haven.

Although there was much of the journey still to travel I had to respect Ellen's decision to stop at this point, and as planned we reviewed the situation the following term. Ellen said she was managing the school work well, though missing the art therapy sessions. She gained good grades in the GCSE examinations and only one or two were lower than expected.

Kate

Kate was referred for art therapy because of declining school attendance; in educational terms she was becoming a school-refuser. Such students are difficult for teachers to understand because there seems no 'good' reason for staying away. Problems had started in Year 9 (13 years), following an alleged bullying incident in her form, but extra support had brought no signs of improvement. She was part way through Year 10, and GCSE examinations drew nearer. When coming to school became unbearable for Kate, and her family, an art therapy referral was made.

I have worked with about a dozen school-refusers, with varying degrees of success; almost all have had attachment difficulties with a parent, usually the mother. Because of the quiet, non-challenging nature of their neediness, they are more easily overlooked in a busy school and early support can be delayed:

'Even when teachers do recognise that a girl is in difficulties, they do not know what to do to help her, especially if the problem is complex. Even when a student is referred to other agencies, these agencies may only respond to an aspect of the problem, thereby compartmentalising it' (Osler *et al.* 2002: 58).

Kate lived with her mother (English) and her older sister, directly opposite the lower school. Following a bitter divorce, when Kate was 7 and her sister 8, her father (Irish) left, and moved two miles away. The girls continued to see him regularly.

In school Kate was quiet and rather timid; a tall, pretty girl of average ability but her poor attendance meant increasing isolation. She was marginalised, lonely and unseen.

The therapy

Through a selection of images I describe how art therapy helped to contain Kate's anger against her mother; that containment, and being understood, lessened her guilt and allowed her to move out slowly from the Oedipal relationship she maintained with her father. Although Kate's attendance did not improve, the goodwill of the teachers and art therapy provision enabled Kate to keep a vital, though tentative, hold on school. This eventually led to a place at college and a new beginning.

Kate was creative and at ease with art materials (she was studying GCSE art), and although initially shy, her voice could be forceful in the sessions. The first painting revealed much of her story, and together we explored the symbolism (Figure 11.5).

Kate is the tree, with outstretched branches, and her mother and sister are the bushes, pressing in on either side. The largest bush to the left, separated by the empty bench and warmed by the sun, symbolises her father. This is her divided family. The tree dominates the picture, just as Kate's school-refusal dominates and terrorises the family. She is powerful and manipulative, desperate to be seen.

Because of the discord between her parents it was unlikely that Kate had introjected an integrated couple; she had no experience of a triadic relationship. An unhealthy division had developed, whereby Kate formed a couple with her father, and her sister formed a unit with her mother (dyadic relationships). Kate was stuck in the Oedipal phase and remained the little girl, idealising her father; his departure, not consciously remembered, changed the family dynamics, and Kate was marginalised at home (mirrored later in school). Not going to school was a fierce attack against her parents, particularly her mother, and it unleashed primitive anger in all three females. Kate felt persecuted and guilty.

At the beginning of therapy Kate expressed her anger in explosive images and words. She wanted me to know how much she loathed her mother,

14/11/04

Figure 11.5 Divided family.

choosing words like bad, stupid, weak, jealous and childish. It was important for Kate to know that I could look at her images, and hear her words, in an uncritical manner.

As Kate's understanding increased, she acknowledged her need to move from the child to the adolescent. This was a major challenge to her sexuality which, if accepted, would alter the relationship with her father. She moved into a depressive period and attendance at school ground to a halt; only the art therapy held. A referral was made to CAMHS, and family therapy commenced; I liaised closely with the worker.

Kate's father was a self-employed plasterer; kind and well-meaning, who tried to treat both daughters fairly. But he lacked insight and blamed the school for Kate's problems, unlike Kate's mother and sister, who blamed her. He was having a house built in Ireland, close to his parents, and he and Kate went regularly. There she could have her father all to herself, as her sister was a rare visitor.

The heavy, fragmented painting shown in Figure 11.6, with a darkened sun, reflects Kate's desolation on returning home from the long summer holiday in Ireland; a part of her father's unfinished house stands in the corner. Kate, now a Year 11 student, rarely attended school. She was lonely and depressed. Life was bleak, but in common with her peers, and with her agreement, three weeks' work experience was arranged at a local primary school. After much persuasion from her year head, Kate went (art therapy still continued). Although she was not always present, the children liked her, and their acceptance was affirming. Kate received a good report from the school and the headteacher kept her one day a week for the rest of the school year: '. . . there has been an appreciation that frequently, lasting therapeutic benefits are likely to depend on altering real life circumstances as well as on developing better ways of dealing with them' (Rutter 1990: 4).

Kate's anger slowly diminished but her depression lingered. She recalled occasions at school when she had felt lonely and worthless and on returning home had cried bitterly, but her mother always left her alone. There was no comfort and no understanding.

Bion's work on 'containing' relates to Kate's need for an empathetic mother, described here by Martha Harris (1970: 36):

> he talks of the infant's need of a mother who will receive the evacuation of his distress, consider it and respond appropriately. If this happens, the infant has an experience of being understood as well as of being comforted . . . The mother's failure to respond to his distress results in the introjection of an object which is hostile to understanding, together with that frightened part of himself which is divested of meaning through not eliciting a response.

As Kate continued to experience being understood, her depression slowly

Figure 11.6 Ireland.

lifted, and although on occasion she retreated to the safety of the young child, she slowly moved forward.

Plate 12 is a peaceful scene, standing in contrast to Figure 11.5. The leafy, weeping tree has room to grow; it stands firm, sustained by sun and water and protected by hills. Like Kate's growing insight, it has a depth lacking in the first image. But this tree stands alone, and Kate knew that art therapy would finish in two months' time, when she left school.

Year 11 had gone on study leave, and Kate, like her peers, was now legitimately at home. She no longer attended sessions in school uniform, but in the typical adolescent uniform of tops and jeans. This change in outward appearance, from schoolgirl to young woman, modelled the inner change we worked towards in therapy.

However, the coloured-pencil drawing (Plate 13) shows a naked, asexual figure, vulnerable to the gaze of the faceless onlookers. It is the only time Kate depicts a figure. She sees it as herself, and the joined part-figures as her accusing mother and sister. It mirrored my own countertransference to Kate as a helpless child in search of a satisfying mother. The image posed the recurring question: 'Would Kate move forward into maturity or remain the child?'

In spite of long-term absence, Kate sat four GCSE subjects (in a room on her own), attended a careers interview and considered courses at local colleges. Her family was surprised.

Working towards an ending with Kate was difficult. She missed two consecutive sessions and on her return reverted to the little girl. But before we met again, London had suffered the July bombings and with society's emotions unlocked, Kate had asked her grandfather, on one of his frequent visits, about her mother's childhood. She learned that her grandmother (deceased) had been confined to bed for long periods of time suffering from severe depression. She had been physically and emotionally unavailable for Kate's mother as a child, who had thought it all her fault. Some of that pattern had been repeated with Kate. This intergenerational knowledge lessened Kate's anger and guilt towards her mother; she felt less persecuted, and developed a greater acceptance of herself. (Kate's mother had been the only daughter between two brothers, and the Oedipal attachment made with her father as a child still remained.)

Kate said, 'Doing this [art therapy] has taught me to think. I don't think my mother ever thinks. I can manage so much better now.'

The last session

Kate arrived 30 minutes late, having somehow forgotten, she said. It was a painful ending; only the date appeared on her final piece of work. I arranged to review the situation with her after the holiday, and this we did. She informed me that her father had sold his house, and had bought a larger property some miles away; Kate was going to live with him. Her examination results had been good enough to secure a place at a nearby college, and I learnt some time later that she had started the course.

Conclusion

Having an acknowledged therapeutic presence within a school raises staff awareness as to the importance of mental health in relation to learning; such an understanding is essential in a nation presently obsessed with examination results: '. . . the lasting foundations of high achievement are security, joyousness and creativity, not fear and robotics' (James 2006: 20).

Students are referred for art therapy from across the many ethnic groupings. I see few students from the Asian communities while there is always a steady stream of Afro-Caribbean and white girls. I remember the first words from a 12-year-old mixed-race student, an only child: 'I don't know anybody else like me. My father is Jamaican and my mother Greek Cypriot.'

It would be tempting to pay little heed to the historical past of oppressed racial and cultural groups and to deal only with the here and now in school, but this would be short-sighted. Schaverien (1998), through art psychotherapy groups, describes how powerfully the memory of the collective unconscious continues to transmit trauma and grief through the generations. This is so in the experience of a number of our students. But each girl has her own story to tell, and the provision of art therapy gives them the time and space in which to tell it.

> Whereas the abiding sense of personal incapacity that characterizes alienation is defined by 'discrepancy,' the creative process is determined by 'synthesis,' by encounter with oneself and with one's world. In its synthetic, integrative insistence on commitment and engagement, creativity stands in contrast to alienation, and therefore is recognized as a potent container with which to work change.
>
> (Estelle 1990: 112)

Art therapy has now been part of the school for 14 years; it has reached mid-adolescence. Its positive identity is due to the ongoing support of the headteacher and the senior management team, without whom, like some of the students, it would be difficult to survive.

References

Adams, H.B. (1907) *The Education of Henry Adams*. Boston, MA: Houghton Mifflin Co.

Blos, P. (1967) The second individuation process of adolescence, *Psychoanalytic Study of Childhood*, 22: 162–86.

Champernowne, I. (1968) Art therapy as an adjunct to psychotherapy – script of lecture given at Cumberland Lodge.

DfES (Department for Education and Skills) (2003) *Every Child Matters*. London: DfES.

Eliot, T.S. (1963) *Four Quartets*, 'East Coker', in *Collected Poems 1909–1962*. London: Faber & Faber.

Erikson, E. (1968) *Identity: Youth and Crisis*. New York: W.W. Norton & Co.

Estelle, C.J. (1990) Contrasting creativity and alienation in adolescent experience, *The Arts in Psychotherapy*, 17.

Freud, A. (1958) Adolescence, *Psychoanalytic Study of Childhood*, 13: 255–78.

Gibbons, O. ([1612] 1975) *Penguin book of English Madrigals*. Harmondsworth: Penguin.

Harris, M. (1970) Some notes on maternal containment in 'good enough' mothering, *Journal of Child Psychotherapy*, 4.

James, O. (2006) Mrs Mac's elementary lesson, *The Times*, 2 October.

Klein, M. (1986) *The Selected Melanie Klein*. Harmondsworth: Penguin.

Osler, A., Street, C., Lall, M. and Vincent, K. (2002) *Not a Problem? Girls and School Exclusion*. London: National Children's Bureau.

Rutter, M. (1990) Vulnerable children: opportunity or disaster? The challenge of change. Text of Robina Addis Memorial Lecture, *YoungMinds* newsletter, 9: 1–5.

Rutter, M. and Rutter, M. (1993) *Early Child Development: Challenge and Continuity across the Lifespan*. New York: Basic Books.

Schaverien, J. (1998) Inheritance: Jewish identity and the legacy of the Holocaust mediated through art psychotherapy groups, *British Journal of Psychotherapy*, 15(1).

Sinason, V. (1991) Emotion and importance of therapies in school, *BAAT Newsletter Supplement – Art Therapy in Education*.

Winnicott, D.W. (1971) *Playing and Reality*. Harmondsworth: Penguin.

Winnicott, D.W. (1986) *Home is Where We Start From*. Harmondsworth: Penguin.

'I wonder if I exist?': a multi-family approach to the treatment of anorexia in adolescence

Tessa Dalley

Introduction

> The development of anorexia is so closely related to abnormal patterns
> of family interaction that successful treatment must always involve reso-
> lution of the underlying family problems, which may not be identifiable
> as open conflicts; on the contrary, quite often excessive closeness and
> over intense involvements lie at the roots.
>
> (Bruch 1978: 106)

Bruch goes on to suggest that clarification of the underlying family problems
is a necessary part of treatment because all anorexics are involved with their
families in such a way that they have failed to achieve independence and a
separate sense of self as developing young women. Enmeshment between
mother and daughter is a common dynamic in the aetiology and persistence
of this pervasive disorder.

This chapter explores the use of multi-family groups in the treatment of
anorexia. Working as a member of the multi-disciplinary team, the art
therapist took the lead in introducing creative activity as part of the therapeutic programme. Using clay for sculpting family members enabled different
dynamics to emerge. In particular, the clay forms facilitated clarification of
the anorexic predicament in terms of her precarious sense of self and her
relationship to other family members, especially her mother. The sense that
she did not exist in the family sculpt was expressed by the difficulty of creating a body image. The families could 'see' this in the aesthetic response to the
clay work, which provided a way of communicating the experience by giving
it form (Case and Dalley 2006). As parents of anorexic adolescents tend to
present family life as more harmonious than it actually is, or they deny difficulties altogether, this was a significant experience for the whole family
promoting separateness, symbolic thought and change.

Understanding anorexia

Anorexia is becoming increasingly common among adolescent girls in the western world. Most anorexics are female with age of onset commonly between 12 and 23. For a diagnosis of anorexia nervosa to be made, the young woman's body mass index (BMI) must be less than 18. She is amenor-rhoeic, has a preoccupation with food and a morbid fear of becoming fat. Anorexics overevaluate their shape and weight and judge their self-worth largely, or even exclusively, in terms of their ability to control this.

Anorexia nervosa is particularly difficult to treat due to uncertainty about the underlying cause of the illness. While Lask and Bryant-Waugh (2000) provide a comprehensive overview of the aetiology, assessment and treatment, there are a variety of views from clinicians regarding the disorder. As early as 1895, Freud made a link between anorexia nervosa and melancholia, focusing on loss of appetite, whereas others focused on not eating as a defence against greed (Berlin *et al.* 1951). Palazzoli (1963) points to parental failure in under-standing their developing child as an individual in her own right, while Crisp (1980) describes an intense fear of becoming physically and emotionally mature. The emphasis on disturbance in body image is taken up, from a feminist perspective, by Orbach (1978) in her book *Fat is a Feminist Issue*. Understanding anorexia from the angle of the family as a system (Minuchin *et al.* 1978), Palazzoli (1978) suggested that, through her symptom of starving herself, a child with anorexia nervosa is trying to negotiate control and autonomy with her family.

Mothers and daughters

There is general agreement that the anorexic has a nearly delusional misper-ception of her body. Her disturbed body image makes her confused about body sensations and the refusal to eat may be understood in terms of the symbolic attachment to her mother. For example, Birksted-Breen (1997) sug-gests anorexia is a disturbance in the area of symbolisation connected with the lack of transitional space between mother and daughter. Weinreich *et al.* (1985) describe mother's devaluation of her daughter's attempt to be an adult and Sours (1974) speaks of the narcissistic use of the child to maintain the mother's own sense of self.

The desire to re-merge, to fuse with the mother, carries with it the fear of being engulfed, swallowed up or annihilated. Due to lack of differentiation between herself and her mother, the anorexic achieves this through her own omnipotence. Lacking the flexibility to negotiate her own separateness, she creates for herself an 'in myself space' (Levens 1995). She fears her mother will enter this inner space which is carefully guarded by the anorexic to ensure her sense of survival. There is no transitional space for her and so she develops (metaphorically) without a skin (Bick 1968).

Raphael-Leff (1986) suggests that anorexic young women have never successfully made the crucial early distinction between themselves and their mothers. A mother who herself cannot come to terms with separateness may blur the boundaries between herself and her baby, resisting the process of differentiation. If the body boundary between the baby and mother does not become fully established, the baby cannot accurately locate the mother as provider of bodily satisfactions. The mother is then experienced as 'absent' or empty, and the anorexic develops a self-container to protect herself against this experience of emptiness. Especially at risk of this are female babies, who are 'symbolically interchangeable', that is, they share the female form. This is why, Raphael-Leff suggests, there are more girls than boys who develop the condition. Such a daughter tries to claim control over what goes in and comes out of her body due to anxiety about what is inside and what is outside. In this way she also rejects the development of a full sexual identity with a feminine body and an inner world that can contain a baby.

Along with this defective self-concept, her inner emptiness has to be hidden. The anorexic is adept at concealment because she is over-compliant to others' wishes. There is a façade of perfection and high achievement for which she receives praise. Magagna (2000) suggests that a sense of fatness when the child is emaciated is linked to lack of an inner mental structure. Such structures give meaning to emotional experiences and put them into manageable psychological form. Instead of an inner mental structure the child with anorexia holds herself together through attachment to a 'pseudo autonomous' self which barricades itself against accepting nurture, both psychological and emotional (Magagna 2000: 228).

Those who have suffered from the condition have made a significant contribution to the literature (Bruch 1978; Sours 1980; Malan 1997).

> Willy-nilly, nature is impressing upon the girl the sexual function in society. By refusing food either she is subconsciously rejecting the function and finding escape in starvation so what she loses are the two assets peculiar to women, breasts and fertility; or she does not yet feel mentally equipped for it. Nature is getting out of hand; it has to be slowed down.
>
> (Dunseith 1978: 169)

The recourse to anorexia indicates a failure in an ability to symbolise and verbalise inner conflicts, resulting in her becoming what Jeammet (1981) describes as a 'prisoner of her own identification object'. The eating disorder is an attempt to be in control of her own life and to acquire an identity. Macleod (1981: 83), another sufferer, writes: '. . . driven as I was towards success by anxiety and the fear of failure. In reality I was back where I had started – in a position of helplessness and hopelessness – but with one important exception. I had something that I could call my own; my disease. My unique neurosis, which I perceived as my thinness.'

Art therapy literature and treatment approaches

Art therapists have written extensively about their work with young people with anorexia (Murphy 1984; Luzzatto 1994; Schaverien 1994; Waller 1994; Levens 1995; Maclagan 1998; Rehavia-Hanauer 2003). Wood (1996) provides a comprehensive overview of the literature and Gilroy (2006) gives a helpful summary of the qualitative research on art therapy with patients with eating disorders.

Usually anorexics do not see anorexia as a problem. Resistance to understanding the seriousness of the condition can lead to a difficulty in forming a therapeutic alliance because of the repetitive and deeply suicidal nature of the pathology. Anorexics are caught in destructive cycles of 'defiance, defence and ambivalence' (Waller 1994: 76) and have a 'desperate unwillingness to change' (Luzzatto 1994: 60). They arouse powerful reactions of anger and disappointment, sometimes in the wake of rescuing fantasies by those closely involved in their treatment.

Some art therapists have noticed common themes that emerge in the art work of their patients. For example, Murphy (1984) remarked on the consistency of recurrent imagery, spontaneously produced in individual sessions. Luzzatto (1994) observed themes connected to images of 'double trap' which recur as the young person presents herself as small and vulnerable, within an imprisoning situation, threatened by something persecutory in the external world from which she cannot escape. Luzzatto points out the unique double transference to the therapist and to the art work. Frightening negative transference can be contained within the image while more benign transference processes become manifest through the relationship with the therapist. As this split can be contained in the therapeutic work until there is a readiness for integration, the therapeutic alliance is maintained, which prevents premature termination of treatment.

Levens (1995) also noticed that themes became apparent with regard to the content of her patients' art and their associations to it. In particular, numerous images portrayed a person or an animal eating another with themes of being potentially 'swallowed up' in a relationship. Levens discusses the idea of magical thinking which is linked to the anorexic's desperate attempts to be in ultimate control of her body. She addresses the basic paradox in the following question: 'Why does the patient dwell in a world where the mere existence of food is experienced as persecutor, an ever-present monster which is ready to devour her immediately she dares to allow herself to want to eat it?' (Levens 1995: viii). Levens emphasises the relevance of the body boundary and how the development of a relationship with another person strongly threatens the integrity of an anorexic's identity. This threat comes to be expressed concretely in terms of the potential annihilation of the individual's existence. Food and the body appear to be both the source of the threat and the means by which the patient protects herself against the threat.

Developing these ideas, other art therapists describe how art-making within a therapeutic relationship offers an alternative means to develop a capacity to relate to another person. For example, Schaverien (1994) equates the material sensory experience of making art with bodily sensations, which is a process that takes time to engage. The unconscious enactments through food become conscious enactments through art. The capacity for symbolisation and relating can develop as art offers a medium through which a relationship can be ensured first with the self and then with another. By engaging in the art process there is movement in and out of the internal and external world experience. Levens (1995) describes how the 'artist' steps back from her image to gain a perspective and then goes closer to 'create illusion'. At certain moments the onlooker feels at one with her work and no longer remains outside of herself. The art objects are used as significant visual feedback to the maker. The 'doing' at a concrete level enables development of the observing self and a move from acting out through the body towards symbolic thought. Art-making can, in this way, provide an alternative language, particularly when words are often used defensively with these young people who tend to be highly articulate but concrete in their thinking.

Using clay

The therapeutic properties of clay are described in some depth in this volume (see Chapter 4). Foster (1997) and Killick (1993), who use clay with people in psychotic states of mind, suggest that the importance of clay lies in the concrete properties and its three-dimensional, as opposed to two-dimensional, form. Their ideas are helpful when considering the anorexic who, in a similar delusional state to those described by Foster, has profound difficulties due to fear of direct emotional connecting and intimacy. Foster suggests that the fear of making a three-dimensional object is linked to the fear of the likelihood of creating a container for persecutory forces and a resemblance of bad body parts. However, she points out how the clay may come to represent a concrete sense of control over the body and its (affective) contents:

> New and therapeutic experiences with body-like and life-like objects become possible because the objects are self-made, controllable and concretely changeable in interactions which are 'touching and forming'. The psychotic anxieties about the dangerous inside of Self and an Other can thus be worked with dynamically.
>
> (Foster 1997: 68)

In this sense, making three-dimensional forms in a clay or plastic medium offers the anorexic an experience of boundaries of the self that do not engulf her. Using the clay medium provides the possibility of acting on external reality as well as exploring a physical sense of her own body. Internal conflicts and anxieties are projected into the clay and externalised to reflect disowned aspects of self which are easier to 'see' for oneself than to take in from another person. The clay object 'provides a medium between the self-created world and external reality. This medium is considered to be essential for the development of object relationship' (Milner 1952: 4–9).

Family therapy

The predicament of the anorexic is highly complex. Her conflicts are internal as well as located externally within her family system, in particular in the relationship with her mother. This raises the question of whether individual treatment or family work is helpful for a patient who is highly defended and resistant to change but at the same time is dangerously ill, sometimes critically so. Like food, the anorexic is resistant to take in anything in the context of a therapeutic relationship. Eisler *et al.* (1997) suggest that family therapy is the most effective treatment for the early onset of anorexia. A family, like a social system, has adaptive mechanisms which maintain stability as well as accommodating the changing needs of individual family members. The aim of family therapy is to make use of these adaptive interactions. In the presence of serious and persistent problems such as anorexia, these mechanisms become increasingly challenged and unavailable (Eisler 2005).

Multi-family groups

Multi-family group work involves working together with a number of families with similar clinical presentation. Most parents with an anorexic child experience a complex set of feelings including failure, guilt, fear and embarrassment. While family therapy is effective in making use of the whole family's own resources and coping strategies, McFarlane (1982) observed that traditional 'insight' by the family or its individual members into their problems was not essential for therapeutic change to occur. Instead he believed that families might learn by seeing parts of themselves in others – including their own 'dysfunctions'. Multi-family work enables families to learn from each other and provide support and encouragement, which helps their sense of isolation (Sholz *et al.* 2003).

The idea of treating a number of families together was first pioneered more than 40 years ago by Laqueur *et al.* (1964), working with patients with schizophrenia. Subsequently the multiple family model has been applied to other psychiatric disorders such as drug and alcohol abuse, child abuse and eating disorders. It was the encounter with seemingly 'impossible' families which generated the idea of creating an institution specialising in promoting change for multi-problem and multi-agency families, developed by Alan Cooklin at the Marlborough Family Centre (Asen *et al.* 1982, 2001; Cooklin *et al.*

1983). Asen (2002), who helped to pioneer this work, describes how, from the beginning, multiple family therapy was a blend of group therapy and family therapy, using psychodynamic practices and attachment theory. The aim was to improve inter- and intra-family communication to help to understand some of the troubled behaviour of the identified patient:

> By focusing not only on their ill relative, but also on the symptomatic members of other families, each family member could potentially re-examine their own lives from different and new perspectives. Through the exchange of ideas and experiences with other relatives and members of other families it seemed possible to compare notes and to learn from one another.
>
> (Asen 2002: 4)

The first experiments of applying multiple family therapy to eating-disordered teenagers were pioneered in Dresden (Scholz and Asen 2001) and London (Dare and Eisler 2000). Asen *et al.* (2001) describe how this approach seemed highly relevant since it directly addressed the parents' sense of struggling away in isolation and having to rely heavily on the input of doctors and therapists. Involving parents directly was an important step for them to become expert themselves. Parents are put in charge of feeding their child to help reduce the hold that this disorder has on their daughter. This is considered crucial for successful treatment because, as long as self-starvation remains, the adolescent with anorexia is not capable of making rational decisions about food and weight. Although she is functioning like a much younger child in need of help, this, however, sets up extreme ambivalence to treatment by the young person who wants to take control of her own life.

The original groups in Dresden and London began with a four-day block running from 9.00 a.m. to 5.00 p.m. and subsequently on a monthly basis for up to six months. The various phases of the treatment process, which involved the use of a communal family meal as an important part of the multi-family group, is described in the *Treatment Manual for Multi-Family Therapy with Anorexia Nervosa* (Scholz *et al.* 2003). The role of the therapist is that of a catalyst, enabling families to connect with one another and encouraging mutual curiosity and feedback. Professionals are in the minority which contributes to a 'family' rather than a 'medical' atmosphere. With a number of families in the room the therapists enable interactions to happen using structural techniques such as 'enactment' and 'intensification' (Minuchin and Fishman 1981). 'Enacting' the eating problems concretely, with families taking part in meals together, creates conflicts which can be addressed and worked through at the time. There are plenty of 'co-therapists' in the shape of the family members who are consultant to each other (Stevens *et al.* 1983).

A clinical example of a multi-family group

The multi-family group described here in detail took place within a Child and Adolescent Mental Health Service (CAMHS) team. The model of working relied heavily on the format devised by Scholz *et al.* (2003), although making family meals together was not possible as there were no kitchen facilities. The group was adapted to the clinic context and took place over four sessions of two hours duration every two weeks. The programme was devised with a different activity each week. Following an introductory time at the beginning of the group, there was a break for 15 minutes in which tea, coffee, fruit juice and biscuits were brought in and then removed from the room. The activity continued with the whole group meeting together at the end.

The staff group consisted of five members of the multi-disciplinary team (consultant psychiatrist, child psychotherapist with a dual qualification in art therapy and child psychotherapy, systemic family therapist, clinical social worker with a dual qualification in social work and psychodrama, and a social work student). All staff were present at the beginning and ending of sessions and during the breaks. It was agreed at the planning stage which two staff members would lead the group with particular activities while the others observed behind a one-way screen.

The group

This group comprised of four families, A, B, C and D (for reasons of confidentiality, details of the family circumstances have been changed). The ages of the anorexic young people, all girls, ranged from 13 to 16. Families A, B and C had both parents living in the household. Family A were Welsh. Daughter A, aged 15, was the only child living at home, as her brother, ten years older, had left home and was living in Wales. The age gap between the siblings was due to daughter A's mother suffering from a number of miscarriages. Family B were white British. Daughter B was also 15 and her brother, two years younger, had a diagnosis of attention-deficit hyperactivity disorder (ADHD). The mother of family C came from Switzerland and her own mother was still living with the family. Family C had a similar composition to family B in that their daughter, C, aged 16, was the oldest child with a brother two years younger. In family D, who were white British, the parents separated five years before when the father left the home. He attended three out of the four sessions due to work commitments. Daughter D, aged 13, was the youngest child in the group. She had a sister, four years older, who attended every session. All family members were invited but none of the boys attended, which became a prominent dynamic in the group.

Session one

As an introduction to the first session, the consultant psychiatrist provided a psycho-educational summary of anorexia and its biological, environmental and genetic components. This forum also set the scene for thinking together and establishing ground rules for the group. It was important that the families, understandably anxious, were reassured that they did not have to say anything that they did not want to. The staff introduced themselves and explained that some of them would be behind the screen for some activities. The families were invited to see for themselves so that 'secrets' and 'hiding' did not become an issue within the group.

Following introductions, the families were asked to do a family tree or genogram in their family groups. After the break, each family shared their family tree with the whole group. A 'goldfish bowl' discussion followed, firstly with the young people and then the parents, who shared similarities and differences with regard to their family trees and any thoughts arising from the exercise.

In this first session there was little mention of anorexia except by mother from family D who said she had had an eating disorder as a teenager. The main theme that emerged from the young people's discussion was how they were hardworking and conscientious. They shared the experience of their mothers' overpowering anxiety, leaving them feeling scrutinised and over-monitored. In the parents' discussion, the mothers acknowledged how much they worried about their daughters. They also voiced their inhibition and resistance about attending but felt more relaxed having met the other families in the group. Another general theme that arose was alcoholism in relation to some of the members of their extended families.

Session two

The second session involved the 'paper plate exercise'. Working in their family units, using cuttings from magazines, paper plates and glue, the parents were asked to make a meal that 'they would like their daughter to eat for dinner'. The young people were invited to make a plate of food for the same meal. During the task, the observing staff team noticed the fathers were not so involved with the activity, leaving the mothers to take the lead with their daughters. The mothers, in particular, spoke about feeling drained over the endless battling and negotiation during mealtimes. Weights and measures had become important to all the families, trying to stick to their meal plan, which was acknowledged as a helpful, independent and neutral guideline. Stories of hiding food, tricks to fool their parents such as feeding the dog, the constant battles and violence in the household – daughter D described trashing her room – were all shared by the young people. The reflecting staff team asked the group whether these battles went on before the onset of anorexia and reflected on how tired everyone must be of the conflict. Daughter C said that she was not sure she wanted to get better and be normal as she felt she got more attention when she was thin. Before she had been overweight but continued dieting and was now unable to stop.

Following this session, in the post-group discussion, the staff group were encouraged by the increased openness in sharing issues but noticed that expression of feelings was still measured and guarded. The focus of the discussion kept coming back to food. The families used this to hide deeper underlying feelings as it was safer to talk about battles over food rather than feelings between each other.

Session three

In the third session, each member of the group was given the task 'to sculpt their family out of clay'. A lump of clay on a paper plate was provided for each person. The family units were asked to split up and work in groups of children, mothers and fathers. All members of the group were anxious, asking for further instructions and clarification. There was a sense of feeling inhibited and nervous as they were out of their normal structures and family systems. The mothers immediately assumed a comfortable rapport, working on their clay with enthusiasm, talking together about anorexia, sharing ideas together, such as good books. In contrast, the fathers were tense and inhibited, looking around for guidance, working silently with an odd comment passing between them about work. The young people had a good laugh together, swapping stories about school, with a sense of liberation, perhaps feeling that they could regress and make a mess.

The mood dramatically changed on discussion of the clay forms. One mother (family D) presented her family as an idealised unit. She portrayed how she wanted things to be – sunny, going out to play tennis with her two children. The father was not represented. Another mother (family A) presented her family as figures in a boat-like shape, protected from the outside, drifting along with no one in particular driving or steering. The family were all together and no one was in charge. The father of this family created three heads with long snake-like necks, intertwined, with their daughter in front and parents behind. He wanted to show how important it was to stay together as one unit which was 'not intended to be suffocating'.

Father B lined up his family in height order. They were flat on the plate (not standing up), with hands linked up. There was, however, a large lump of unused clay placed like a boulder behind the flimsy figures. His partner also placed the family in height order in a circle with a ring of clay around them which she said protected them from the outside world. They were all looking inwards at each other. She noticed that she made her daughter smaller than her, although in reality she was taller, and she spoke of her awareness of her daughter growing up and becoming a young woman. This brought to mind the siblings, prompting speculation about the missing brothers and why they were not able to be present to think with them in the group. Anger and resentment was expressed by the girls and the feeling that because they were boys they did not need to come. Daughter B, whose brother had the diagnosis of ADHD, expressed her exasperation that he got all the attention at home but, 'He is not here!' All the parents were surprised at the pressure they experienced for their sons to attend, in spite of the fact that they were included in the family sculpts, which raised a question about the different roles of the siblings in the families.

Mother C made her family, including her mother, as a cluster of fir trees, the different sizes representing each member of the family. She came to realise how this may represent her native Switzerland but, more significantly, that all the nutrients and food would be taken from the ground and therefore none of the family required feeding by her. Mother A, who made the boat, remarked that the trees would not move, just grow taller, which developed into a discussion about fear of their daughters growing up, becoming independent and sexually active young women.

During the break, mother D offered her daughter a banana. This provoked an angry response and daughter D withdrew from the circle. The rest of the young people described their pieces. Daughter A said she had spent a lot of time and care on making an accurate figure of her mother, which she had made first. The figure of her father was less carefully created. She then added that she made herself last, just as a 'blob – rather sluglike'. She only put herself in at the last minute but acknowledged that she did not know why.

Daughter D's sister made their dog as big as the adults, while she made her anorexic sister very small. Both children from this family spoke about their father's need to be in control. He had previously spoken about how there was no negotiation or discussion over food. Like her sister, D made her father very big although she made her mother first. She remained angry and withdrawn, very reluctant to speak, but then realised that she had not put herself into the model at all. This led to daughter B realising that she had also left herself out of her family sculpt. B was surprised to discover this, saying that she had forgotten, although she was quick to point out that she did consider herself as part of the family. She went on to acknowledge that she was unable to see herself and therefore avoided creating herself by 'forgetting'. Daughter A echoed this sentiment, speaking about the difficulties she had in 'creating' herself as she was worried that people would over-analyse it, considering it either too fat or too thin. She had created herself as a lump of clay – an afterthought.

The central theme that became clear was the difficulty that the anorexic girls had in modelling themselves with a body, to 'see' themselves in a representational female form. This was a striking feature that emerged from the clay images. Size and body image then became the focus of the discussion and some differences in the group began to emerge. For example, mother D said that she had purposely made her daughter very thin whereas the other families disagreed, saying they had not thought twice about the actual size and body shape of their child. Daughter C went on to say how she felt lonely and anxious and did not want to be helped. D echoed how angry she felt, saying that no one understood her feelings and how difficult it was for her to eat. She used her anger to keep people out or away. This was helped by feeling that she did not exist. The realisation that their daughters had left themselves out of the family units was a shock for all the families. The intensity of feeling emerged from the sense that the girls had no voice, no sense of self and that they did not exist. This was dramatically conveyed by the clay objects that had brought these feelings into the consciousness of the group.

Session four

In the final session, the families were offered the opportunity to reflect further on the experience of the clay sculpt. Family B in particular expressed their dismay and how much they struggled with the fact that their daughter had not included herself. However, since the last group, they reported that this had opened up avenues for discussion and allowed them to speak together about emotions and body image as a family. This led to a discussion among all the families about what had triggered anorexia. Daughter A spoke about her anger with her parents and how food and starving herself was something she had control over. She described how she could focus solely on this and ignore everything else, but understood the obsessional behaviour that had taken over her life was not helpful. Daughter B felt that her triggers were about body image and feeling fat as a size 12, while her friends were all size 6/8 (as was her mother). She said she did not show any emotions before she had anorexia. However, she felt she had found a voice in the group and was more able to express herself now. Control of eating was important for D who, after her parents divorced and her grandfather died, felt a loss of control over her life, and food was something she could control. It was acknowledged that D's withdrawn and angry state had taken on the angry role for the group, which released further helpful sharing of feelings about anger, resentment and disappointment. In this final meeting, D came to the group in a very different mood, expressing her relief that others could hear her unhappiness, despair and anger.

Another theme that emerged was that the families found it hard to imagine life without anorexia and discussed how things would change if the condition was not present. The girls expressed feeling over-monitored and that small accomplishments were not recognised or praised. It was agreed that changes needed to be made by the adults as well as the young people if things were going to improve.

Discussion

The importance of addressing the family dynamics through the multi-family framework set the scene for changes for all participants. Working with individual creative processes and family systems addressed the complex experience of the anorexic and her family at many different levels. Using the clay as part of the therapeutic programme enabled unconscious thoughts and feelings to reach expression symbolically, in three-dimensional form. Both the internal conflicts of the anorexic, and those located within the family dynamics, could be put into words. The problematic relationship between daughter and mother, and the role this occupied in maintaining the dysfunction of the family became clearer.

> If a person's identity is constructed in language (Lacan 1977), then perhaps the refusal to talk, so characteristic of anorexics, is also a refusal to take on an identity (as female) and a refusal to be defined (as adult). The anorexic girl is continually attempting to achieve a separate identity in the fact of this lack of differentiation but not the one which is structured for her and she maintains a state in which she is in phantasy, both fused with mother and not like her.
>
> (Birksted-Breen 1997: 106)

The clay family sculpts provided powerful communication for the whole family. The reality of the clay forms enabled the families to 'see' for themselves the bleakness of the anorexic experience. The formation of the self as 'absent', non-existent or merely a 'lump' with no form or shape was an expression of the sense of wishing no body shape, either fat or thin, with no sense of identity. The clay pieces created 'the body that had been lost' (Levens 1995: 71), which could contain dangerous and unwanted projections for both mothers and daughter. (Killick 1993; Foster 1997). Using the clay enabled thinking to take place about how the family system continued to support the presence of anorexia. Paradoxically, it had become understood how definition of the body through anorexia was the only way for the daughters to establish a sense of separateness and a feeling of existence (Krueger 2001).

Making art within the multi-family group created a structure which required a necessarily separate space as each pursued their own creative act. As the clay forms could stand alone, the young person had the experience that her feelings belonged only to her. The group allowed for these feelings to be processed in an environment in which the anorexic could not control the group and destroy the potential for separateness. The momentum of the group was taken over by the families who felt empowered by each other in the acknowledgement of their shared situation. In this 'family' environment, the therapists were experienced as separate and non-invasive. This enabled both the family and the anorexic to take things in and begin to develop a voice and a sense of self.

Some therapists working with anorexics warn of the dangers of using only verbal interpretation in their therapeutic approach. Symbolic interpretations can be experienced too concretely, as a psychic assault, which recreates the feeling of being invaded by an all-powerful parent (Bruch 1988; Luzzatto 1994). It was noticeable at the beginning how the mothers tended to speak for their daughters' experience. There was a considerable shift in this dynamic during the process of the group as the girls found their own voices by conveying their experience. This brought about a change to the anorexic's passivity which can be compounded by her sense that her mother has always known what she felt.

Conclusion

It is clear that anorexia is a complex disorder, the origins of which are almost certainly multi-factorial. In this chapter, anorexia has been thought of as fulfilling a number of functions for the young person and also her family. These include retreat from adult sexuality, a defence against aggression and an attempt to assert control over a chaotic intra- and interpersonal world. The anorexic develops a complex psychic structure which organises her inner world and protects her from intolerable emotions. It is in effect a 'psychic retreat' (Steiner 1993). The suggestion that anorexia functions as a defence which protects the growing young woman from unwanted projections, and in particular from the mother, became evident in the multi-family setting. It was clear how, if mother and daughter maintained a state of fusion, this made it impossible to develop a sense of separateness.

Eigen (1999: 1) suggests that the rejection of food, sometimes called 'toxic nourishment', represents symbolic rejection of these maternal projections. The serious consequences of anorexia, both psychological and physical, are a measure of the anorexic's desperate need to protect herself from these 'toxic' maternal projections as they are associated with either anxiety or anger. Williams (1997) describes how this helps to defend the child from being 'invaded' and 'broken into' and how the child is used as a 'receptacle of projections of a parent's anxieties which have not been metabolized or digested by the parent' (p. 121). This dilemma is 'solved' by not taking in anything at all and, as expressed in the group, not representing the self.

Without the capacity to take in or 'introject' parental role models that are required to establish a sense of identity, the anorexic is left with a profound inner emptiness and an inability to develop adult relationships. Working with the whole group dynamics and the other activities of the multi-family setting, the family sculpts conveyed the stark reality of the anorexic's struggle to find a representation of herself. The activity of making provided a transitional space in the creative arena for separation and development of a 'me-not-me' experience. (Winnicott 1971). The clay forms provided expression of bodily experience and, as such, a playground for rudimentary object relationships. It was possible to create a structure for both a sense of self and a body image necessary for the capacity to enter into symbolic relating.

Acknowledgements

I would like to thank Eia Asen for his enthusiasm and support in helping us to develop this work, also my colleagues in the CAMHS team who worked so creatively together.

References

Asen, E. (2002) Multiple family therapy: an overview, *Journal of Family Therapy*, 24: 3–16.

Asen, K.E., Stein, R., Stevens, A., McHugh, B., Greenwood, J. and Cooklin, A. (1982) A day unit for families, *Journal of Family Therapy*, 4: 345–58.

Asen, K.E, Dawson, N. and McHugh, B. (2001) *Multiple Family Therapy: The Marlborough Model and its Wider Applications*. London: Karnac.

Berlin, I., Boatman, M., Sheimo, S. and Szurek, S. (1951) Adolescent alternation of anorexia and obesity, *American Journal of Orthopsychiatry*, 21: 387–419.

Bick, E. (1968) The experience of skin in early object relations, *International Journal of Psychoanalysis*, 49: 484–6.

Birksted-Breen, D. (1997) Working with an anorexic patient, in J. Raphael-Leff and R. Perelberg (eds) *Female Experience: Three Generations of British Women Psychoanalysts on Work with Women*. London: Routledge.

Bruch, H. (1978) *The Golden Cage: The Enigma of Anorexia Nervosa*. Cambridge, MA: Harvard University Press.

Bruch, H. (1988) *Conversations with Anorexics: A Compassionate and Hopeful Journey through the Therapeutic Process*. Northvale, NJ: Jason Aronson.

Case, C. and Dalley, T. (2006) *The Handbook of Art Therapy*, 2nd edn. London: Routledge.

Cooklin, A., Miller, A. and McHugh, B. (1983) An institution for change: developing a family day unit, *Family Process*, 22: 453–68.

Crisp, A. (1980) *Let Me Be*. Hove/Hillsdale. Lawrence Erlbaum.

Dare, C. and Eisler, I. (2000) A multi-family group day treatment programme of adolescent eating disorder, *Euopean Eating Disorders Review*, 8: 4–18.

Dunseith, B.L. (1978) Personal view, *British Medical Journal*, 24 June:169.

Eigen, M. (1999) *Toxic Nourishment*. London: Karnac.

Eisler, I. (2005) The empirical and theoretical base of family therapy and multiple family day therapy for adolescent anorexia nervosa, *Journal of Family Therapy*, 27(2): 105–31.

Eisler, I., Dare, C., Russell, G., Szmukler, G., le Granve, D. and Dodge, E. (1997) Family and individual therapy in anorexia nervosa: a five-year follow up, *Archives of General Psychiatry*, 54: 1025–30.

Foster, F. (1997) Fear of three-dimensionality, in K. Killick and J. Schaverien (eds) *Art, Psychotherapy and Psychosis*. London: Routledge.

Freud, S. (1895) Extracts from the Fleiss papers, draft G, *Standard Edition*, vol. 1. London: Hogarth Press.

Gilroy, A. (2006) *Art Therapy and Evidence Based Practice*. London: Sage.

Jeammet, P. (1981) The anorexic stance, *Journal of Adolescence*, 4(2): 113–29.

Killick, K. (1993) Working with psychotic processes in art therapy, *Psychoanalytic Psychotherapy*, 7: 25–38.

Krueger, D.W. (2001) Body self: development, psychopathologies and psychoanalytic significance, *The Psychoanalytic Study of the Child*, 56: 238–59.

Lacan, J. (1977) *Ecrits*. London: Tavistock.

Laqueur, H.P., La Burt, H.A. and Morong, E. (1964) Multiple family therapy: a multidimensional approach, *Family Process*, 13: 95–110.

Lask, B. and Bryant-Waugh, R. (2000) *Anorexia Nervosa and Related Eating Disorders in Childhood and Adolescence*. Hove: Psychology Press.

Levens, M. (1995) *Eating Disorders and Magical Control of the Body: Treatment Through Art Therapy*. London: Routledge.

Luzzatto, P. (1994) Art therapy and anorexia: the mental double trap of the anorexic patient – the use of art therapy to facilitate psychic change, in D. Dokter (ed.) *Arts Therapies with Clients with Eating Disorders: Fragile Board*. London: Jessica Kingsley.

Maclagan, D. (1998) Anorexia: the struggle with incarnation and the negative sublime, in D. Sandle (ed.) *Development and Diversity: New Applications in Art Therapy*. London: Jessica Kingsley.

Macleod, S. (1981) *The Art of Starvation*. London: Virago.

Magagna, J. (2000) Individual psychotherapy, in B. Lask and R. Bryant-Waugh (eds) *Anorexia Nervosa and Related Eating Disorders in Childhood and Adolescence*. Hove: Psychology Press.

Malan, D.H. (1997) *Anorexia, Murder and Suicide*. Oxford: Butterworth-Heinemann.

McFarlane, W.R. (1982) Multiple family in the psychiatric hospital, in H. Harbin (ed.) *The Psychiatric Hospital and the Family*. New York: Spectrum.

Milner, M. (1952) Aspects of symbolism in comprehension of the not-self, *International Journal of Psychoanalysis*, 33.

Minuchin, S. and Fishman. C.H. (1981) *Family Therapy Techniques*. Cambridge, MA: Harvard University Press.

Minuchin, S., Rosman, B. and Baker, L. (1978) Psychosomatic Families: Anorexia Nervosa in Context. New York: Harvard University Press.

Murphy, J. (1984) Art therapy in the treatment of Anorexia nervosa, in T. Dalley (ed,) *Art as Therapy: An Introduction to the Use of Art as a Therapeutic Technique*. London: Routledge.

Orbach, S. (1978) *Fat is a Feminist Issue*. New York: Paddington Press.

Palazzoli, M.S. (1963) *Self-Starvation: From the Intrapsychic to the Transpersonal Approach to Anorexia Nervosa*. Haywards Heath: Human Context Books.

Palazzoli, M.S. (1978) *Self Starvation in the Treatment of Anorexia Nervosa*. New York: Jason Aronson.

Raphael-Leff, J. (1986) *Vogue*, June.

Rehavia-Hanauer, D. (2003) Identifying conflicts of anorexia nervosa as manifested in the art therapy process, *Arts in Psychotherapy*, 30: 137–49.

Schaverien, J. (1994) The picture as transactional object in the treatment of anorexia, in D. Dokter (ed.) *Arts Therapies with Clients with Eating Disorders: Fragile Board*. London: Jessica Kingsley.

Scholz, M. and Asen, E. (2001) Multiple family therapy with eating disordered adolescents: concepts and preliminary results, *European Eating Disorders Review*, 9: 33–42.

Scholz, M., Rix, M., Hegewald, K. and Gantchev, K. (2003) *Treatment Manual for Multi-Family Therapy with Anorexia Nervosa*. Vienna: Maudrich Verlag.

Sours, J. (1974) The anorexia nervosa syndrome, *International Journal of Psychoanalysis*, 55: 567–76.

Sours, J. (1980) *Starving to Death in a Sea of Objects*. Northvale, NJ: Jason Aaronson.

Steiner, J. (1993) *Psychic Retreats: Pathologicl Organisations in Psychotic, Neurotic and Borderline Patients*. London: Routeldge.

Stevens, A., Garriga, X. and Epstein, C. (1983) Proximity and distance: a technique used by family day unit workers, *Journal of Family Therapy*, 5: 295–305.

Waller, D. (1994) The power of food: some explorations and transcultural experiences in relation to eating disorders, in D. Dokter (ed.) *Arts Therapies with Clients with Eating Disorders: Fragile Board*. London: Jessica Kingsley.

Weinreich, P., Harris, P. and Doherty, L. (1985) Empirical assessment of identity syndromes in anorexia and bulimia nervosa, *Journal of Psychiatric Research*, 19: 297–302.

Williams, G. (1997) *Internal Landscape and Foreign Bodies: Eating Disorders and Other Pathologies*. London: Karnac.

Winnicott, D.W. (1971) *Playing and Reality*. Harmondsworth: Penguin.

Wood, M. (1996) Art therapy and eating disorders: theory and practice in Britain, *Inscape*, 1(1): 13–19.

Chapter 13

'Other people have a secret that I do not know': art psychotherapy in private practice with an adolescent girl with Asperger's syndrome

Julia Meyerowitz-Katz

Introduction

In the sentence used in the title to this chapter, Sally, my client, referred to her painful and difficult perception that there was something that she did not understand that excluded her from ordinary human relatedness. This chapter will describe how, in our work together, she became more able to process emotion and to think about her difference. Sally was referred, at the age of 15, to my private practice for art psychotherapy shortly after having been diagnosed with mild autistic spectrum disorder/Asperger's syndrome.

She attended regular art psychotherapy sessions with me over two years. Parental consultations took place every six to eight weeks. The role of the art materials, art processes and resulting art works and the rhythm between verbal and non-verbal communication were significant elements in the therapeutic process. The clinical work will be contextualised by a discussion of the relevant art therapy and psychotherapy literature, as well as relevant themes in the contemporary literature addressing mild autistic spectrum disorder/Asperger's syndrome. This is followed by a description of the clinical process, and discussion of the ways in which Sally and her family changed. Finally, I will consider the role played by the context of the work in affecting the course of the therapy as well as some implications for art therapy emerging out of this case.

Theoretical background

Autism and Asperger's syndrome

There is a substantial amount of research and debate concerning the aetiology of autism and Asperger's syndrome and their relationship to each other and to psychosis (Spensely 1995; Tustin 2002; Hodges 2004; Molloy and Vasil 2004; Rhode and Klauber 2004; Simpson 2004; Houzel and Rhode 2005; Bogdashina 2006). The literature refers to the complexity of these conditions in which personality, developmental issues, environment and genetics can all play a part.

Asperger considered that the syndrome that he identified was a disorder of personality development (Asperger 1944, cited in Simpson 2004). Tustin (1992) postulated psychogenic causes. Baron-Cohen (1995, cited in Bog-dashina 2006) proposes that the distinguishing feature of autism is lack of a theory of mind, i.e., an inability to understand the motivations or predict the actions of others as well as an inability to understand one's own mind; while Happe (1994, cited in Hodges 2004) suggests that Asperger's syndrome may be distinguished from autism by the partial development or partial preservation of theory of mind. Bogdashina (2006) points out that 'mind-blindness' works both ways and that the actions of non-autistic people are confusing for autistic people, but that equally, non-autistic people find autistic people difficult to understand.

While evidence as to the aetiology of these conditions is inconclusive (Alvarez 2004; Houzel and Rhode 2005), it is possible to identify a group of people who are recognisably 'different' in the ways in which they relate to others, but who still manage a certain level of functioning in the world. Although they do wish to engage on an interpersonal level, their ability to do so is impaired (Hobson 2002, cited in Hodges 2004), and they are excluded from human ordinariness (Shuttleworth 1999). Although they do not fit neat categories (Molloy and Vasil 2004; Rhode 2004) they manifest a particular quality of difference in their way of being that other people recognise and that they themselves are aware of (Jackson 2002; Molloy and Vasil 2004).

Art therapy

Art therapy has been offered as a form of treatment to children on the autistic spectrum since the 1960s (Evans and Dubowski 2001). In this context it is suggested that art therapy can foster an individual's capacity to understand symbols and to have meaningful relationships with the world (Dubowski and James 1998; Fox 1998). Stack (1998) refers to her patients' fear of therapy, linked with a fear of becoming connected to feelings, and she describes how the art therapy process allows for movement between areas of vulnerability and self-protective autistic defences so that new boundaries of self can be established alongside the comforting safety of autistic states.

Theorists suggest that working with this client group can be challenging in particular ways. Tipple (2003), writing about working with children on the autistic spectrum, refers to our subjectivity in trying to understand the meaning of art works made in art therapy and points out that the constructs with which we frame our thinking affect how we understand the work, implying the need for thoughtfulness when approaching art processes and art works made in therapy. Evans (1998) writes that when working with individuals on the autistic spectrum, it may be difficult for an art therapist to develop a therapeutic relationship based on the assumption that the art is made within a shared area of meaning. She considers that the impaired communication skills commonly experienced by this group may make early stages of art therapy challenging for art therapists. She refers to studies which suggest that sophisticated-looking work may actually be schematic, rigid and formula driven.

Central to art therapy theory are ideas that art-making processes and art objects are intrinsic to the art psychotherapeutic relationship, providing opportunities for communication between therapist and patient, as well as providing opportunities for understanding the nature of these communications (Case and Dalley 1990, Meyerowitz-Katz 2003, Schaverien 1999, 2000). If the boundaries and structures remain consistent, then any changes, including changes in the way art materials are used, are likely to reflect changes within the internal worlds of the child and the therapist and in the changing relationship between them (Meyerowitz-Katz 2003; Case 2005). Theorists suggest that art materials and processes can provide an intermediary area of experience in which the unprocessed emotional experience associated with primitive states of mind can be contained and transformed into thoughts (Evans 1998; Dalley 2000; Killick 2000; Meyerowitz-Katz 2003; Case 2005). A space is thereby created in which a shared relationship between the therapist and patient can emerge which can foster the patient's development of an internal space in which emotional experience can be processed, thereby fostering the development of the capacity to symbolise and the ability to think. This means that thinking develops out of an emotionally connected experience with another person.

Schaverien (1999, 2000) has identified two kinds of image which can occur within the art therapy process, and that are associated with different internal processes when they are made: diagrammatic images which are made as conscious communications, designed to help relate a feeling state, dream or memory; and embodied images, which convey a feeling state that cannot be described in words and which often reveals previously unconscious elements in the psyche; such states often involve complex images which engage aesthetic responses and so influence the countertransference. During the making of embodied images, a process of internal transformation occurs that facilitates the patient's development.

Other theoretical and clinical approaches

Research suggests that the interactional rhythms and modification of emotion intrinsic to the interaction between infant and mother result in neurophysiological activity that leads to brain development (Shuttleworth 1999; Case 2005). Houzel and Rhode (2005) point out that there is an obvious link between this neurological formulation and Bion's (1962) model of the containing function. It is postulated that the comparable dynamics between therapist and patient can lead to changes in brain development that would support the patient's ability to manage their lives better, by improving their thinking capacity and symbol formation (Hobson 2002; Houzel and Rhode 2005).

Alvarez (2004) postulates that an early deficit in the ability to interact meaningfully within personal relationships causes ongoing deficits in communication with other people and a self-feeding cycle of impairment develops. Polmear (2004) suggests that people with Asperger's syndrome feel impinged on by their own emotions as well as by the external world. She considers that Asperger's patients, rather than being 'mindless', experience a 'mind body over-fullness' (p. 99) in which other people's feelings are experienced as if they were located in the patient's body and the patient feels attacked by these feelings that cannot be contained or moderated and therefore need to be avoided or expunged. She suggests that language can be used both as a communication and as a barrier.

Many theorists suggest that the therapist's verbalisation to the patient of what she observes in the sessions can be a useful technique that can support a good therapeutic outcome. Pozzi (cited in Rhode 2004) suggests describing what the patient's body is doing, while Youell (1999) attests to the value of the therapist's efforts in understanding feeling states, as well as in verbalising, describing and even creating feeling states. She understands this process to be part of normal maternal functioning as well as a clinical method, part of Alvarez's (1992) term 'reclamation'. The child's favourite objects/images used initially to sustain autistic states can become more meaningful with the development of a richer internal world (Youell 1999).

Autistic traits may distort the effects of normal pubertal changes in adolescence, thus complicating the process of this developmental stage (Klauber 1999). Klauber (2004) suggests that adolescents with Asperger's try to control an unpredictable and frightening external world by refusing to allow other people's responses and by trying to avoid meaningful links or experiencing strong emotions. She suggests that, within the therapeutic relationship, the physical and psychological upheaval of adolescence can provide a window for renegotiating impaired developmental, physical and emotional experiences.

There is some evidence that a psychodynamic form of treatment can be helpful in facilitating improved quality of life for children with these conditions (Rhode and Klauber 2004). However, Alvarez (2004) and Polmear (2004) note that although Asperger's patients may become less dependent on soothing and comforting autistic-like behaviours when they feel more secure and are able to be open to other experiences, they may revert to those behaviours to calm themselves whenever their feelings threaten to overwhelm them. Rustin (2004) writes that it is important for therapists to accept the limits within which psychotherapy can help patients with Asperger's. She uses the term 'hard-wire' to refer to aspects of problems in thinking and in understanding the world that remain unchanged in spite of the considerable changes that can occur in a patient's emotional life.

The impact of a diagnosis of autism in a child can be experienced by parents as traumatic. Alvarez (2005) stresses that work with the individual child cannot proceed without work with the parents. The loss of a healthy child must be mourned, and ways must be found to work with the healthy part of the child (Klauber 1999). As the child changes, the environment around him will need to change in order to accommodate these changes, and support is needed in order to do this. Shuttleworth (1999) suggests explaining and naming to parents that the strangeness in their child is due to an impaired ability to manage relationships with other people, as well as managing his own mental states. She recommends fostering intimacy within the parent-child relationship as well as the parents' capacity to nurture their child, by supporting parents' recovery from feeling burnt out and overwhelmed.

Background to the clinical work

Sally was referred to me as she turned 15. She was the eldest by four years of two children. Her younger brother was severely autistic and attended a special school. There were concerns that Sally was depressed and isolated. I agreed to meet her parents in order to explore the possibility that I would take Sally on as a patient.

During our preliminary meeting, Mr and Mrs Thomas described their concerns; they felt that Sally was suffering and that she was lonely and depressed. It seemed that although their worry about her was shared, they were finding it difficult to share in her parenting. They disagreed with each other in their understanding of why she was in this position. When they disagreed, Mrs Thomas always took Sally's side and seemed overly identified with her. She spoke almost constantly in a stream of anxiety, taking up a lot of the space, and in the session I found it difficult to think. She described feeling claustrophobic and desperate within her relationship with Sally but was unable to change anything. It seemed that their relationship had always been like this. Mr Thomas described an unusual closeness between Mrs Thomas and Sally during Sally's infancy, from which he had been excluded.

He was noticeably silent much of the time and seemed depressed. He described how he had had a good relationship with Sally when she was younger, but that he was now shut out and could not reach her. Sally no longer spoke to him and would leave any room that he entered. He felt that he had lost his daughter, as well as his son, to autism.

Both parents were very proud of Sally's drawing ability, describing her as a talented cartoonist. We agreed that I would begin seeing Sally on a weekly basis and that the three of us would meet at regular intervals. They hoped that Sally's engagement in art therapy would lead to lessening of her depression, acceptance of growing up, gaining independence, and improved confidence. They hoped that she would take on more adult responsibilities, improve her communication and that relationships at home would improve.

Art therapy sessions

My first impressions of Sally were of a tall, stooped teenager with long blonde hair, dressed in dowdy unflattering clothes; when standing next to her mother at the door, she seemed to be trying to hide inside her. It was apparent that she had great difficulty with ordinary communication such as making eye contact and expressing herself verbally. She responded to me monosyllabically in a hesitant, babyish voice. I ascertained that she liked the idea of art therapy and wanted to come. She did not express any curiosity about me or the room or what we were to do in our time together and kept her head bowed with her gaze focused on her lap. She was keen to use the materials and to engage with me in making a folder. When it was made, she carefully poured paints into a palette and used a large brush to confidently decorate her folder with her name. She used up all the paint that she had poured, leaving the palette clean and hardly discoloured the water in the jar. I was struck by how she somehow managed to foreclose the possibility of mess and of any messy engagement with the materials. It was as if her engagement with the materials hardly left a trace that she had been there. I had a sense that Sally had somehow learned to be with another person in a way that made her almost invisible.

Early sessions

Sally's early sessions dragged on in almost total silence. Her images would emerge on the paper as if she was following a template; she almost never used an eraser and rarely seemed to feel that she had made a mistake. Figure 13.1 is an example of images that she created early in her therapy and is typical in its lack of background context, its resemblance to internet and computer game characters and its lack of narrative or reference to lived experience. While she worked, I found it increasingly difficult to stay alert, becoming very sleepy. In response to my wonderings, Sally did not offer a narrative or explanation as to the meaning of her images for her. I struggled to have meaningful associations with these images; they seemed to contain a 'secret' that I could not unlock and it seemed as if both her art-making and the resultant images were separating us.

Middle period

As her therapy progressed, there were changes in the relationship between us, and it seemed that she was trying to find ways of reaching me. Interspersed among the silent, mind-numbing sessions were sessions in which she would talk to me, in her tiny babyish voice, although she never looked at me.

I learned that she was very preoccupied with her identity and how she fitted into the world; she thought she was 'a bit autistic'. She described flapping her arms like her brother did, to comfort herself. She also described finding

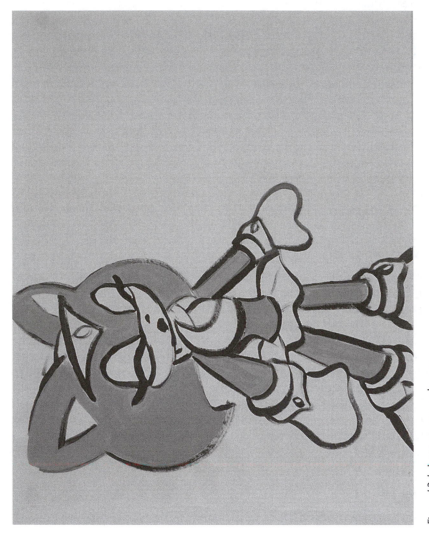

Figure 13.1 Internet game character.

talking frightening and said that she did not like to look people in the eye because then her 'thoughts stopped'. She was fearful of making people angry with her. She spoke about her difficulties at school that were both academic and social; school was frightening. She described her loneliness, her perception that other children found her weird and made fun of her. She spoke about dying and wanting to be dead.

It seemed that Sally was describing living in a frightening and hostile world in which the withdrawal of autism seemed soothing, safe and useful. I understood her talk of death and dying as a clear communication that she was reaching out for help. I noticed that her speech was changing; there were times when it was babyish, and other times it was more grown up. I also noticed that there were times during the sessions when I felt more awake and interested.

In a session just before a break, Sally did a drawing of a computer game character, a cartoon-like fox, lying with its tail over its tummy, fast asleep (Plate 14). She was very particular about how it was to look and, unusually, used an eraser. She did not like the first attempt and restarted. Then she was very particular about wanting to use crayons to colour it in. She coloured in very intensely, it took a long time and she was worried that she would not finish; we discussed her finishing next time, however she said she would not like to do that. I understood that perhaps it was difficult for her to imagine links between sessions; it felt to me as if each session was like a self-contained bubble.

In this session it seemed that Sally was able to engage with the materials in a way that was less controlled; she allowed some vulnerability and confusion, by making mistakes, and she was able to engage with me at the same time as she was working. There was a more alive quality to my experience of being with her as she worked. Making the image seemed to bring her father to mind. She felt he hated her, because he would reprimand her for not speaking. Her thinking seemed to be rigid and concrete and lacked any sense of the possibility of understanding another person's point of view.

I found that I had several associations with this image of the fox. I wondered if the cartoon-like sleeping fox represented the part of her that was going to go to sleep during the break so that she did not miss me; if perhaps the sleeping fox was tied up with dormant angry feelings that were connected to her relationship with her father; and further, whether the sleeping fox introduced an aspect of Sally that had not wanted to engage but that was emerging and becoming available for shared thinking. I felt that the significance of this image lay in her tolerating some vulnerability and confusion while she made it and the fact that I had some meaningful associations to it, whereas I had struggled to find meaning in her previous images. Although in this session Sally and I were able to discuss her relationship with her father, she did not respond to my interpretations about her image. I was left wondering if I was inventing meaning because as an art psychotherapist I was looking for it and expecting it to be there.

During a subsequent meeting with Mr and Mrs Thomas, six months into the therapy, I noticed a change in their relationship and heard that a lot had changed in the family. I observed that Mr and Mrs Thomas could now think and talk jointly about Sally. They made good eye contact and seemed to have a loving and bonded relationship. Mr Thomas seemed to have reclaimed his role in Sally's life to some extent. He very emotionally described spending time with Sally in nightly Scrabble games and discussions about her cartoons. There had been a family outing during which Sally had asked to sit next to him. He said that he felt he had his daughter back and that it was wonderful to be spending time with her. Mrs Thomas expressed her feelings of being burnt out, and not feeling able to do anything more for Sally. Mr Thomas seemed to have become more engaged in thinking about Sally's care. They reported that as well as developing a 'school phobia' (their words) Sally was refusing to leave the house unless accompanied by Mrs Thomas. They subsequently made a decision to take Sally out of school and home tutor her.

I noticed that Sally was beginning to take more of an interest in her appearance and that she was wearing more colourful, if childish, clothes. Sometimes she rushed into my room, bursting to talk and would begin speaking even before I had reached my chair. We were able to have discussions about her anger, about how when she was angry with people and couldn't express it to them, she turned on herself – for example by drawing on her body, or not eating. Sometimes the atmosphere in her sessions was fraught and tense, as if there was a battle going on, although Sally would vehemently deny this if I commented on it. She was rigid in her thinking and was unable to see things from any but her point of view. She insisted that she was a child and not a teenager.

In spite of our conversations, each session still felt to me like a bubble, separate from all the others, and there were still sessions in which I felt numbed and found Sally difficult to reach and could not feel connected to her art work. It was as if she had a secret that I could not share. During supervision the idea of a second weekly session emerged. We thought that it would help Sally link sessions, keep our communication going, deepen her engagement and provide more holding for her as she was having such a difficult time. A decision to increase her sessions to twice weekly was made jointly, in a meeting with Mr and Mrs Thomas, and through discussion between Sally and myself during her sessions.

Twice-weekly sessions

During her twice-weekly sessions Sally began using a greater range of materials and began to explore the painterly property of paints – creating images that included paint that was flicked or dripped onto the surface. She became more confident, although her use of the materials remained largely concrete, such as a clay internet game character, a decorated box and a tube which did not stand for anything else. She also began to paint images from her imagination. During one session in this period she made three paintings of storms (Plate 15). There was a quiet, industrious atmosphere while she was working and a shared liveliness. She worked intently and quickly. When she was finished she noticed some paint splatters on the wall and the tables and anxiously asked me whether she had made them. She spent some time cleaning the walls and other surfaces, trying to ensure that there was no damage. I linked her desperate cleaning up with her anxiety about her own destructive forces and the difficulty of staying with strong messy feelings – they had to be cleared away as soon as possible.

Although she never looked at me, she sometimes looked around the room or turned her head in my direction when I spoke. She demonstrated a certain amount of self-insight and explored her ambivalence about growing up. As her engagement with the process of her therapy deepened, I was able to make interpretations about what I thought was happening between the two of us. Her anxiety rose correspondingly and she clung to more autistic modes. In her art work she would repeat images of cartoon and internet game characters and I found it difficult to keep my thoughts in my mind while she worked. There were times when she asked me if I could please make her severely autistic. On a conscious level this was connected to her wanting to have a place to belong to (a place in the family and a special school, like her brother). On an unconscious level, I felt that it was an expression of how painful it was for her to negotiate the messiness of her own emotional life and of interpersonal relating.

Sally found the idea of approaching breaks increasingly difficult. She did not want to be separate from me and expressed a lot of anger towards her parents for taking her on holiday, but could not allow any anger towards me – she could not tolerate thoughts that I might instigate a break. However, she did express ambivalent feelings about her therapy. It felt as if the ongoingness of her therapy, and correspondingly the development of her inner world, was under constant threat. She expressed these anxieties in conversations about wanting to be autistic, her family moving to another part of the country, and her not deserving to have her mother spend money on her therapy.

During her first session after a break, nine months into therapy, Sally brought her digital camera and showed me her holiday pictures. Then she made a painting of her favourite one, which depicted a night sky over the sea with the moon reflected in the water. The photograph had been taken on an evening walk with her father during their holiday, and she described standing next to him gazing at the view and feeling happy and peaceful. During the following session that week, she completed her image and cut the edges because she wanted it to be neater (Plate 16).

Several things occurred to me when considering this image. It was a depiction of a real experience that had happened outside and that she was bringing into her therapy, thus linking inner and outer. There were further links in her being able to continue working on an image over two sessions. And the image was about being happy to be with her father. The picture reminded me of how she liked her world to be – with smooth uncomplicated surfaces, away from the light and with a sense that the world was ordered and under her control. There was no hint in the picture of any feelings associated with being away from me.

Sally began to grapple with ordinary adolescent issues. She came to a session in the shortest mini-skirt imaginable, knee-high high fashion boots and her favourite multi-coloured cardigan. She sat down and asked if she could take off her boots – she did not like them, her mother made her buy them – and we discussed her annoyance with her mother, who did not want her to wear such a short skirt. When the conversation became intense and strong feelings began to emerge, she suddenly got up, fetched a pencil and drew a cartoon-like cat. It seemed clear that making the image had provided her with an autistic escape route from her difficult feelings. In response to my wonderings, she said that the image was a copy of something she had seen. Then she asked, 'Can people be made severely autistic?' We had a discussion about how difficult it was for her to accept her non-autistic side because of the feelings that emerge and how autism sometimes seems attractive.

A year into therapy and after five months of twice-weekly sessions, Mr and Mrs Thomas reported positive changes in Sally and in family life. They had had their first ever weekend away without their children, leaving them in the care of a family friend. There had been several family outings, to the theatre and to restaurants. Sally was taking the dog for walks on her own and would go shopping alone. Mr Thomas had noticed that she was losing her baby voice, and we discussed how therapy had been addressing her ambivalence about growing up. Mr and Mrs Thomas were able to discuss their relationship with Sally with each other. Mr Thomas described his hurt during the times when he felt unsupported when Mrs Thomas defended Sally's position, and described his pain and depression when his own daughter would have nothing to do with him. The family were still avoiding difficult situations, and were struggling to manage angry feelings. There was some ambivalence about continuing with the second weekly session and it was decided that we would review that in a meeting after the Christmas break.

Loss of the second session

After the Christmas break Mrs Thomas phoned me to say that they were going to 'drop' the second session. I was unable to persuade her to wait until we could meet and then think about this together, or to prolong the decision until Sally had time to adjust to the loss. This felt like an attack on the therapy and on the part of Sally that was trying to evolve in a non-autistic way. I wondered whether the family was finding the changes in Sally too difficult to adjust to and what I could have done to prevent this from happening.

Sally came to her session later that day and reported that she was no longer going to be coming twice a week. She said that she did not understand why, because she liked coming. She seemed very confused and bewildered and discussed loss, losing things, being sad, wanting something different from what made her dad happy, wanting to please her dad, and trying to make him happy by doing what he wanted. She moved from this to attacking herself, saying that she was ugly and did not have proper breasts, and asked whether I could ask her parents to let her have plastic surgery. She made a mess when pouring paint directly onto the paper and then felt very bad about the mess, worrying that I would be angry with her. This was an extremely painful session and I was greatly encouraged by her capacity to use me and the materials to stay with the difficult feelings and not hide behind a safe cartoon image. I felt that her difficulties in managing puberty in relation to her father were clearly apparent, as were her internal processes of identifying with the assault on her inner world, feeling overwhelmed with her own destructive feelings and then asking me to rescue her by intervening concretely.

At this time Sally produced several images that reflected her growing capacity to allow uncertainty, mess and confusion, and to draw on her own imagination – for example, a spoon that seemed to emerge out of her unconscious in an uncensored way and involved a deeper and more messy engagement with the paint (Figure 13.2). My associations with the spoon were as a teaspoon. As such it is an obvious symbol of feeding and being fed, it is the container for the food that passes between mother and infant, and as such is experienced in a transitional space. I wondered if Sally's spoon painting was communicating something of an unconscious awareness that the art-making was providing a transitional area for her, both in terms of her relationship with me, being able to take in symbolic food, and in terms of her negotiating the tension between the pull towards autism and the pull towards relationship in her art making.

At other times she continued to draw cartoon figures. Sometimes it seemed as if she was stylistically trying to combine her two main themes, the autistic-like encapsulated images and the more painterly expressive ones. It was as if on one level she was trying to find a way to condense both sessions into one, to somehow make up the 'lost' sessions, and on another level, to try and integrate her non-autistic side with her autistic side.

Sally agreed to attend the meetings I held with her parents. She came to her first meeting full of anger, some of which was linked to the lost second session, which the family found difficult to address. She was argumentative, continually disagreeing with, denying or disparaging views expressed by her parents. She angrily expressed the view that she was worthless and undeserving several times, deeply upsetting her parents. She described being angry with everyone and at times in the meeting she refused to speak. She continued to use the family meetings to express her anger, as well as to communicate her thoughts and feelings about other important issues.

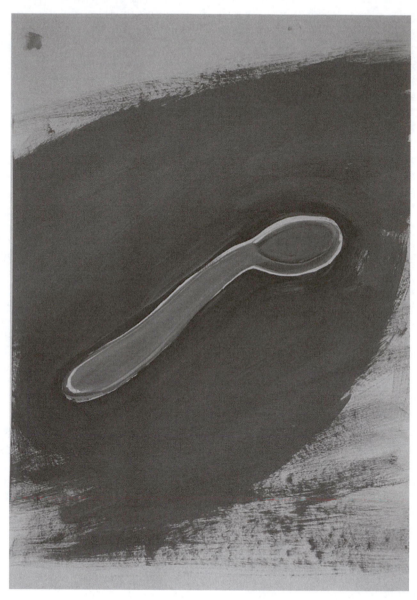

Figure 13.2 Spoon.

In spite of all the progress, there were still many sessions in which Sally would sit in silence, examining her hair and breaking off split ends, effectively pushing us both back into our bubbles with sleepiness between us, and foreclosing the possibility of thoughtfulness. I decided to respond by verbalising my observations of what she was doing, reminding her that I was thinking about her and that I was wondering what her thoughts were. The following is what happened in one particular session.

The atmosphere became loaded with anguished primitive erotic need; it was almost unbearable. As I continued commenting, Sally changed her activity with her hair, pushing some of it behind her left ear so that half of her face was exposed. She leant her head on her right hand, and her elbow on the arm of the chair, with her thumb in her mouth and closed her eyes. She sucked on her thumb. She began rocking the chair, still with her eyes closed and her thumb in her mouth. I commented that she reminded me of a baby being rocked while her mum thought about her. This went on for quite a while, and I continued to verbalise my observations of her behaviour as well as telling her that I continued to think about her. She continued to alternately rock in her chair and fiddle with her hair.

Later in the session she said that she did not think that she had autism or Asperger's syndrome, explaining that she had been with autistic and Asperger's people and she was not like them. She said that she no longer wanted to be autistic but she thought that there was something wrong with her because 'other people have a secret that I do not know'. We talked about what that secret might be and that it might be linked to understanding other people's feelings and thoughts. On reflection I wondered whether she was beginning to understand that autism and Asperger's syndrome, rather than being attractive and safe options, could actually make life more difficult, and whether she wanted to deny that she was in any way like that.

It seemed in this session, and others like it, that my verbalisation of what I observed her doing validated her experience, providing her with a profound experience of being seen, and of being the focus of someone else's mind. This encouraged her to communicate early primitive unconscious experience that I could contain, thus supporting the growth and development of her emotional life and fostering her ability to think.

Ending phase

Soon after, I learned that my personal circumstances were to change and that Sally's art therapy would have to end a few months later. I told Sally of this at the beginning of a session. She responded with immediate anxiety about what would happen to her art work, and then spent the session reviewing her images. It seemed that she had made a strong connection between her unconscious life and her art works and I felt that in worrying about the fate of her art works, she was also worrying about how she was going to manage mediating between her inner world and the outside without me.

In a subsequent session, during a long silence, I realised that I was deep in thought. Sally was sitting in her chair, very still and relaxed, her hair behind her ears. Sometimes she looked around the room. I commented that we were sitting together sharing a thinking space while thinking our thoughts. She considered that and then engaged in more conversation. Our discussion moved to her describing a game that she played where there is a 'meanie' that throws boulders at you that you have to smash. She denied any links that I tried to make between this game and feelings about our relationship. She said she was sad I was leaving, but not angry.

In a session towards the end of her therapy, Sally drew and then painted what she described as a chocolate chip cookie. She was very involved with the materials in the process, spending ages trying to get the texture right and then she painted a swirl of colour around it and splattered paint on to the finished picture. She was pleased with her picture. She described how she loved chocolate and chocolate chip cookies. Although she consciously made an image about desired, good food, which I understood was a communication about the goodness that she had experienced with me, the image also reminded me of the boulders thrown by the 'meanie' in the game that she had described in the previous session, as well as having associations with faeces. I linked the image to anger about the approaching ending. It seemed to me to be a satisfying image in its capacity to hold opposing associations.

In her last session we talked about how she was sad that I was leaving. We discussed her anxiety about managing her inner world herself in the form of how she was going to look after her images. We talked about how hard she had worked in trying to understand things with me, how much she had valued our conversations and thinking together with me about things and about how much she had changed. She said that she was less depressed although she occasionally still had thoughts about death and dying. She talked about aspects of herself that she liked, and how she liked to wear a little make-up. She described how she still wanted to remain a little girl, but she was doing things that teenagers did too.

She said that she might forget me but not for a very long time; when thinking of me she would feel a mixture of happiness and sadness. She said that she would like to live in my consulting room, after I left, because she liked it. When I made an interpretation about her imagining living in my consulting room as a way of feeling close to me when I had gone, she became confused because how could she feel close to me when I was not there? And I was reminded again, that in spite of all the progress she had made, there was a concrete aspect to her thinking that had not shifted.

Before her therapy ended, I arranged for Sally to meet a therapist who facilitated communication and social skills groups for teenagers with Asperger's syndrome. I was encouraged because Sally had been to meet her, and was excited about the prospect of joining a group of teenage girls with whom she might make friends.

Discussion

I have described my work with Sally within the context of my private art psychotherapy practice. There are several implications for art psychotherapy in this context and I think that the work described here highlights some of them. The therapist is working in isolation and has to hold cases that in other settings would be held by a team within an institution. The value of supervision, as well as participation in regular peer discussion groups can't be underestimated. Private practice, particularly when offered in a private home, offers clients a more personal environment that lacks the formality and hierarchical feel of an institutional setting; it offers an ordinary context that perhaps makes therapy feel part of everyday life.

Work with parents can be experienced as a joint collaborative effort; it is crucial in supporting the progress of the therapy. In this case, parent consultations provided opportunities for a shared thinking space to develop in which Mr and Mrs Thomas could strengthen their parental partnership, mourn the loss of their healthy child, accept and understand Sally's oddness and find ways of nurturing their relationship with her and think together about her future.

However, parents of children seen in this context are employing the therapist and have the power to unilaterally terminate the therapy, or as in the case of Sally's second weekly session, to interfere with the structure of the therapy. When this happens the therapist is presented with a very difficult dilemma of how to hold the boundaries and protect the work with the child without antagonising the parents and risk seeing the therapy terminated by them in a destructive manner, or causing the child to become painfully caught between therapist and their parents.

Sally and I experienced the decision to 'drop' the second session as a devastating assault on her therapy and the development of her internal world, and I wondered whether the umbrella of an institution, and a team approach to the work, might have made any difference, or whether it would have been any different had Mr and Mrs Thomas been meeting with a different therapist. I felt responsible and wondered what I could have done differently in order to prevent it from happening. Although I think that to a certain extent I became identified with the part of Sally that was being attacked and felt impotent, my experience told me that there was very little I could do without causing Sally to become caught between her parents and myself, and so I had to go along with their decision.

It was helpful to consider this event in terms of the larger family dynamics. It gave me a first-hand experience of something that Sally had probably experienced before, and shed new light on the difficulty she faced in trying to develop her non-autistic side. Sally had an opportunity to work through her responses to a devastating experience of loss with an ally in a contained and mindful setting and she was able to use the experience to ultimately strengthen her internal world.

The growth and development of Sally's internal world was facilitated by the art psychotherapy setting in a complex way. A significant aspect of the work was that the meaning held in the form of Sally's verbal and non-verbal communications, as well as the content of these communications, changed, within individual sessions and over the course of her therapy. Art-making in this setting facilitated Sally's improvement because it provided an in-built safe place, the necessary 'autistic' safety, to which she could retreat, and out of which she could emerge, reaching out into relationship, when it felt safe enough to do so. Art-making provided her with a flexible form of communication. As her therapy progressed, and with repeated experiences of containment, there was a gradual movement toward relationship, evidenced through transference dynamics, conversations and by art-making and art works that allowed uncertainty, confusion and a certain amount of mess. Sally was enabled to develop her emotional connectedness and engage with the artmaking process within a shared area of meaning to produce both diagrammatic and embodied art works. Changes within her therapy resulted in her growing confidence and her interest in ordinary adolescent issues as well as in her ability to think about her identity, particularly in relation to autism and Asperger's syndrome.

Concluding thoughts

Other than brief personal accounts of setting up in private practice by two art therapists in a British Association of Art Therapists' *Newsbriefing* (De Heger 2006; Wilson 2006), I haven't found any references in the literature to art therapy in this context. I hope that this contribution will stimulate further thinking and discussion about art therapists working in private practice. Most of the art therapy literature on working with children tends to focus on work with the children and does not address working with parents or carers. I think that this case illustrates how valuable work with parents and carers can be, and I think this is an area that deserves our attention. Equally important are considerations about frequency of sessions. My experience of teaching on training courses is that the model that is offered to students is of weekly sessions. My experience as a supervisor suggests that practising art therapists tend to continue with this structure. Perhaps we might consider that this is not a structure that we should adhere to rigidly, as it seems that increasing the frequency of sessions can significantly support therapeutic growth.

References

Alvarez, A. (1992) *Live Company: Psychoanalytic Psychotherapy with Autistic, Borderline, Deprived and Abused Children*. London: Routledge.

Alvarez, A. (2004) Issues in assessment: Asperger syndrome and personality, in M. Rhode and T. Klauber (eds) *The Many Faces of Asperger's Syndrome*. London: Karnac.

Alvarez, A. (2005) Autism and psychosis, in D. Houzel, and M. Rhode (eds) *Invisible Boundaries. Psychosis and Autism in Children and Adolescents*. London: Karnac.

Bion, W. (1962) *Learning From Experience*. London: Maresfield Reprints.

Bogdashina, O. (2006) *Theory of Mind and the Triad of Perspectives on Autism and Asperger Syndrome. A View from the Bridge*. London: Jessica Kingsley.

Case, C. (2005) *Imagining Animals: Art, Psychotherapy and Primitive States of Mind*. London Routledge.

Case, C. and Dalley, T. (1990) *Working with Children in Art Therapy*. London: Routledge.

Dalley, T. (2000) Back to the future: thinking about theoretical developments in art therapy, in A. Gilroy and G. McNeilly (eds) *The Changing Shape of Art Therapy. New Developments in Theory and Practice*. London: Jessica Kingsley.

De Heger (2006) From employed art therapist to self-employed, *Newsbriefing*, Spring: 10–11.

Dubowski, J. and James, J. (1998) Arts therapies with children with learning disabilities, in D. Sandle (ed.) *Development and Diversity: New Applications in Art Therapy*. London: Free Association Books.

Evans, K. (1998) Shaping experience and sharing meaning: art therapy for children with autism, *The Journal of the British Association of Art Therapists, Inscape*, 3(1): 17–25.

Evans, K. and Dubowski, J. (2001) *Art Therapy with Children on the Autistic Spectrum: Beyond Words*. London: Jessica Kingsley.

Fox, L. (1998) Lost in space: the relevance of art therapy with clients who have autism or autistic features, in M. Rees (ed.) *Drawing on Difference. Art Therapy with People who have Learning Difficulties*. London: Routledge.

Hodges, S. (2004) A psychological perspective on theories of Asperger's syndrome, in M. Rhode and T. Klauber (eds) (2004) *The Many Faces of Asperger's Syndrome*. London: Karnac.

Hobson, R.P. (2002) *The Cradle of Thought*. Basingstoke: Macmillan.

Houzel, D. and Rhode, M. (eds) (2005) *Invisible Boundaries: Psychosis and Autism in Children and Adolescents*. London: Karnac.

Jackson, L. (2002) *Freaks, Geeks and Asperger Syndrome*. London: Jessica Kingsley.

Killick, K. (2000) The art room as container in analytical art psychotherapy with patients in psychotic states, in A. Gilroy and G. McNeilly (eds) *The Changing Shape of Art Therapy: New Developments in Theory and Practice*. London: Jessica Kingsley.

Klauber, T. (1999) The significance of trauma and other factors in work with the parents of children with autism, in A. Alvarez and S. Reid (eds) *Autism and Personality: Findings from the Tavistock Autism Workshop*. London: Routledge.

Klauber, T. (2004) A child psychotherapist's commentary on Hans Asperger's 1944 paper, 'Autistic psychopathy in childhood', in M. Rhode and T. Klauber (eds) *The Many Faces of Asperger's Syndrome*. London: Karnac.

Meyerowitz-Katz, J. (2003) Art materials and processes: a place of meeting. Art psychotherapy with a four-year old boy, *Inscape: The Journal of the British Association of Art Therapy*, 8(2): 60–9.

Molloy, H. and Vasil, L. (2004) *Asperger Syndrome, Adolescence and Identity: Looking Beyond the Label*. London: Jessica Kingsley.

Polmear, C. (2004) Finding the bridge: psychoanalytic work with Asperger's syndrome adults. in M. Rhode and T. Klauber (eds) *The Many Faces of Asperger's Syndrome*. London: Karnac.

Rhode, M. (2004) Introduction, in M. Rhode and T. Klauber (eds) *The Many Faces of Asperger's Syndrome*. London: Karnac.

Rhode M. and Klauber, T. (eds) (2004) *The Many Faces of Asperger's Syndrome*. London: Karnac.

Rustin, M. (2004) Psychotherapy and community care, in M. Rhode and T. Klauber (eds) *The Many Faces of Asperger's Syndrome*. London: Karnac.

Schaverien, J. (1999) *The Revealing Image: Analytical Art Psychotherapy in Theory and Practice*. London: Routledge.

Schaverien, J. (2000) The triangular relationship and the aesthetic countertransference in Analytical art psychotherapy, in A. Gilroy and G. McNeilly (eds) *The Changing Shape of Art Therapy. New Developments in Theory and Practice*. London: Jessica Kingsley.

Shuttleworth, J. (1999) The suffering of Asperger children and the challenge they present to psychoanalytic thinking, *Journal of Child Psychotherapy*, 25(2): 239–65.

Simpson, D. (2004) Asperger's syndrome and autism: distinct syndromes with important similarities, in M. Rhode and T. Klauber (eds) *The Many Faces of Asperger's Syndrome*. London: Karnak.

Spensley, S. (1995) *Francis Tustin*. London: Routledge.

Stack, M. (1998) Humpty Dumpty's shell: working with autistic defence mechanisms in art therapy, in M. Rees (ed.) *Drawing on Difference: Art Therapy with People who have Learning Difficulties*. London: Routledge.

Tipple, R. (2003) The interpretation of children's artwork in a paediatric disability setting, *The Journal of the British Association of Art Therapists, Inscape*, 8(2): 48–59.

Tustin, F. (1992) *Autistic States in Children*. Cambridge: Cambridge University Press.

Tustin, F. (2002) *Autistic States in Children*, revised edn. London: Routledge.

Wilson, P. (2006) From employed art therapist to self-employed, *Newsbriefing*, Spring: 12–13.

Youell, B. (1999) Matthew: from numbers to numeracy: from knowledge to knowing in a ten year old boy with Asperger's syndrome, in A. Alvarez and S. Reid (eds) *Autism and Personality*. London: Routledge.

Further reading: selected books and papers on art therapy with children and adolescents

Specific

Adolescence

Bissonnet, J. (1998) Group work for adolescent boys in a social service setting, in D. Sandle (ed.) *Development and Diversity: New Applications in Art Therapy*. London: Free Association Books.

Brown, A. and Latimer, M. (2001) Between images and thoughts: an art psycho-therapy group for sexually abused adolescent girls, in J. Murphy (ed.) *Lost for Words: Art Therapy with Young Survivors of Sexual Abuse*. London: Routledge.

Cregeen, S. (1992) Seizure as symbol: an exploration of the symbolic meaning of an epileptic seizure within a therapy relationship, *Inscape*, spring: 17–26.

Milia, D. (2000) *Self Mutilation and Art Therapy: Violent Creation*. London: Jessica Kingsley.

Riley, S. (1999) *Contemporary Art Therapy with Adolescents*. London: Jessica Kingsley.

Welsby, C. (1998) A part of the whole: art therapy in a comprehensive school, *Inscape*, 3(1): 37–40.

Assessment

Case, C. (1998) Brief encounters: thinking about images in assessment, *Inscape*, 3(1): 26–33.

Douglass, L. (2001) Nobody hears: how assessment using art as well as play therapy can help children disclose past and present sexual abuse, in J. Murphy (ed.) *Lost for Words: Art Therapy with Young Survivors of Sexual Abuse*. London: Routledge.

Tipple, R. (2003) The interpretation of children's artwork in a paediatric disability setting, *Inscape*, 8(2): 48–59.

Autistic and psychotic states of mind

Case, C. (2003) Authenticity and survival: working with children in chaos, *Inscape*, 8(1): 17–28.

Case, C. (2005) *Imagining Animals: Art, Psychotherapy and Primitive States of Mind*. London: Routledge.

Evans, K. (1998) Sharing experience and sharing meaning: art therapy for children with autism, *Inscape* 3(1): 17–25.

Evans, K. and Dubowski, D. (2001) *Art Therapy with Children on the Autistic Spectrum: Beyond Words*. London: Jessica Kingsley.

Evans, K. and Rutten-Saris, M. (1998) Shaping vitality affects, enriching communication: art therapy for children with autism, in D. Sandle (ed.) *Development and Diversity: New Applications in Art Therapy*. London: Free Association Books.

Fox, L. (1998) Lost in space: the relevance of art therapy with clients who have autism or autistic features, in M. Rees (ed.) *Drawing on Difference: Art Therapy with People who have Learning Difficulties*. London: Routledge.

Henley, D. (1994) Art of annihilation: early onset schizophrenia and related disorders of childhood, *American Journal of Art Therapy*, 32(4): 99–107.

Henley, D. (2001) Annihilation anxiety and fantasy in the art of children with Asperger's syndrome and others on the autistic spectrum, *American Journal of Art Therapy*, 39: 113–21.

Hermelin, B. (2001) *Bright Splinters of the Mind: A Personal Story of Research with Autistic Savants*. London: Jessica Kingsley.

McGregor, I. (1990) Unusual drawing development in children: what does it reveal about children's art? in C. Case and T. Dalley (eds) *Working with Children in Art Therapy*. London: Tavistock/Routledge.

Stack, M. (1998) Humpty Dumpty's shell: working with autistic defence mechanisms in art therapy, in M. Rees (ed.) *Drawing on Difference*. London: Routledge.

Eating disorders

Levens, M. (1995) *Eating Disorders and the Magical Control: Treatment through Art Therapy*. London: Routledge.

Maclagan, D. (1998) Anorexia: the struggle with incarnation and the negative sublime, in D. Sandle (ed.) *Development and Diversity: New Applications in Art Therapy*. London: Free Association Books.

Education

Arguile, R. (1990) 'I show you': children in art therapy, in C. Case and T. Dalley (eds) *Working with Children in Art Therapy*. London: Routledge.

Arguile, R. (1992) Art therapy with children and adolescents, in D. Waller, and A. Gilroy (eds) *Art Therapy: A Handbook*. Buckingham: Open University Press.

Boronska, T. (1995) 'Art psychotherapy with children in a special school setting, *Young Minds Newsletter*, 21 (April).

Gersch, I. and Goncalves, S. (2006) Creative therapies and educational psychology: let's get together, *Inscape*, 11(1): 22–32.

Karkou, V. (1999) Art therapy in education, *Inscape*, 4(2): 62–70.

Nicol, A.R. (1987) Psychotherapy and the school: an update, *Journal of Child Psychology and Psychiatry*, 28(5): 657–65.

Ross, C. (1996) Conflict at school: the use of an art therapy approach to support children who are bullied, in M. Liebmann (ed.) *Art Approaches to Conflict*. London: Jessica Kingsley.

Group work

Dalley, T. (1993) Art psychotherapy groups for children, in K. Dwivedi (ed.) *Groupwork for Children and Adolescents*. London: Jessica Kingsley.

Henley, D. (1998) Art therapy in a socialization programe for childen with ADHD, *American Journal of Art Therapy*, 37: 2–12.

Henley, D. (1999) Facilitating socialization within a therapeutic camp setting for children with attention deficits utilizing the expressive therapies, *American Journal of Art Therapy*, 38: 40–50.

Liebmann, M. (2004) *Art Therapy for Groups: A Handbook of Themes, Games and Exercises*, 2nd edn. London: Routledge.

Murphy, J., Paisley, D. and Pardoe, L. (2004) An art therapy group for impulsive children, *Inscape*, 9(2): 59–68.

Prokofiev, F. (1998) Adapting the art therapy group for children, in S. Skaife and V. Huet (eds) *Art Psychotherapy Groups: Between Pictures and Words*. London: Routledge.

Skaife, S. and Huet, V. (eds) (1998) *Art Psychotherapy Groups: Between Pictures and Words*. London: Routledge.

Waller, D. (1993) *Group Interactive Art Therapy: Its Use in Training and Treatment*. London: Routledge.

Health

Lillitos, A. (1990) Control, uncontrol, order and chaos: working with children with intestinal motility problems, in C. Case and T. Dalley (eds) *Working with Children in Art Therapy*. London: Routledge.

Malchiodi, C. (1998) *Medical Art Therapy with Children*. London: Jessica Kingsley.

Vasarhelyi, V. (1990) The cat, the fish, the man and the bird: or how to be a nothing. Illness behaviour in children: the case study of a 10 year old girl, in C. Case and T. Dalley (eds) *Working with Children in Art Therapy*. London: Routledge.

Vasarhelyi, V. (1991) How Snerp, the snake-dragon and his friends, Starlight and the two Bridgets, decided to join the United Nations of feelings, *Inscape*, summer: 18–29.

Learning difficulties

Dubowski, J. and James, J. (1998) Arts therapies with children who have learning difficulties, in D. Sandle (ed.) *Development and Diversity: New Applications in Art Therapy*. London: Free Association Books.

Rabiger, S. (1990) Art therapy as a container, in C. Case and T. Dalley (eds) *Working with Children in Art Therapy*. London: Routledge.

Rabiger, S. (1998) Is art therapy? Some issues arising in working with children with severe learning difficulties, in M. Rees (ed.) *Drawing on Difference: Art Therapy with People who have Learning Difficulties*. London: Routledge.

Rees, M. (ed.) *Drawing on Difference: Art Therapy with People who have Learning Difficulties.*, London: Routledge.

Looked-after children

Aldridge, F. (1998) Chocolate or shit: aesthetics and cultural poverty in art therapy with children, *Inscape*, 3: 2–9.
Boronska, T. (2000) Art therapy with two sibling groups using an attachment framework, *Inscape*, 5(1): 2–10.
Case, C. (1987) A search for meaning: loss and transition in art therapy, in T. Dalley, C. Case, J. Schaverien, F. Weir, D. Halliday, P. Nowell Hall and D. Waller (eds) *Images of Art Therapy: New Developments in Theory and Practice*. London: Tavistock.
Case, C. (1990) Reflections and shadows: an exploration of the world of the rejected girl, in C. Case and T. Dalley (eds) *Working with Children in Art Therapy*. London: Routledge.
Case, C. (2005) *Imagining Animals: Art, Psychotherapy and Primitive States of Mind*. London: Routledge.
Case, C. (2005) The Mermaid: moving towards reality after trauma, *Journal of Child Psychotherapy*, 31(3): 335–51.
Knight, S. (1989) Art therapy and the importance of skin when working with attachment difficulties, in D. Sandle (ed.) *Development and Diversity: New Applications in Art Therapy*. London: Free Association Books.
O'Brien, F. (2003) Bella and the white water rapids, *Inscape*, 8(1): 29–41.
O'Brien, F. (2004) The making of mess in art therapy: attachment and the brain, *Inscape*, 9(1): 2–13.

Physical abuse

Case, C. (1994) Art therapy in analysis: advance/retreat in the belly of the spider, *Inscape*, 1: 3–10.
Case, C. (2002) Animation and the location of beauty, *Journal of Child Psychotherapy*, 28(3): 327–43.
Malchiodi, C. (1990) *Breaking the Silence: Art Therapy with Children from Violent Homes*. New York: Brunner-Mazel.

Race and culture

Case, C. (1999) Foreign images: images of race and culture in therapy with children, in J. Campbell, M. Liebmann, F. Brooks, J. Jones and C. Ward (eds) *Art Therapy, Race and Culture*. London: Jessica Kingsley.
Dalley, T. (1990) Images and integration: art therapy in a multi-cultural school, in C. Case and T. Dalley (eds) *Working with Children in Art Therapy*. London: Routledge.
Hiscox, A. and Calisch, A. (eds) (1998) *Tapestry of Cultural Issues in Art Therapy*. London: Jessica Kingsley.
Solomon, G. (2005) Development of art therapy in South Africa: dominant narratives and marginalised stories, *Inscape*, 10(1): 3–14.

Research

Gilroy, A. (2006) The evidence base for art therapy with children and adolescents, in A. Gilroy, *Art Therapy, Research and Evidence-based Practice*. London: Sage.

Sexual abuse

Buckland, R. and Murphy, J. (2001) Jumping over it: group therapy with young girls, in J. Murphy (ed.) *Lost for Words: Art Therapy with Young Survivors of Sexual Abuse*. London: Routledge.

Hagood, M. (1992) Status of child sexual abuse in the UK and implications for British art therapists, *Inscape*, spring: 27–33.

Hagood, M. (2000) *The Use of Art in Counselling Child and Adult Survivors of Sexual Abuse*. London: Jessica Kingsley.

Murphy, J. (1998) Art therapy with sexually abused children and young people, *Inscape*, 3(1): 10–16.

Murphy, J. (ed.) (2001) *Lost for Words: Art Therapy with Young Survivors of Sexual Abuse*. London: Routledge.

Sagar, C. (1990) Working with cases of child sexual abuse, in C. Case and T. Dalley (eds) *Working with Children in Art Therapy*. London: Routledge.

Thomas, L. (1998) From re-presentations to representations of sexual abuse, in D. Sandle (ed.) *Development and Diversity: New Applications in Art Therapy*. London: Free Association Books.

Supervision of child art therapy

Case, C. (2007) Imagery in supervision: the non-verbal narrative of knowing, in J. Schaverien and C. Case (eds) *Supervision in Art Psychotherapy*. London: Routledge.

Dalley, T. (2007) Piecing together the jigsaw puzzle: thinking about the clinical supervision of art therapists working with children and young people, in J. Schaverien and C. Case (eds) *Supervision in Art Psychotherapy*. London: Routledge.

Henley, D. (2007) Supervisory responses to child art therapy: assessment, intervention and outcome, in J. Schaverien and C. Case (eds) *Supervision in Art Psychotherapy*. London: Routledge.

Symbolisation, process and mediums

Boronska, T. (1995) The werewolf and the wrestling ring: exploring unconscious process through the use of metaphor, *Inscape*, 1: 19–25.

Burkitt, E. and Newell, T. (2005) Effects of human figure type on children's use of colour to depict sadness and happiness, *Inscape*, 10(1): 15–23.

Case, C. (1990) Heart forms: the image as mediator, *Inscape*, winter: 20–6.

Case, C. (1995) Silence in progress: on being, dumb, empty, or silent in therapy, *Inscape*, 1: 21–6.

Case, C. (1996) On the aesthetic moment in the transference, *Inscape*, 1(2): 39–45.

Case, C. (2000) Our lady of the queen: journeys around the maternal object, in

A. Gilroy and G. McNeilly (eds) *The Changing Shape of Art Therapy*. London: Jessica Kingsley.

Case, C. (2000) Santa's grotto: an exploration of the Christmas break in therapy, *Inscape*, 5(1): 11–18.

Case, C. (2006) Observations of children cutting up, cutting out, and sticking down, *Inscape*, 10(2).

Goldberg, D. (1991) From monsters to moons: universal and culturally-specific symbols in psychotherapy, *Inscape*, summer: 5–11.

Simon, R. (1992) *The Symbolism of Style*. London: Routledge.

Weir, F. (1987) The role of symbolic expression in its relation to art therapy: a Kleinian approach, in T. Dalley, C. Case, J. Schaverien, F. Weir, D. Halliday, P. Nowell Hall and D. Waller (eds) *Images of Art Therapy: New Developments in Theory and Practice*. London: Tavistock.

Wood, M. (1984) The child and art therapy, in T. Dalley (ed.) *Art as Therapy*. London: Tavistock.

Trauma of war

Kalmanowitz, D. and Lloyd, B. (eds) (2005) *Art Therapy and Political Violence: With Art. Without Illusion*. London: Brunner-Routledge.

Wise, S. (2005) A time for healing: art therapy for children, post September 11, New York, in D. Kalmanowitz and B. Lloyd (eds) *Art Therapy and Political Violence: With Art. Without Illusion*. London: Brunner-Routledge.

Under 5s

Deco, S. (1990) A family centre: a structural family therapy approach, in C. Case and T. Dalley (eds) *Working with Children in Art Therapy*. London: Routledge.

Dubowski, J. (1990) Art versus language: separate development during childhood, in C. Case and T. Dalley (eds) *Working with Children in Art Therapy*. London: Routledge.

Hosea, H. (2006) The brush's footmarks: parents and infants paint together in a small community art therapy group, *Inscape*, 11(2).

Matthews, J. (1989) How young children give meaning to drawing, in A. Gilroy and T. Dalley (eds) *Pictures at an Exhibition: Selected Essays on Art and Art Therapy*. London: Routledge.

Meyerowitz-Katz, J. (2003) Art materials and processes – a place of meeting: art psychotherapy with a four year old boy, *Inscape*, 8(2): 60–9.

Proulx, L. (2002) *Strengthening Emotional Ties through Parent-Child Dyad Art Therapy: Interventions with Infants and Pre-schoolers*. London: Jessica Kingsley.

Reddick, D. (1999) Baby-bear monster, *Inscape*, 4(1): 20–8.

General

Case, C. and Dalley, T. (eds) (1990) *Working with Children in Art Therapy*. London: Routledge.

Case, C. and Dalley, T. (2006) *The Handbook of Art Therapy*, 2nd edn. London: Routledge.

Dalley, T. (2000) Back to the future: thinking about theoretical developments in art therapy, in A. Gilroy and G. McNeilly (eds) *The Changing Shape of Art Therapy*. London: Jessica Kingsley.

Dalley, T., Case, C., Schaverien, J., Weir, F., Halliday, D., Nowell Hall, P. and Waller, D. (1987) *Images of Art therapy: New Developments in Theory and Practice*. London: Tavistock.

Gardner, H. (1985) *Frames of Mind: The Theory of Multiple Intelligences*, London: Paladin.

Halliday, D. (1987) Peak experiences: the individuation of children, in T. Dalley, C. Case, J. Schaverien, F. Weir, D. Halliday, P. Nowell Hall and D. Waller (eds) *Images of Art Therapy: New Developments in Theory and Practice*. London: Tavistock.

Henley, D. (2002) *Clayworks in Art Therapy*. London: Jessica Kingsley.

Kramer, E. (1971) *Art as Therapy with Children*. New York: Schocken Books.

Kramer, E. (1979) *Childhood and Art Therapy: Notes on Theory and Application*. New York: Schocken Books.

Lyddiatt, E.M. (1971) *Spontaneous Painting and Modelling*. London: Constable.

Naumberg, M. (1973) *An Introduction to Art Therapy*. New York: Teachers College Press.

Rubin, J. (1978) *Child Art Therapy*. New York: Van Nostrand Reinhold.

Safran, D. (2002) *Art Therapy and AD/HD: Diagnostic and Therapeutic Approaches*. London: Jessica Kingsley.

Index